P9-CFV-198

Lady Catherine, the Earl, AND THE
Real Downton Abbey

ALSO BY THE COUNTESS OF CARNARVON

Lady Almina and the Real Downton Abbey:
The Lost Legacy of Highclere Castle

Lady Catherine, the Earl, AND THE Real Downton Abbey

THE COUNTESS *of* CARNARVON

B\D\W\Y
Broadway Books
New York

B CARNARVON

Copyright © 2013 by 8th Countess of Carnarvon

All rights reserved.

Published in the United States by Broadway Books, an imprint of the
Crown Publishing Group, a division of Random House LLC,
a Penguin Random House Company, New York.
www.crownpublishing.com

Broadway Books and its logo, B \ D \ W \ Y,
are trademarks of Random House LLC.

Originally published in hardcover in Great Britain by Hadder &
Sloughton, a Hachette U.K. company, London, in 2013.

Downton Abbey is a registered trademark of Carnival Films Ltd.

Library of Congress Cataloging-in-Publication Data

Carnarvon, Fiona, Countess of.
Lady Catherine, the earl, and the real Downton Abbey / the Countess
of Carnarvon.—First edition.
1. Great Britain—Social life and customs—20th century.
2. Highclere Castle—History—20th century. 3. Carnarvon, Henry
George Alfred Herbert, Earl of, 1898–1987. 4. World War, 1939–1945—
Great Britain. 5. Nobility—Great Britain—Biography. I. Carnarvon,
Catherine, Countess of, 1900–1977. II. Title.
DA578.C29 2013
941.082092—dc23
[B]   2013028842

ISBN 978-0-385-34496-8
eBook ISBN 978-0-385-34497-5

Printed in the United States of America

Cover design by Laura Klynstra
Cover photograph and painting: © Highclere Castle Enterprises LLP 2013
Author photograph: © Tobi Corney Photography

10 9 8 7 6 5 4 3 2 1

First U.S. Edition

For my darling husband and son,
Geordie and Edward,
and my beloved sisters,
Sarah, Lucy, Alex, Penny and Georgie.

Hancock Lee, Born 1653 died 25th May 1709 at "Ditchley, Northumberland Co".

SARAH ALLERTON, dau of Isaac Allerton, Granddau of Fear Brewster and Isaac Allerton of the Mayflower from who descended ZACHARY TAYLOR, 12th president of the U.S., and General Richard Taylor, CSA, and the ditchley line.

FRANCIS LIGHTFOOT LEE, Born at Stratford 14 October 1734, died at "Menokin" in Jan 1797, bur^d at Mt. Airy. Burgess from both Loudoun and Richmond Counties, co-founder of Leesburg, and Signer of the Declaration of Independence.

Matilda Lee, dau of Philip Ludwell Lee.

HENRY LEE, born at Leesylvania afsd. 29 Jan 1756, died at "Dungeness", Cumberland Island, Ca. 25th March 1818 Bur^d in Lee Chapel, Lexington, VA. Brilliant cavalry leader in the Revolution, three times Governor of Virginia, Member of Confederation and U.S. Congress, died a martyr to freedom of the press.

ⓜ Ann Hill Carter, dau of Charles Carter of "Shirley", born 24 Mar 1773, married at "Shirley" 18 Jun 1793, died 10 Jul 1829 at "Ravensworth", Farfax Co., Bur^d Lee Chapel.

ROBERT EDWARD LEE, born at Stratford 19 Jan 1807, died at Lexington 12th Oct 1870. Graduate of West Point, Superintendent of West Point, Colonel U.S. 2d Cavlary, Commanding General, Army of Northern Viginia, C.S.A., and the Armies of the Confederacy. President of Washington College, Bur^d in Lee Chapel, Lexington.

ⓜ Mary Ann Randolp Custis, dau of George Washington Parke Custis of Arlington House, Alexandria County.

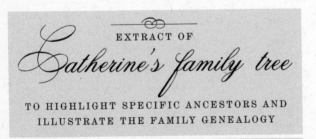

EXTRACT OF

Catherine's family tree

TO HIGHLIGHT SPECIFIC ANCESTORS AND ILLUSTRATE THE FAMILY GENEALOGY

or | ↑ Denotes ancestors or descendants	⋮ Direct but not immediate descendant	ⓜ Married

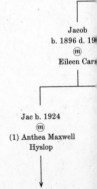

Jacob b. 1896 d. 19
ⓜ
Eileen Car

Jac b. 1924
ⓜ
(1) Anthea Maxwell Hyslop

William Lee, born at Stratford 31st Aug 1739 died at Greenspring 27th Jun 1795, bur^d at Jamestown. Merchant in London, first American Alderman of London, Commercial Agent of the Continental Congress to France, and its representative at the Courts of Berlin and Vienna.

Arthur Lee, born Stratford 21st December 1740, died 12th December 1792 at "Lansdowne", Middlesex Co. Holder of degress in both medicine and law, he was appointment Commissioner to France in 1776 and signed the treaty of Alliance with France in 1778. Member of the Confederation Congress and Chairman of the Board of the Treasury (Secretary of the Treasury) from 1784 to 1789. Never married.

HENRY LEE, born 1729 at "Lee Hall" afsd died 15 Aug 1787 at "Sully", Fairfax County, bur^d at "Leesylvania". Burgess, County Lieutenant and State Senator From whom descended the Leesylvania Line.

Mary Lee, born at Leesylvania 9 Jul 1764, died 10 Nov 1827 at Alexandria. Sister of "Lighthouse" Harry, Father of General Robert Edward Lee

ⓜ

Philip Richard Fendall grandson of Philip Lee of Blenheim, afsd.

Philip Richard Fendall Jnr b ? d 1827
ⓜ
Mary Elizabeth Young 1804

Philip Fendall
ⓜ
Anne Treddick

Descended from Wendall, Lowell and Gerrish families

MARIAN FENDALL
ⓜ
JACOB WENDELL 1895

Henry 4th Earl of Carnarvon (1831-1890)
ⓜ
1. Lady Evelyn Stanhope
2. Elizabeth Howard

George 5th Earl of Carnarvon (1866-1923)
ⓜ
Almina Wombwell (Rothschild)

Reginald Lee b. 1898 d. 1928

Philippa b. 1904 d. 1973 12th Earl of Gallloway

CATHERINE B. 1900 D. 1978 ⓜ

1. 6TH EARL OF CARNARVON *(2 children)*
2. GEOFFERY GRENFELL *(no children)*
3. DON MOMAND *(no children)*

June b. 1927
ⓜ
Peter Prescott 1954 (Brigadier)

HENRY 7th Earl of Carnarvon b. 1924
ⓜ
JEAN WALLOP

Penelope b. 1925 d. 1990
ⓜ
Gerrit van der Woude (son of Mary Wendell)

GEORDIE ⓜ FIONA
8th Earl and Countess of Carnarvon

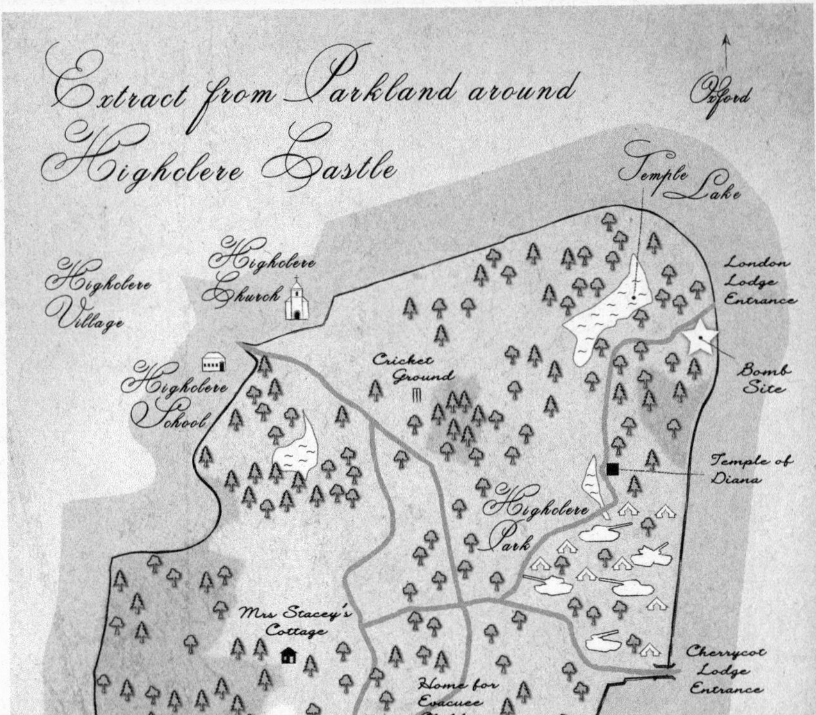

Extract from Parkland around
Highclere Castle

Oxford

Highclere
Village

Highclere
Church

Temple Lake

London
Lodge
Entrance

Highclere
School

Cricket
Ground

Bomb
Site

Temple of
Diana

Highclere
Park

Mrs Stacey's
Cottage

Home for
Evacuee
Children

Cherrycot
Lodge
Entrance

← Bristol

London →

Highclere Castle

Sidown
Vale

Rifle
Range
Practice

B17 Plane

Heavens
Gate

Sidown
Hill

Lightning plane

Mosquito Plane

Home guard lookout

Golf
Course

Bombing Valley

Highclere
Stud

Southampton ↓

N

Contents

Prologue

This book describes the lives of the family who lived at Highclere Castle from 1923 to 1945, in particular the beautiful Anglo-American Catherine Wendell and the man she married, who became the 6th Earl of Carnarvon. Like its predecessor, about Almina the 5th Countess of Carnarvon, it is intended more as a narrative of the time than a work of history. Nonetheless, it is the product of many months of research in the Castle's archives as well as conversation with those surviving family members who knew the people involved. It is based on diaries, memoirs, letters, household accounts and photographs, the guestbook that records those who came to stay and the recollections of those who worked here.

In Britain, the inter-war years were marked by the legacy of the First World War, which had exacted a terrible price on young men's lives and bequeathed economic turbulence and political change. The fabric of the old society was loosening and a new spirit of personal liberty was in the air. Many of the great houses of England declined as their owners became impoverished. Highclere's survival as the family home of the Carnarvons was very much in the balance. Increasingly, so was peace between the nations of Europe.

The new young 6th Earl and Countess of Carnarvon were initially burdened by their responsibilities, but soon enough they were swept up in the freedom and gaiety of the 1920s. Catherine was a beautiful, vivacious but thoughtful woman, loved by everybody; her husband was a generous and amusing host, an excellent judge of racehorses, and a kind and proud father. Unfortunately for Catherine, however, he grew increasingly fond of the glamour of London, of its clubs, its fast society and its romantic diversions.

The book features a cast of well-known people, friends of the Carnarvons, who played a part in shaping the politics of the 1920s and 1930s. At the outbreak of the Second World War, a new generation of the people who lived at Highclere were swept up into global conflict. The Castle became home to evacuee children and teachers, and the estate provided a training ground for soldiers from all over the world. Catherine's son, the heir to Highclere, played his part in one of the most brutal campaigns of the war.

Despite the trials of these years, Highclere Castle and the community of people who lived and worked here survived; the house remains the home of the Earl and Countess of Carnarvon. Via its television alter ego 'Downton Abbey', Highclere Castle has achieved new renown on a global scale and thrilled millions of viewers in hundreds of countries.

I hope that you enjoy this book and its insights into the history of the Real Downton Abbey. My husband Geordie and I love this house, the landscape and the people who work here with us. It is an extraordinary place, full of wonderful stories.

Lady Catherine, the Earl, AND THE
Real Downton Abbey

I

India, March 1923

It was a stifling afternoon at the Wheeler Polo Club in Meerut, northern India. The waves of heat still distorted the view over the five first-class polo grounds, but Catherine was much relieved that the most oppressive part of the day was over. She was sitting on a white-canopied dais with the Viceroy, Lord Reading, and Lord Inchcape, the chairman of the P&O line, their wives, Lady Reading and Lady Inchcape, and some other friends. Behind them, on the long, whitewashed verandahs, several hundred of the team members' families and guests were watching the afternoon's match.

Catherine's husband, Lord Porchester, was playing number two and the game was level. She had never seen a polo match until she arrived in India two months ago, although her husband, a keen rider, played well. It was part of army life in a cavalry regiment. There were other amusements, beyond the polo grounds was a racecourse and her husband—who was known to family and friends all his life as Porchey—also enjoyed plenty of snipe, duck and black partridge shooting with his fellow officers.

Catherine was a favourite with all Porchey's friends. Very pretty, with an entrancing smile, she was flirtatious and fun. She was always impeccably stylish in the latest fashions. Even sitting under the huge canopy she would wear one of her charming wide-brimmed hats to protect her complexion from the relentless sun. March was not the hottest month in Meerut by any means; Catherine knew it would become uncomfortable as the spring turned to summer. But it was so beguiling, so different from the narrow grey skies between the houses in Mayfair, London. She loved the scents of the great Neem trees, the different herbs and spices that flavoured the air and the vastness and colours of India. It was all a world away from her experience.

Despite playing a significant part in the British Army during the First World War, time had stood still for the Army of British India. The cavalryman reigned supreme and his regiment trained and drilled in between dressing for supper and dining off silver plates in full mess kit. Servants were legion. Each officer occupied a bungalow with his wife and family and was attended by a *khitmatgar* (butler) and a *bhisti* (bearer). Catherine was born in Maine and had spent her first twelve years in New York and New Hampshire. Now she was adjusting to a very different environment, with its Old World customs, its bougainvillea-filled gardens and manicured lawns that had to be watered carefully every day.

It was the last chukka and Lord Porchester's stick tangled with an opponent's, but he managed to push the ball towards the mouth of the goal. For a moment it seemed to hesitate, but good luck spun it over the line. Catherine leapt up, smiling and clapping with excitement. When he came to write his memoirs, more than forty years later, Porchey recalled his moment of triumph. 'My beloved wife Catherine was probably the most excited of our many supporters.' There was tremendous applause. The exhausted teams presented themselves to the Viceroy and Catherine smiled proudly as her husband received a commemorative cup from Lady Mansfield. Her husband was not the bookish type like his father. He loved the racing and sporting worlds, was a noted horseman, a soldier and superb raconteur; he was enormous fun to be with.

A tall *chuprassi*, one of the messengers from the Viceroy's bodyguard, dressed in white and beturbaned, stepped forward to hand something to the dishevelled Lord Porchester. 'Sahib, a priority telegram from Egypt.'

Porchey turned to the Viceroy for permission to open it. 'Of course, dear boy. More news of your dear father and his wonderful discovery, I imagine.' Catherine smiled at her husband. Porchey's father, Lord Carnarvon, had uncovered the tomb of Tutankhamun just before Christmas; in fact, just before they sailed to India. It had been front-page news around the world and was the culmination of more than sixteen years of painstaking excavation in the hills around the Valley of the Kings in Luxor, Egypt.

Catherine liked her father-in-law very much. He was totally different to his son: he loved to pore over scholarly texts about Egyptology, was passionate about Egypt's culture and possessed one of the finest collections of Ancient Egyptian works of art in the world.

Porchey slipped open the telegram. Catherine stepped towards him as he stood motionless. Then he read aloud, 'From Sir John Maxwell, Commander in Chief Egypt to Sir Charles Monroe, Commander in Chief India. Urgent. Will you please expedite an immediate passage for Lord Porchester to the Continental Hotel Cairo, where his father Lord Carnarvon is seriously ill. Three months compassionate leave.'

Catherine leaned in to her husband. 'Darling, I am so sorry.'

The match was forgotten. Lord Inchcape cleared his throat. 'Look here Porchester, the *Narkunda* sails tomorrow and will be calling at Suez. She's full to the gunnels but I could instruct the Captain to have a junior officer's cabin made available.' Lord Reading turned to one of his ADCs and said, 'I've an idea. We should put Porchester on my train down to Bombay tonight; that will give him ample time to board the *Narkunda*.'

Porchey was tremendously grateful to them both. He turned to Catherine and the two of them went to sit down and discuss their plans. 'I hate to leave you alone here, darling, but I don't see we have any choice.'

Catherine had never seen her husband cast so low. She took his hand. 'I shall be perfectly fine, really. I'm sure all our friends will be a wonderful help. I'll make a start on closing up the house.' Porchey nodded. Though they didn't acknowledge it, they both felt that somehow he would not be coming back to India and that this part of their lives was over. Catherine would return to their bungalow, Bronx Hall, in Mhow. He would send a telegram as soon as he arrived in Egypt.

Porchey brightened. 'I'm sure my mother will already have set out for Cairo, so all may not be lost.' Almina, 5th Countess of Carnarvon, was an extraordinarily skilled and gifted nurse. If anyone could save her husband, she could.

Porchey arrived at the Continental Hotel a week later to find that his mother was already there. She had hired a small biplane and flown to her husband's bedside, accompanied by the family's personal doctor, Dr Johnnie. This was even better than Porchey had hoped for. His mother's determination never ceased to amaze him. She and Dr Johnnie had arrived in two days rather than the two weeks it would have taken by train and sea.

Porchey went straight to his father's rooms and tapped on the door. A nurse drew him into the dimly lit space. Everything was quiet. She whispered to him, 'Thank goodness you've come, Lord Porchester. Your mother is exhausted. She's had several sleepless nights now and we've had to insist that she gets some rest.'

Porchey nodded. 'How is he? Can I see him?'

'Of course,' replied the nurse, 'though I'm afraid he may not recognise you.'

Porchey trod softly across to the bed. His father was unshaven and seemed so angular, his pulse visibly beating erratically. Porchey touched his hand, which felt burning hot. 'Papa, this is your son, Henry, I've come from India to see you.' His father's eyes turned towards him but they were blank. He seemed delirious. Porchey felt overwhelmed by sadness. He had been away at school, away at war and then away in India. Now he could feel that it was too late for both of them. Suddenly he felt exhausted.

That evening he had supper with his father's colleague, Howard Carter, and his sister Evelyn. Eve had been out in Egypt with their father for weeks and was already very strained by the extraordinary events that had overtaken the 5th Earl's investigations in the Valley of the Kings. Eve had been at his side to witness the momentous unsealing of Tutankhamun's tomb, an event that generated massive excitement all over the world. After nearly twenty years of excavations in the desert, the 5th Earl of Carnarvon and

Howard Carter, the brilliant Egyptologist, had made a discovery that would rewrite historians' understanding of Ancient Egypt and fascinate people for generations to come. Now, just six weeks after stepping into the Shrine Room and Treasury, the first man to enter the tomb of the boy king in three thousand years lay desperately ill.

Porchey had hardly fallen asleep when he heard the knock. It was nearly two in the morning. One of the nurses put her head around his door. 'Lord Porchester, hurry. I'm so sorry, your father has just died. Your mother has closed his eyes and would like you to go in and say a prayer.'

Porchey scrambled into a dressing gown and headed for his father's rooms. Suddenly the hotel was plunged into darkness. Carefully he made his way along the corridor and into the suite. He could just make out his mother, on her knees at his father's bedside, crying softly. He knelt down beside her and put his arm around her as he offered a small prayer of his own. 'He fought so hard to live,' whispered Almina, between tears, 'but just at the end he said, "I have heard the call; I am preparing."'

Porchey stayed a few minutes and then decided to leave his mother alone. He retreated from the bedroom to the sitting room where Eve, Dr Johnnie and Howard Carter had gathered. Somebody had brought a torch. A few minutes later, much to their relief, the lights came on again. Porchey and Eve hugged one another. Everyone was desperately upset, their faces showing exhaustion and sadness. Each of them, in their different way, had loved the 5th Earl.

In the days to come, the world's newspapers would work themselves into a state of feverish excitement over the Earl's death. 'The curse of Tutankhamun', shrieked the headlines. The press took great delight in suggesting that at the moment of Lord Carnarvon's passing, the lights throughout Cairo had been extinguished by ghostly command of King Tut. The reality was more prosaic: power shortages were common in Cairo and the Earl had died of blood poisoning contracted from a mosquito bite that he had nicked while shaving. The cut festered in the Egyptian heat and the illness seeped steadily through his body.

Lord Porchester was about to assume the role and responsibilities to which he had been born. It was a terrible shock. He was just twenty-five years old and, though his father's health had never been robust, the 5th Earl was only fifty-six when he died. Lord Porchester had not expected to inherit for many years; he had just rejoined his regiment on the assumption that he had a long army career ahead of him. Porchey and Catherine had been married for less than a year and they must have expected that they had plenty of time to really get to know each other and establish themselves in their marriage before the duties attached to being the heads of the household claimed them.

Porchey sent a telegram to Catherine—their intuition had indeed been correct. She should sail for England as soon as possible. Though she had half expected this news, it must have been difficult to take in. In addition to the grief and the worry for her husband, Catherine had to prepare herself for a new life. She was no longer the wife of an army officer. Catherine had just become the chatelaine of Highclere Castle, one of the loveliest and most famous country houses in England. She and Porchey were now the 6th Earl and Countess of Carnarvon.

2

A Very English American

Catherine could never, as a child growing up in New York State, have expected to live in India, much less Highclere Castle. Then again, by the time she married Lord Porchester, she had already lived through a great deal of disruptive change. Catherine was the daughter of Jacob Wendell Jnr and his wife, Marian, née Fendall, and had been born Anne Catherine Tredick Wendell on 25 November 1900 in a house called Willowbank in Kittery, Maine—one of the family's many homes. Her father wrote a teasing but evidently pleased-as-Punch letter to his Aunt Sallie to tell her the news. 'I don't know whether you'd call it a pretty baby or not: it reminded me more of a plucked turkey than anything else. Its eyes are blue and what hair it has is light. Marian is as happy as can be and delighted with her little daughter.'

Catherine was the third of four children and had two

older brothers, Jacob and Reginald; five years later, she would also have a younger sister called Philippa. At the time of Catherine's birth, her family were, if not quite in the ranks of the American super-rich, then certainly extremely wealthy.

Her father, Jacob (Jac) Wendell Jnr, was born in 1869 into one of New York City's foremost families. The Wendells were of Dutch descent and among the original settlers of Manhattan Island. Catherine's paternal grandfather had increased his family fortune through trade, and her father had followed in his footsteps, making his own success by going into business with a college friend to form a railway supplies company.

Wendell Jnr seemed to be a chip off the old block: reliable and savvy as well as jovial company, a man beloved by his many friends. He was a prominent member of the Harvard class of 1891, and caroused with Mark Twain and Ralph Waldo Emerson during his European tour after graduation. At the inaugural dinner of the Harvard Club of Rome in April 1892, he entertained these friends with comic songs and impressions that had them all in gales of laughter. He was excessively charming, witty, kindly and eligible, an altogether excellent match for Marian Fendall, who married him in her hometown of Washington DC on 16 April 1895.

Where the Wendells were an old family that had made money through business, the Fendalls could boast equally longstanding and even more illustrious lineage. Jac and Marian's wedding breakfast was held at the home of the bride's aunt, Miss Mary Lee Fendall. Catherine was descended on her mother's side from the Lee families of Virginia, which made her practically aristocracy in the United States. Her great-great-grandfather was Philip Richard Fendall, a cousin of Revolutionary War hero and eulogiser of George Washington, Henry Lee III. The Lee-Fendall clan was extensive and extensively involved in politics at the highest levels. The best known of all was Catherine's distant cousin, General Robert Lee, the commander of the Confederate Army and one of the most lauded military leaders in US history.

The marriage of Catherine's parents brought together two great families, and appears to have been, besides, a very happy one. As well as the house in Maine where she was born, Catherine grew up between her paternal grandparents' town house in New York City and Frostfields, her mother's country house in the tiny and picturesque town of Newcastle on the outskirts of Portsmouth, New Hampshire. The photos of Marian, Jac and their four children in the gardens at Frostfields show an informal group, seemingly caught in a moment between expeditions to play in the rock pools, or run down to the beach with the dogs. Frostfields was a modern seaside villa, imposingly large but not grand, unlike the New York headquarters of the Wendell family with its dark Victorian furniture and heavy drapes at the windows.

Catherine's childhood was typical of a monied East Coast family, shuttling between the great hub of New York City and the country retreat at Portsmouth. There were long mornings with her governess followed by dancing and music lessons in town, tennis parties and ponies in the countryside. She saw far more of her parents than many of her British contemporaries, especially at the weekends, though Jac and Marian—or Gar as the children called her—also had their own busy social lives to lead. They were often out at balls, trips to the theatre, dinners with friends, or enjoying any of the other sources of gaiety available to the wealthy in the most prosperous city on earth.

The family was of the class that cherished its history and cultivated the sense of confident purpose that came from having been successful over the course of generations.

Catherine's parents were well matched and affectionate with each other and their children. She was close to all three of her siblings; most particularly in these early years her two older brothers. It appears that until she was ten, Catherine was a happy child living a charmed life.

Then, in 1910, her father lost his entire fortune in one supremely unlucky (or badly judged, depending on one's point of view) stroke. Jac Wendell Jnr's business was in railway supplies. For the best part of twenty years he and his partner sold equipment to the companies that were expanding the urban railway network in cities all over the States. They exported to countries around the world. With such a diverse and successful business of two decades' standing, it is somewhat mystifying that Wendell Jnr should have elected to invest everything in a single railway stock. When its value crashed months later, he lost his entire business and, with it, the Wendells' centuries-old winning streak.

The flip side to the United States' economic dream factory, to the busy creation of all that staggering wealth, was this: risky manoeuvres that could bring whole fortunes tumbling down, and with them the livelihoods and prospects of hundreds of people, all the way from proprietor to lowliest employee. Fortunately for Catherine's family, if not for the employees, her father had lost only his money, not Marian's. The fact that Catherine's mother was independently wealthy saved the Wendells from ruin, though their circumstances were inevitably much reduced.

In the wake of this financial disaster, Jac Wendell did something surprising. He took the opportunity to pursue a long-cherished dream and reinvented himself as a professional actor. It was a significantly left-field action for the scion of a New York dynasty with a young family to maintain, but it was also the flowering of a lifelong passion to entertain.

Jac had been a key member of the Hasty Pudding Club, Harvard's dramatic society, and was described by some who saw him there as the best amateur actor of his generation. For the Harvard Class of 1891 Fifth Report, produced in 1911, Jac wrote that, 'My "play" has now become my work and I am working at that with enthusiasm.' In his first season at the New Theater in New York, he played Agrippa in *Antony and Cleopatra* and Feste in *Twelfth Night*. He also played a dog and a half-witted boy in other productions which, as he wrote, 'shows that there are some histrionic advantages that go with a college education.'

Perhaps Jac believed he would become one of the great professional actors of his generation. Unless he had ambitions to be an actor-manager or, better still, a big producer, he cannot have imagined he would make much money. It is tempting to wonder whether the peculiar recklessness that led to his financial ruin did not stem from a subconscious drive to eradicate his old life and thus free himself to pursue the one he had always wanted. Or, at least, it would be if the loss of his fortune hadn't subsequently caused him so much distress. What is certain is that, with Marian's money backing him up, in the wake of the disaster he was able to opt for something rather more Bohemian than the life he had lived previously. His boldness seemed initially to pay off: his second season at the theatre saw him cast as the leading man in *What the Doctor Ordered*.

Then a misfortune infinitely greater than the mere loss of a twenty-year endeavour befell the Wendells. Jac became seriously ill. For all his gaiety and determination to make the most of things, the worry about the impact of his decisions on his family had caused him to have a nervous breakdown. He was utterly exhausted. During the theatrical tour he contracted pneumonia.

Many encouraging notes from his friends were dispatched. Theodore Roosevelt wrote, 'Jack Wendell here's to you, oh incarnation of the pudding! We miss you greatly and we are deeply concerned to know that you are so sick. May you soon be well is the earnest hope of your friends and well wishers.' In the archives at Highclere there is a tiny note Jac wrote to his wife in a spidery hand, which begins, 'Goodbye my darling . . . '

Despite all the prayers and hopes, by the time the Harvard Class of 1891 Fifth Report came out, Jacob Wendell Jnr was dead. Where most of his classmates' entries are more or less ironic accounts of their quiet lives, no longer than three paragraphs, Jacob's entry is a five-page-long obituary, a tribute to a man so well loved by his college contemporaries that there is still a seat that bears his name at the Harvard Club.

In the course of just over a year, Catherine's idyllic childhood had been obliterated. The confident expectations, the luxury, the secure social status, the happiness of a charmed circle: all were gone. Her father was gone.

Marian Wendell lost little time to grief. Though she and Jac seem to have been a sincerely close couple and his sudden death at the age of forty-two must have been shattering, she had practical questions to resolve. New York high society in the first decade of the twentieth century was not an easy place to be a young widow with four children and depleted finances. It was a world unchanged since Edith Wharton had described the gilded cages of rigid conventions that bound women's lives. In New York a widow had no independent status. With the loss of her husband, she was effectively demoted. Marian had some money of her own and her house at Frostfields but, without marrying again, which she evidently had no desire to do, she and her children would be cut off from the lifeline of the city and its society.

She decided it was time for a fresh start and wrote to her cousin, Gertrude Tredick Griffiths, who ten years before had married an Englishman and gone to live in London.

Gertrude and Marian had been fond of one another when they were growing up, and Gertrude had been a bridesmaid at Marian's wedding, but they hadn't seen each other since Gertrude's move. The affection must have been deep and sincere though, because, in an act of significant generosity, Gertrude and Percy Griffiths invited Marian and all four of her children to live with them. He was a partner at the accountancy firm of Deloitte and a fanatical collector of rare furniture. They had a London house in Bryanston Square and spent the weekends at Sandridgebury, their home just outside St Albans, a small cathedral city twenty miles north of London.

Catherine left the States behind when she was twelve years old. She never lived there again.

Marian and Gertrude seem to have worked together to establish clear routines for the children almost from the moment of their arrival. Jac, the eldest boy, was sent to school at Repton. Reggie, two years younger, went to Eton. He was a direct contemporary of Porchey, Catherine's future husband, and only the second American ever to be elected to Pop, the school's society of senior boys, a body very roughly analogous to prefects. Catherine and Philippa were educated at day schools in London. At weekends Marian, Gertrude, Percy and the girls decamped the short distance to Sandridgebury, where they were joined in the school holidays by Jac and Reggie.

The arrangement seems to have worked very well. The only note of discord occurred when Gertrude, who had no children of her own, wished to adopt Philippa. Marian was quite firm in her refusal. Despite this sticky moment, the Griffiths were unfailingly kind and generous. It must have been an enormous change for them, as a childless couple used to pleasing themselves, and with two houses full of precious furniture; not a combination that would necessarily work well with four boisterous children.

In 1910 the *Portsmouth Herald*, the local paper of the New Hampshire town where Catherine had spent much of her first ten years, had run a rather breathless front-page profile of 'Mrs Gertrude Tredick Griffiths and her success'. It claimed her as a brilliant society arbiter and 'leader of the American colony in London.' In truth, the Griffiths did not move in the most exalted social realm, though they were well connected among the wealthy professional classes that felt perfectly at ease mingling with the gentry, and had extensive contacts with other well-off Americans living in London. Marian Wendell might have reflected that, if life was perhaps a little less glamorous than it had been in New York before Jac's death, she had at least achieved the reinvention of her family's story. In London Marian was not just Jac's widow, she was also Gertrude's cousin. She was part of a solidly comfortable upper-middle-class world that, in practice, afforded greater social mobility than the New York high society she had left behind.

It's impossible to say for sure what impact her family's change in circumstances and country, to say nothing of the loss of her father, had on Catherine. Her mother's efficient management of the move, the financial cushion of her wealth and the ready-made social circle that awaited the Wendells in London must surely have helped. So, too, must the companionship of her siblings. If they had been fond of each other before, after their arrival in England the four Wendell children were devoted to one another. Jac took his role as the eldest very seriously all his life, looking out for his sisters in particular. Catherine adored both him and her brother

Reggie and regarded Philippa as her natural companion in fun. They were all very close to their mother, Gar.

As they grew up and settled more comfortably into London society, the family acquired a reputation for being excellent company. They all loved to dance, but Jac and Philippa were considered among the best dancers in London. Catherine and Philippa were growing into very attractive girls, fun and flirtatious, much in demand. Catherine had a soft prettiness, Philippa a dark-haired, dark-eyed intensity. A press photo of her in the Spanish dancer's costume she wore to a ball at Claridge's, not long after Catherine's marriage, shows her looking extremely sassy, staring at the camera from beneath her flat black hat, arms on hips and shawl slung across her body.

The family worshipped at St Mark's Church on North Audley Street in Mayfair. Catherine and her sister would sweep in on a Sunday morning, one on each of Gar's arms, smiling and greeting their numerous friends from among London's smart set. The Wendell sisters were charming, and were invited everywhere.

The Wendells' adolescence seems to have been a lot of fun, despite the horrific events that were decimating the generation of young people among whom they were living. The war in Europe broke out two years after they arrived, and one can only imagine Marian's relief that, as Americans, her boys were exempt from conscription. Reggie, born in 1898, was also just too young, but Jac was not. In 1915 he was sent a white feather, the gesture of contempt towards those so-called cowards who had not joined up. In fact, he, like so many, was desperate to go.

It can be difficult to grasp the eagerness that young men felt, even once the scale of the carnage and its seeming futility had become apparent. Alfred Duff Cooper, who served as a Grenadier Guard and was later a Conservative MP and opponent of Neville Chamberlain's appeasement policy, as well as a friend of Catherine and her husband and a great visitor to Highclere, wrote in his memoir *Old Men Forget*, that for 'normal young men' in wartime, 'joining the army was plainly the decent thing to do, like giving up a seat to an old lady or taking off one's hat in a holy place.' He acknowledged that some really did struggle with their conscience, but implied strongly that they were the odd ones. There was a combination of basic decency and the boldness of youth that swept most young men off to face the war's long hours of fatigue and boredom and horrors.

In 1916, Jac joined Professor Richard Norton's American Volunteer Motor Ambulance Corps. If part of Marian had hoped she would be spared this, she was also immensely proud. The Ambulance Corps was already legendary. It was founded in London in autumn 1914 by Norton, an eminent archaeologist and friend of Henry James and Edith Wharton, both of whom raised funds for the body. It began with two cars and four drivers. By the time it was taken over by the American Army when the United States entered the war in 1917, there were 600 American volunteer drivers and 300 ambulances. They worked alongside the British Red Cross and were initially under the command of the British Army. The French Army was, however, even worse served by ambulance units than the British, so they were promptly switched to work with the French.

The Ambulance Corps, or *les voitures américaines* as the French called it, was noted for exceptional bravery, rescuing men from right under the noses of the enemy and amidst heavy barrages. They were collectively awarded the Croix de Guerre, the French military honour created in late 1914 to recognise the unprecedented valour being displayed in the field. Richard Norton died of meningitis in 1917, but was nonetheless France's most highly decorated non-Frenchman of the war.

Jac served in the seventh section of the Ambulance Corps, which received four collective citations in French honours. He was also cited individually. Despite being wounded at Verdun, he, unlike the unfortunate Norton and so many of his friends and contemporaries in the Army, who were dying in their dozens every day, survived the war. Once the United States joined the conflict in 1917, he became an aide-de-camp to General Pershing. He was clearly an asset to the US Army. For one thing, Jac, like Catherine and all the Wendell siblings, was fluent in French. He had also spent over a year on the ground in France and proved himself to be both supremely able and brave. That white feather must have felt like a ridiculous joke from another lifetime.

In 1918, with her beloved older brother safely back, Catherine threw herself into the rapturous celebrations of the end of the war. The social whirl had been maintained, as far as possible, throughout. It was felt that when the young men were on leave they needed to have as much fun as possible: champagne at dinner, the conversation of charming young ladies such as the Wendell sisters, and then for some (though never for the Wendells, who were well guarded from such scandalous activities) dancing in nightclubs till dawn.

Now the festivities ratcheted up a gear. There was a heady sense of liberation, of relief and possibility. Duff Cooper remembered that both during and for some time after the conflict, there was a sense that it was almost a duty to be not just cheerful, but as happy as possible. 'Among my own friends it became a point of honour never to show a sad face at the feast. And if we wept—as weep we did—we wept in secret.'

Stoicism, indeed gaiety, was the virtue and the necessity of the age, but it can't have been easy. Duff Cooper had very few friends left; they had been wiped out, one by one. Of the eight young men who made a trip to Venice in 1913, he was the only survivor. Each week there was another telegram, another friend dead.

Catherine's future husband was partially shielded from the impact of this carnage by being posted to India and thence to Mesopotamia rather than the killing fields of northern France. Lord Porchester—Porchey—was eighteen years old when on Boxing Day 1916 he sailed for Bombay to join his regiment and complete his military training. The 7th Queen's Own Hussars were a cavalry regiment and attracted the dashing sons of the aristocracy and the gentry. Porchey had joined up in a mood of boisterous patriotism and had the typical young man's conviction that nothing bad could possibly happen to him. Training in Mhow appeared to bear this out. There were sword-play exercises, mounted combat with lances, polo games to improve horsemanship and four kit changes a day. Full dress uniform was obligatory at dinner, which was served off silver that would not have been out of place at Highclere, Porchey's beloved childhood home.

Porchey was desperate to see action and serve his country. Finally, in autumn 1917, he got his wish when the regiment was sent to Mesopotamia to fight the Turks. They landed at Basra and marched 500 miles in blistering, spirit-sapping heat to Baghdad, where they had been ordered to join reinforcements to mop up the retreating Ottoman Army. Porchey and his men mounted an ambush on the Aleppo Road as another unit rode into the desert to cut off the flank of the enemy troops. The operation was a total success and the Ottoman 50th Division was duly defeated. Porchey had played his part well and with courage, surviving some near escapes. Lives were of course lost and he and his men had seen terrible suffering among the Arab civilian population that moved them profoundly. But overall, the Hussars' experiences were more like a boys'-own adventure story than anything resembling the grinding horrors of the Western Front or the blood bath that was Gallipoli.

Porchey made it back to London in June 1919, exhausted and (according to his mother) in need of a good delousing, but unharmed. Almina, the Countess of Carnarvon, knew a great deal about the afflictions of returning soldiers. She had spent the last four years nursing wounded and traumatised officers, providing a level of care that was singled out as exceptional by the highest military authorities. At the outbreak of war, Almina had turned Highclere Castle into a hospital and nursing home, before moving the bulk of activities to Bryanston Square in London in 1916. When the amnesty was signed she packed up, exhausted but convinced she had found her life's vocation. She nearly didn't live to fulfil it. At the end of 1918 she fell ill with the Spanish flu, the deadly virus that raged around the world and claimed even more lives than the conflict that had just ended. Almina was fortunate, and strong. She survived to read the letters that poured in from grateful ex-patients who wrote that without the superb care they had received at her hospitals, they would have lost legs, or their minds, or hope.

Now the Castle was once again a home, but the houses of the aristocracy had to justify their existence as never before, and privilege was no longer taken for granted to quite the same extent. For the Carnarvons and the wider community of Highclere, as for families and communities from every walk of life up and down the land, the post-war years saw an uneasy return to normality in a changed world.

For everyone, there was grief and relief. There was also,

initially at least, a sense that, however ghastly it had been, it had all been worth it. In the immediate aftermath of the Allied victory, and as the Versailles Peace Conference got under way, the opinion in victorious nations was that a decisive blow for peace and stability had been struck. It took a decade or so for that optimism to wear off and the scale of the war's tragic consequences to emerge. By 1929, the certainty that the Allies had won a war to end all wars was being shaken, but in 1918 all of that was to come. For now, life had to go on, had—in fact – to be appreciated as never before. For those lucky enough to survive, it was time to live a little.

Porchey suffered appendicitis just after getting back, but his mother leapt into action and nursed him back to health after the operation. Then, as he waited to hear about his next posting with the 7th Hussars, he abandoned himself to the huge party that London society was throwing, seemingly every night of the week. Catherine Wendell was doing something similar. The spring and summer of 1919 were riotous with dinners, dances and gaiety of all kind. They must have criss-crossed the streets of London's fashionable districts on the same nights, going from one ball to another without ever quite being at the same party at the same time. It was not in a ballroom in Mayfair that Catherine met Porchey, but on a harbourside in the Mediterranean.

3

The Girl in the Yellow Dress

In May 1919, Miss Catherine Wendell appeared in a light entertainment whimsically entitled *In a Persian Garden*, organised by Lady Allington. The event took place at London's Palace Theatre and was to raise money for the Church of England's Waifs and Strays Society. Such *tableaux vivants* in aid of a good cause were tremendously popular among the smart set well into the Thirties. The daughters of London high society were enlisted to do good and to amuse themselves with dressing up and amateur dramatics at the same time. One imagines that such a divertingly exotic spectacle as a Persian garden must have proved very appealing to the young gentlemen in the audience.

Catherine, whose father had so loved acting, and whose siblings were famously good dancers, evidently treasured her time on the stage, since she kept the programme and the press photos from the event in her personal scrapbook, which is still at Highclere. She was one of an ensemble of dancers and sadly there is no photo of her in costume, but it was her headshot, alongside that of another participant, Miss Lois Sturt, that the press chose to illustrate their brief report. Her fair hair is waved and bobbed, her expression guileless and tranquil, except for a hint of a smile at the eyes. Catherine, like her siblings, seems to have inherited some of the physical charisma of their father. Eileen Carr, who was later to marry Catherine's brother, Jac, remembered going to one dance and seeing this pretty blonde girl absolutely surrounded by young men. She asked her dance partner who she was. 'Don't you know? That's Catherine Wendell. It's said she has had thirteen proposals of marriage and I'm thinking of being the fourteenth!'

By the time she met Porchey, in Gibraltar in the autumn of 1920, Catherine had certainly bewitched many of London's most eligible young men. Louis, Lord Mountbatten was an admirer, as was Prince George, a younger son of King George V and Queen Mary, who remained a friend for life. There seems to have been something about her that inspired devotion. She was a tremendous flirt, fun and pretty, but also totally innocent and very sweet, and she had indeed received numerous proposals of marriage before her engagement to Porchey. They ranged from the inconsequential to one that seems to have been accepted and possibly even announced in the press in the States in early 1919, before it was subsequently broken off. Francis Collingwood Drake was a neighbour of Catherine's, the son of Mr and Mrs John Ramsey Drake of Batchwood Hall in St Albans. There is nothing to suggest what occasioned the break, but perhaps Catherine, somewhat dazzled by so much attention, simply realised she had been hasty.

In any case, her mother decided, in 1920, that it was time

for Catherine to see a little more of the world. Catherine and Marian set off together on a trip around Europe and the Levant, leaving Philippa in the care of her brothers, and cousin Gertrude.

Arriving in the south of Spain, Mrs and Miss Wendell were invited to Gibraltar by Lord Inverclyde, who was one of the Governor of Gibraltar's two aides-de-camp. The other was Lord Porchester, who had been appointed a few weeks previously. The posting was a very welcome change of scene from the damp chill of the regimental barracks in Catterick, Yorkshire, where he had spent much of the previous six months.

One of Porchey's first tasks was to organise the annual Governor's Ball, which had occasioned Lord Inverclyde's invitation to the Wendells. Lord Inverclyde asked Porchey, as a favour, to collect his guests from the mainland. Ever obliging, Porchey made his way to the Wendells' hotel and found himself face to face with a lovely girl with beautiful eyes and a delicious wide smile. He was captivated. They chatted as they strolled down to the quayside to board the boat for the crossing to the Rock, and Porchey noticed the faintest trace of an American accent. Catherine felt totally relaxed in this dapper young gentleman's company. She had been rather glad of the break from the London social scene and, since she was so close to her mother, had been enjoying herself immensely, but it was refreshing to meet someone new, especially someone so charming.

Two days later, 150 guests dined in the courtyard of the Governor's residence. The gardens were strung with lanterns entwined in the flowers and all the men looked resplendent in their uniforms. Catherine was besieged by hopeful partners who wanted to dance the night away, and was much admired by all. She wore a pale yellow dress that her mother had helped her to choose, and to some others' chagrin, spent much of the evening gliding across the dance floor in Lord Porchester's arms, chatting as they danced. Marian sat on one of the little gilt chairs that lined the walls of the ballroom with the other chaperones, proudly looking on and noting Lord Porchester's evident interest.

It seems probable that Catherine and Porchey must have spoken again before his sudden departure in the days shortly after the ball, as over the months that followed they began a correspondence. They had evidently made quite an impression on one another but, much to his irritation, Porchey was not in a position to stay and further the acquaintance. The British Army was engaged in cost cutting, and henceforth the Governor would have to manage with only one ADC.

Porchey had arrived in Gibraltar determined to have a good time, and it had far exceeded his hopes. Now he expected to be returned to his regiment, which had been sent back to India, but to his surprise he was offered another, rather intriguing posting, this time on secondment to the British Embassy in Constantinople. When he arrived he discovered that his principal role was to do a spot of spying on a certain high-profile critic of the British position in the Middle East. Whoever had arranged this mission was either inept or running an expert double bluff. Porchey's target was none other than his uncle, Aubrey Herbert, his father's younger brother. Aubrey was a renowned expert on the Balkans and Turkish affairs, and very much *persona grata* with the Sultan. He was also an energetic eccentric, who had twice been offered the throne of Albania in recognition of his outstanding work in the region and, consequently, just the sort of man from whom His Majesty's government did not wish to hear criticism.

Porchey was not really the mastermind sleuth type, so he had accepted the brief in the spirit of adventure rather than

willingly. It was with relief as well as delight in the ridiculousness of the situation that he met Aubrey for dinner and
told his uncle all about his role. The two men resolved to
formulate some amusing stories for Porchey to channel to his
superiors.

As well as the spurious information gathering, Porchey
enjoyed various adventures, both amorous and commercial,
and very much made the most of his time in Constantinople.
In between he prepared for the arrival of Catherine and her
mother, whose voyage through Europe and North Africa had
continued after his departure from Gibraltar. Porchey found
that Miss Wendell was still very much on his mind and he
was anxious to arrange some day trips to amuse her while she
was visiting Constantinople. They had been corresponding
ever since he left, though the tone of the letters seems to have
been low key rather than ardent. 'Have you bought a lot of
chic clothes [in Paris]?' he enquired in May 1921. And then,
'Write me a line or send me a wire or do something to cheer
me up as a man cannot live on bread alone.'

One could never have accused Porchey of being a dedicated romantic, but he was superbly amusing company, always
ready to laugh and to entertain. He also formed strong and
sincere attachments to women, and he really could not wait
to see Catherine again (though that was of course no reason
to forswear dalliances in the meantime). As for her part, it
seems very likely that much of his appeal must have have
lain in the way his boisterous anecdotes and sense of fun
reminded her of her father, who had always been ready with
a good story to cheer people up. Though he was perhaps
not the most sophisticated man in society, he possessed a
warmth and a straightforward charm that made him very
attractive to women.

When she arrived, all their favourable impressions of one

another were confirmed. The two of them went riding and attended several dances together. Catherine charmed everyone she met and Porchey found himself totally under her spell. He was dimly aware that she was by no means significantly wealthy, and he suspected that his father would object, but he found himself thinking more and more about what an agreeable life companion Catherine would make. There was something enchanting about her simplicity and sense of fun. When the expected call came for him to return to his regiment in India at the end of the year, Porchey realised that he did not want to go alone. He asked Catherine to marry him and was thrilled when she eventually accepted. According to Catherine's great-niece, he had to ask several times.

It was a grand marriage for her, there can be no doubt, which perhaps accounts for her initial hesitation. The prospect might have seemed like something out of a fairy tale on one hand, but it surely also felt daunting to have to step into the role of Countess. In the end the strength of her feelings overcame any doubts. Catherine was, as later events were to prove, utterly devoted to Porchey.

Marian's feelings on the engagement are not known, but one can surmise that she was pleased. On their return to London in the early autumn, when Catherine told Jac, her oldest brother, he was also enthusiastic for Catherine's sake, but when he subsequently met his future brother-in-law, he slightly reserved his judgement. Perhaps he had deduced something that Catherine and her mother had not, which made him wonder about the degree of Porchey's capacity to support and look after his sister.

Certainly some of the letters that Porchey wrote to Catherine when their engagement was still a private agreement, not yet officially recognised, might have given a different woman pause for thought. He had a tendency to tell her what to do. Learn about polo, he advised, so as to be thought of as interesting and a good sport. 'It's awful to be classed a bore or even a non-entity.' But elsewhere he could be brimful of affection and assurances. 'Oh, C, if you only thought of me as much as I think of you, then you'd have no time to sleep! I have a feeling that next year all my dreams are going to come true, and we will have such fun.'

In any case, the two young people were convinced they were right for one another, and there was no objection from Catherine's side. There was still the matter of Porchey's parents, though. Being of age, Porchey could marry whomsoever he wished, but he had no desire to incur his family's disapproval. Nervously, he delayed his return to India by applying for cavalry training in Wiltshire and set off from Constantinople to return to Britain in late autumn. He dropped in to Highclere en route, to speak to his father.

The interview must have been uncomfortable but it was not a disaster. The 5th Earl expressed exactly the reservations that Porchey had anticipated. He cautioned against marrying an American and, most especially, one with no money. He had done neither, and had enjoyed a very happy and successful marriage. Porchey couldn't have known it, but Lord Carnarvon was already conscious that the vast fortune his wife had brought to their union, which had for twenty-five years seemed unlimited, was, since her father's death, now finite. The 5th Earl had begun to instigate economies but the situation was not yet critical, and he could see that his son was sincere in his affection. Lord Carnarvon was a pragmatist but he had a heart. He suggested that Porchey bring Catherine to London to meet them.

Number 1 Seamore Place was the Carnarvons' home in town, a large and elegant mansion, resplendent with artworks, situated behind Hyde Park Corner and with views onto the park. Both the house and the art collection had been left to Almina three years previously by the man who was generally accepted as her father, Alfred de Rothschild, who had settled a vast sum of money on her when she married.

Catherine must have been unspeakably nervous as she and Porchey stood between the stuccoed columns and waited for Almina's butler, Roberts, to open the heavy black door to them. She could feel sure of her fiancé's love for her, but of very little else. Porchey had asked his sister, Eve, to come along for support. She had helped to get him out of numerous childhood scrapes and was used to mediating between her brother and their parents. Porchey knew that she would be a great friend to Catherine.

The evening passed off as well as it possibly could have done. Almina, doubtless conscious that she herself had undergone the same assessment twenty-seven years previously when she met her prospective parents-in-law, was the perfect hostess, and later pronounced Catherine to be a very sweet girl. Lord Carnarvon admitted to his son when they were alone together after the ladies had retired to the drawing room that Catherine was really quite good looking. He reiterated his concerns, but Porchey could tell that his beloved Catherine's powerful charm had worked again. His father was not going to object. The wedding was set for the following summer.

When the engagement was announced, in June 1922, the New York papers noted that Lord Porchester was wealthy as well as aristocratic and would inherit some 50,000 acres of land, including real estate in Melbourne, Australia, and property in London. The jewel of the inheritance was of course Highclere Castle, described as 'one of the most magnificent country seats in England . . . set in a glorious old park 13 miles in circumference, celebrated far and wide.' They also proudly reported that the bride was a descendant of the

Washingtons and the Lees, and claimed (erroneously) that she would also inherit a large property fortune. Porchey had a large square sapphire reset for his bride's engagement ring. The stone had been given by the 5th Earl to his great friend, Prince Victor Duleep Singh, who had then left it in his will to Porchey, who was his godson.

The official engagement photos released to the press show Catherine at her sweetly radiant best, with softly waved bobbed hair, clear eyes and a cupid's bow of a mouth. Her luminescent expression suggests an innocent delight in her circumstances, mingled with perhaps a tiny hint of anxiety.

She and her mother were helped out hugely in the wedding preparations by Almina, who took on the role that had been played for her by Elsie, her husband's stepmother, when she was a nervous bride-to-be of somewhat uncertain parentage. Catherine's ancestry might have been considerably more solid, but she, unlike Almina, did not have the confidence that comes from possession of a vast fortune. Almina found Catherine absolutely charming and could see that she made her son happy, so with her typical disregard for expense or effort, she set about preparing a lavish welcome to the family.

One particular practical problem was just the same for Catherine and her mother as it had been for Almina and hers. Tradition dictated that after the marriage service, the wedding should be celebrated in a house belonging to the bride's family or friends. Mr and Mrs Percy Griffiths' house in town was comfortable but not magnificent or spacious enough to host the wedding breakfast of the future Earl and Countess of Carnarvon. Almina must surely have recalled the sensitive enquiry undertaken by Elsie, in far more delicate circumstances. Almina's mother, Mrs Wombwell, had not been received by the Carnarvons on account of the rumours about Almina's paternity, and it was therefore quite impossible that she should host the occasion in her own home. With the minimum of fuss, Elsie had secured the use of a friend's house in Mayfair, a neutral space for the celebrations. A generation later and the motivation was different but the need was the same. Almina enquired among her many friends, and Lord Leigh very generously offered Mrs Wendell the use of his house in Grosvenor Square.

Three days before the wedding, Almina hosted a show-stopping ball for her daughter, Lady Evelyn Herbert, and Miss Catherine Wendell, at Seamore Place. *The Times* reported that 1,000 people were invited, including HRH Prince George, Lord Louis Mountbatten and his fiancée Miss Edwina Ashley, dukes, marchionesses, earls, ambassadors and all who were considered amusing in the summer of 1922.

On Monday 17 July, Catherine dressed for her wedding in her bedroom at cousin Gertrude's house. She was attended by her mother, cousin and younger sister, Philippa, who was one of her nine bridesmaids. Doll, her maid, bustled in and out of the room, fetching flowers and more hairpins and endless cups of tea. Catherine made use of these moments to prepare herself. The marriage would be celebrated at St Margaret's Westminster, the very same church where, twenty-seven years previously, her soon to be mother-in-law, Almina, had married the 5th Earl of Carnarvon. Many of her own family had made the voyage from the United States and her mother had invited numerous London friends. Nevertheless, most of the 700 guests were connections of the Carnarvons'. Alongside her excitement at the prospect of marrying the man she adored, there was nervousness at being under the spotlight. The press would be there at her entrance and exit from the church and Catherine knew that every detail of her attire and demeanour would be scrutinised, first by the wedding guests, then by the readers of the following morning's papers. But she also knew she had many supporters in Porchey's family and intimate circle. She was especially pleased that Prince George had agreed to be the guest of honour. He was a particular friend of hers and his presence was an honour that gave her confidence a considerable boost.

Catherine's exquisite wedding clothes must have reassured her that she was looking her very best. She wore a softly draped pale ivory satin dress, with wide chiffon sleeves and silver filigree and pearl-encrusted embroidery, and a four-yard-long Court train, complete with a veil of the finest silk tulle, five and a half yards long, which was held in place by 'a classical bandeau of silver and diamond-centred orange blossoms'. Mr Reville of Hanover Square was her couturier, and his skills with draping were declared genius-like by the press. The first articles covering her fashion choices were rushed out to appear in that same day's evening editions, illustrated with one of Mr Reville's sketches.

Catherine was accompanied to the church by her elder brother, Jac, who was to give her away. He had just become engaged to Miss Eileen Carr, by now a great friend of Catherine's, and one of her bridesmaids. He must have allowed his own good mood and Catherine's evident happiness to silence any doubts about his future brother-in-law.

They were met at the church by all nine of Catherine's bridesmaids and her single pageboy, Master Rennie Maudsley. He was the small son of a family friend, whose nominal role was to assist her with her train but whose main purpose was to look terribly sweet. It was a blustery day, to judge from a candid photo of the bridesmaids assembling, their skirts of canary-yellow georgette over satin whipping about their legs. They all wore magnificent broad-brimmed hats trimmed with flowers and yellow ostrich plumes, and carried large bouquets of yellow roses. The lavish flowers had been purchased by Almina at vast expense from one of London's most fashionable florists. Catherine's bouquet was a long trailing creation of yellow and white roses and delicate sprays of foliage that reached almost to the ground.

The bride arrived at the church door to the sound of the 7th Queen's Own Hussars' regimental call and made her graceful progress up the aisle on Jac's arm to greet the groom, who was wearing morning dress. If she felt nervous as she took Porchey's hand and prepared to assume her new role, then the nerves had dissolved by the time she emerged, a married woman, scarcely forty-five minutes later. In the photo of Catherine and Porchey leaving the church after the service they are both laughing, apparently full of that euphoria that results from the combination of great happiness and release from tension.

They proceeded to 31 Grosvenor Square where they and their 700 guests assembled to celebrate. Lord Leigh's house had been filled to bursting with magnificent arrangements of the same yellow roses that were featured in the bridal party's bouquets.

There is a beautiful menu card, festooned with a bower of pink roses, that records the sumptuous wedding breakfast. Guests were served a feast of classical French cuisine, including salmon cutlets and a lobster salad Parisienne, noisettes of lamb, *crèmes de volaille* and truffles, before sandwiches and patisserie. It was all prepared by a small army of staff, an assembly of Lord Leigh's employees and the Seamore Place and Highclere staff, who had been drafted in to provide extra support.

The party was a triumph for Almina, who had masterminded it, as much as for Marian, who was its official hostess. Judging from the expressions of its principal participants, the bride and groom enjoyed themselves immensely. In between all the chat and the artfully prepared delicacies, the wedding party had some official photos taken, many of which appeared in the press the following day. Porchey stands amidst the multitude of behatted bridesmaids with a proud and contented expression. Prince George, an extremely handsome young man, stands beside him as guest of honour wearing the ever so slightly diffident look of a person who is asked to attend—and be photographed at—many of his friends' most important social occasions. Catherine is seated in front of Prince George and smiles radiantly, like a woman filled with joy and excitement.

The following day saw the wedding, also at St Margaret's Westminster, of Lord Louis Mountbatten, great-grandson of Queen Victoria and Prince Albert, and Miss Edwina Ashley. Miss Ashley was the heiress to her grandfather Sir Ernest Cassel's vast fortune. Sir Ernest had been Britain's greatest financier of the Edwardian age, so Edwina was virtually the richest girl in England. Many of the guests at Porchey and Catherine's wedding, including the Duke and Duchess of Marlborough and the Marquess of Milford Haven, stayed in town to attend the Mountbatten–Ashley nuptials. It was an even glitzier occasion than the previous day's, with the Prince of Wales standing as best man.

Lord and Lady Porchester did not attend this wedding. The previous afternoon, even as their wedding guests enjoyed the last of the ices and coffee and petits fours, Catherine had slipped into her going-away costume. She and Porchey set off to motor down to Highclere, where she would spend her first night as a married woman.

Streatfield, the house steward, a tall, venerable, bewhiskered man who remembered when Porchey was in his cradle, was too old to be dashing up to London to assist at the wedding.

He stayed at the house in order to welcome the newly-weds. It was not the first time Catherine had been driven up the gravel drive, handed out of the car by the house steward and then crossed the Saloon to take some supper in the Dining Room. But never before had she afterwards ascended the imposing Oak Staircase in Porchey's company. Streatfield showed them himself to the East Anglia bedroom and left them there to begin their married life in earnest.

4

From Honeymoon to Highclere

On Christmas Day 1922, Porchey and Catherine sailed for India from Tilbury Docks, arriving in Bombay some ten days later. They had spent five months at Highclere after their wedding, but now Porchey was keen to return to his regiment, which had been posted back to Mhow. They left everyone at the castle in a state of tremendous nervous excitement. At the beginning of November, Lord Carnarvon had received a cable from Howard Carter, who was in Luxor, starting on what the men had reluctantly agreed would have to be the last season of excavations. They had spent years searching for a lost tomb, a royal burial site in the Valley of the Kings that had escaped the attentions of grave robbers and held all its secrets and treasures intact. But archaeology was expensive and the Earl was becoming worried about money. He could no longer afford to fund the works, hoping against hope that their efforts would pay off. On 6 November Carter cabled his friend and patron. 'At last have made wonderful discovery in the Valley. A magnificent tomb with seals intact. Recovered same for your arrival. Congratulations.'

Highclere immediately erupted into a frenzy of activity as a jubilant Lord Carnarvon made hasty arrangements to travel to Egypt. He was almost beside himself. If this really was the untouched tomb of a pharaoh, it was the biggest discovery in the history of archaeology and the vindication of everything he had spent the last sixteen years working for. Almina had almost always joined him on his trips to Egypt, but this year she was suffering from chronic pain in her jaw and opted to stay at home. Eve was also an enthusiastic supporter of her father's investigations, and decided to accompany him. Porchey, by contrast, had never shared his father's passion for Egyptology, never been much interested in the artefacts or the endless poring over scholarly reference works. When the telegram announcing Carter's breakthrough arrived, he was pleased for him and for his father but essentially unmoved.

The festivities in Luxor when Lord Carnarvon arrived were magnificent; he threw a lavish party at the Winter Hotel, open to everyone. The scale of the job was becoming apparent, though. Not only were there months' worth of highly technical excavations to carry out, there was also a fund-raising and publicity drive to coordinate. Lord Carnarvon left Carter dealing with the archaeology and returned to England to deal with the press and promotion. He was summoned to Buckingham Palace to tell King George and Queen Mary in person about the implications of the find.

Christmas was spent quietly at Highclere; Porchey and Catherine's departure was something of a sideshow. It seemed probable that the family wouldn't all be together again for at least a couple of years. As it turned out, that was the last time Catherine ever saw her father-in-law. The next time she embraced Eve, both women were in mourning and Catherine had become Lady Carnarvon.

Porchey and Catherine, like the rest of the world, read the newspapers over the next few months as the story spiralled into a media sensation. The tomb was unsealed on 16 February 1923, and readers from New York to Tokyo marvelled at the beautiful objects that were revealed. As the men who had discovered Tutankhamun's tomb, the Earl of Carnarvon and Howard Carter had become as close to overnight global celebrities as was possible in the 1920s. Catherine devoured Eve's letters, fascinated by every description of the latest artefact.

Porchey was thrilled for his father, but his attention was focused on getting settled back into regimental life and helping Catherine to adjust to the new reality of being a soldier's wife overseas. He had assured her before they left that his posting would not be in the slightest bit onerous, but Catherine had no experience of India, its climate or its people's customs. She had admitted to a certain nervousness on the voyage over. For this child of the New World, it must have been rather odd to fetch up in one of the Old World's most politically important dominions.

The 7th Hussars were posted on a three-year tour to India that Porchey expected to be a return to the pre-war idyll of polo, parties and endless gin and tonic on the veranda, interspersed with the occasional bout of military exercises. All his life Porchey was a fanatic for horses, racing and polo, and he couldn't wait to get back to the company of his friends and the familiarity of his regiment.

There are photos of Porchey and Catherine, newly arrived,

visiting Government House, Bombay. She is elegant in the ankle-length, dropped-waist dress and attached cape that was the height of fashion, worn with a cloche hat trimmed with a trailing scarf, a string of pearls around her neck. Porchey is in the three-piece lounge suit of an off-duty officer, with slicked-back hair and neat moustache. They both look rather uncomfortable, perched on the floral armchairs of the Governor's official residence.

From Bombay they travelled by train to Mhow to join the regiment. Marcelle, Catherine's maid, and His Lordship's valet had gone ahead with the luggage, to help the local staff to prepare the bungalow for their arrival. Marcelle had been with Catherine since she was fourteen years old. She was the daughter of Gertrude's French hairdresser, and had been bestowed with the pet name 'Doll' in the early days, when she herself was still a teenager. Doll was as much a confidante as she was a lady's maid.

If one had been a guest at Porchey and Catherine's bungalow, Bronx Hall, with its grand piano, tiger-skin rugs and carefully watered croquet lawns, one might have been forgiven for thinking that the British were living just as they had thirty years previously. Alongside this sense of continuity with the past, though, was a very different future moving ever closer. The impact of the war on India's sense of itself, and on its position on the world stage, had been dramatic. Thousands of members of the Army of British India had fought and died bravely for the Allied cause, alongside Britons, Canadians, Australians and soldiers of other Commonwealth states. In 1920 India had been one of the founding members of the League of Nations, the great post-war political project that was designed to ensure that such a calamitous conflict could never happen again. The long slow process of movement towards independence for India was gathering steam. But on the ground, little had changed. British India was to all intents and purposes still at the height of its pomp and Porchey and Catherine were at the social pinnacle of the Raj.

There are numerous photos taken at the racetrack, polo cups and picnics. Scraps of information in Catherine's flowing hand tell us that Porchey played polo at the Ezra Cup in Calcutta, Rajpipla Cup in Bombay and the Subaltern's Cup in Meerut. There is a snapshot of Porchey and his three teammates dressed in their striped colours and bright white jodhpurs, on horseback, sticks held easily upright in their right hands. In one photo, presumably taken at a picnic, an Indian boy of perhaps fourteen stares straight at the camera, bare-legged, as two Englishmen in jodhpurs and pith helmets lean over a fire on which a pan of water boils. They seem to be supervising the making of tea.

Catherine appears in some pictures, always with a parasol and a hat, a spectator at endless polo games. She rode herself, of course, and is seated side-saddle in one shot, as Porchey holds her horse's head. In another photo he has his arm around her waist and the two of them stare at the camera with the air of people who are not yet accustomed to having snapshots taken together. It is noticeable that when he stands alongside his wife, his face is habitually set in a firm and serious expression, as if he were feeling the weight of his responsibility as a husband. With his friends he seems more at ease, pipe clamped between grinning teeth. Catherine sometimes smiles tentatively.

For all the luxury and gaiety, it must have been a challenge for her—all that heat and new people and new customs. The wife of a soldier stationed abroad is forced into a small world, with other military families for most of her company.

The wife of a British Army officer in India in 1923 was further isolated from her surroundings by class, caste and the full weight of the Empire. Barely had Catherine started to get used to it when Porchey had to rush to his father's sickbed. Ten anxious days later her husband's telegram confirmed her worst fears and told her she had a new name, a new role and a new home. Catherine consoled herself with the thought that she would soon see her beloved mother, Gar, and her sister Philippa. She had missed them both terribly and now, more than ever, she longed to have her family around her.

On a sunny day in August 1923, four months after the 5th Earl's death, the new Countess of Carnarvon sat in the Morning Room at Highclere enjoying a moment of calm. It was a lovely pale pink room with delicate plasterwork on the ceiling, the smallest and cosiest on the ground floor. Catherine loved it, and had already started to call it her 'sitting room'. She typically spent the first couple of hours each day there, sitting on one of the comfortable sofas writing letters and planning or revising the day's meals. The only worry that morning was that her cook, Mrs Oram, had just handed in her notice. She would write to Mrs Hunt's agency for domestic staff and ask them to interview some candidates.

Catherine crossed to the corner of the room and pulled the bell, which was connected to the bell board on the wall of the staff hallway. Downstairs a red disc appeared, identifying the room in question, and the steward's room boy, Marceau, ran off at high speed to find a footman. When Charles appeared she asked him to please bring some coffee. She wanted to finish the most urgent correspondence before her mother and Philippa, who had come to stay, joined her.

Though there was probably no real hurry. Her mother in particular had never been the earliest riser.

Catherine finished her letters and began pasting wedding photos and letters into her personal scrapbook. The heavy, leather-bound album was embossed with the letters CP for 'Catherine Porchester' and had been a gift after her wedding. Now, since her husband's succession, the initials were no longer correct; not that it mattered very much. She looked up as the door opened and her sister appeared.

Philippa was in high spirits since she had recently become engaged to Randolph, the 12th Earl of Galloway. Her wedding was to be in October. The sisters spent a happy hour looking at photos before their mother's arrival necessitated the ordering of more coffee. Gar was beaming, thrilled for both her daughters.

Philippa reported that Reggie had disappeared with Porchey straight after breakfast. As a single lady she had taken her breakfast in the Dining Room with the gentlemen, while both Catherine and Gar had theirs in bed on a tray. 'They've probably gone out for a ride,' said Catherine, with a smile. 'Or perhaps some golf. Just look at this beautiful day.'

Reggie's wit and sunny personality had instantly endeared him to his brother-in-law. Catherine was delighted by their firm friendship. She had detected her older brother Jac's reticence about Porchey, and suspected that so had her husband. Reggie and Porchey, by contrast, enjoyed a warm and easy-going banter that somehow tied everyone closer together and made her love them both even more.

Catherine balanced the album on an embroidered footstool and sorted some clippings into date order as Marian handed them to her. The first dozen or so pages were already full of pieces from both the British and American press covering her engagement and marriage. She had been intending for months to add the many letters of congratulation, but she hadn't got round to finishing the task in the whirl before her departure for India, and since her return she had been far too busy, mostly with more melancholy occupations. Now she wanted to remember, and look forward to, more joyful times.

The last few months had seen such frenzied activity. In the immediate aftermath of Lord Carnarvon's death, Catherine, Evelyn and Porchey had dashed back from India and Egypt to Britain while Almina and Dr Johnnie returned with the 5th Earl's body. It was a sad homecoming for everyone, but for Porchey, Almina and Evelyn, there was at least the distraction of a million things to do. Lord Carnarvon had stipulated that he should be buried quietly, at a private ceremony on Beacon Hill, the site of an Iron Age fort and the highest point on the Highclere estate. The family was determined to carry out his wishes but it had to contend with the enormous public interest that his new fame had brought.

In the first couple of days after her return to Highclere, Catherine felt useless, unsure what she could do to help. She was now technically the Countess, mistress of the house, but in reality she was still very much the new girl. Unlike her mother-in-law, who had arrived as a nineteen-year-old newly-wed having visited only once, Catherine did at least know the house and its staff a little, having lived there. But that had been in very different circumstances. No one had expected her to assume any responsibility. Almina was then the chatelaine of Highclere and she had been running it for twenty-seven years, through peacetime and war, giving children's parties for 500, establishing a hospital, organising weekend house parties for royalty. She could have done it in her sleep. There was no particular need to prepare Catherine for the role. If she thought of it at all prior to the 5th Earl's death, Almina must have concluded that she would be at Highclere for many years yet, and Catherine, who had been raised in the expectation that she would manage a much smaller household, would be able to learn its ways by observing them.

The two women were in many respects not at all alike. Almina was a powerful personality with boundless energy for getting things done. Catherine was far more diffident by nature, with the sort of quiet strength that did not announce itself. She was gregarious among her friends, but she adapted to her surroundings rather than imposing herself upon them.

Fortunately, she had her sister-in-law by her side. Despite Eve's overwhelming grief for the father she adored, she was conscious that Catherine needed a guiding hand. Highclere was Eve's home; she had never had any other. She had known Streatfield all her life, as well as a succession of housekeepers. She assured Catherine that the senior staff were more than capable of keeping everything under control and that it was not a time for worrying about the niceties. When Porchey came down from London, he heartily agreed.

Catherine decided that, for now, her greatest possible contribution was to support her husband. She was experienced enough in the ways of grief to know that he had a uniquely heavy burden. Almina and Evelyn were devastated by their loss, but they had at least enjoyed a loving relationship with Lord Carnarvon; for Porchey it was more complex. He had just lost the opportunity to build an adult relationship with his father that might have consoled them both for their lack of closeness throughout Porchey's childhood and adolescence.

On 30 April, the Earl's coffin was conveyed by army

ambulance from the family chapel to the summit of Beacon Hill. He received the simple ceremony he had wanted, despite the *Daily Express*'s biplane circling overhead, a photographer leaning out perilously.

Standing by the grave, Catherine could see that Porchey was exhausted. They still had to face the memorial service for family, friends and staff at Highclere in two days' time, and then the larger service, open to all, at St Margaret's Westminster, which Almina had arranged for the following week. The 5th Earl's funeral had been conducted exactly in accordance with his wishes, but the man was now a national hero and there were thousands who wished to pay their last respects.

At some point amidst all the worry over Lord Carnarvon's illness, grief at his passing and the pressures of their new reality, something wonderful happened for Porchey and Catherine. She became pregnant. Porchey told her in no uncertain terms that she must stop fussing over him and rest up herself. By the time her mother and sister came to visit Highclere in August, Catherine was blooming, and the Carnarvon and Wendell families had the best possible news to cherish. Nothing could have been a better distraction from their sorrows than a baby's imminent arrival.

The new Earl of Carnarvon had an additional burden: debt. After the burial ceremony on Beacon Hill, Porchey went up to the City of London to see J. R. H. Mullony, the family solicitor, and then to meet with his trustees, who were led by Sir Edward Marshall Hall. Porchey had never really given much thought to his inheritance but he had rather assumed that he would inherit not merely Highclere but the capital to run it. One short afternoon disabused him of all such pleasant notions. Sir Edward informed him that he had no money and he would probably lose Highclere.

'I'm afraid the estate cannot possibly be retained as it is, not with death duties amounting to half a million pounds,' said Sir Edward. 'Highclere will have to go. You can sell off the land, buy a smaller house somewhere.'

Porchey could only stare. Half a million pounds, a sum equivalent to approximately £25 million in today's money.

In a desperately sombre mood he returned to Highclere, turning over and over the question of how the house could be saved. He loved it and could not conceive of losing it, of being the Carnarvon who let the estate be broken up, the great house sold.

Catherine and Eve were both there to meet him. Eve had grown up at Highclere with her brother and understood instinctively how he felt. 'How am I to survive?' he asked. 'How am I to keep our home?'

'By all means possible,' Eve replied.

Low in morale, he knew the one person who could help him was his mother. But Almina was preparing to leave Highclere and was busy going round the castle putting stickers with 'AC' on all her furniture and *objets d'art*, most of which had been given to her by her father, Alfred de Rothschild. She intended to leave some of her china and chairs behind. Porchey couldn't help feeling resentful of her no-nonsense approach and injured by the fact that his father had left her the outstanding and very valuable Egyptian collection and all his racehorses at the stud.

Porchey began by cutting his expenses. Streatfield was infinitely helpful as they discussed ways to trim the household budget, and Lord Carnarvon appreciated the loyalty, even as he hated having to have the conversation.

Porchey could not resolve the question of how to raise the cash he needed without his mother's help, but she was preoccupied with deciding where to live and how to arrange her new life. It didn't seem the right moment to discuss things with her. Porchey decided to speak to her in a couple of months, when they were all feeling less raw.

That summer saw the first of many house parties that Catherine and Porchey gave at Highclere. Porchey in particular was an inherently sociable creature and, despite the sadness and turmoil of the previous few months and the worries over money, they were both young, in love, expecting their first child, and had just come into possession of one of the finest country houses in the realm. One imagines that at some point they must have decided it was time to enjoy themselves a little. The visitors' book records that twelve people stayed for a week, from 9 to 16 July. One of them was their dear friend Prince George, whom they called PG.

Twenty-seven years earlier, in 1896, Almina had earned her reputation as a gracious hostess and cemented her arrival at the height of British society when the Prince of Wales, the future king Edward VII, attended a shooting weekend at Highclere. That visit had been an extraordinary display of the power of wealth. Almina spent the equivalent of £150,000 on new silk wallpapers for his bedroom, on lobsters and wines and confectionery all brought down from London. It was an occasion of precise formality. Almina had displayed an absolute determination that every single detail be a credit to her and to her husband, the 5th Earl.

The party in 1923 was a very different affair. Prince George was not a distant figure with the power to bestow or withhold approval; he was a personal friend. In addition, the 6th Countess had infinitely less to prove than her predecessor. There was nothing like the same need to impress.

Besides, the world had changed. Five years after the end of the Great War, the Labour Party had already overtaken the Liberal Party as the main opposition to the Conservatives and would form a minority government the following year. After years of campaigning by the suffragettes and their supporters, women over the age of thirty had been granted the vote in 1918, though they would have to wait until 1928 to be enfranchised to the same extent as men. Lady Astor, the second woman elected to the British Parliament, and the first to take up her seat, had been sitting in the House of Commons since the end of 1919.

At Highclere, there were no such obviously radical transformations. The house was still a community that depended on a symbiosis between employer and employee. But if the class distinctions that underpinned this relationship were as carefully observed as ever within the working environment, there had nevertheless been a shift in a broader, societal sense. Upstairs, people still spent their days strolling in the park, chatting, reading a book in the Library, playing golf or planning the future of the stud, depending on their sex. Everyone dressed for dinner, the ladies retired afterwards, the gentlemen joined them in the Drawing Room once port and cigars had been consumed and, like as not, a few hands of bridge would be played. The economics that underpinned Highclere had changed, though. The house was no longer purely a symbol of the leisured class. It needed to earn its own way, and Porchey's plottings over the future of the stud were part of his plan to make sure it did. Even the easy friendship between Catherine (Anglo-American, respectably upper-middle class) and Prince George (fifth in line to the throne at his birth), which predated her elevation to the rank of Countess, spoke of a very different world from the one in which Almina had operated.

Downstairs, things were different, too. In 1891, four years before Almina became Countess of Carnarvon, approximately 41 per cent of British women who worked were employed in domestic service, and in areas where there was no factory work available, that percentage rose considerably. By 1923 domestic service was one of several options available to young working-class women, who were increasingly aiming at nursing or clerical work. It would be misleading to suggest that there had been any kind of revolution; even in 1931, domestic service was still by far the largest single sector of women's employment, at 24 per cent. But many women and men alike had fought and worked throughout the war, on the battlefield, in hospitals and munitions factories. They had a greater sense of their own capabilities, their personal identity—and their class identity—than ever before. There was more access to education, and national insurance was increasingly available to cover unemployment or sickness (though domestic servants were not entitled to receive any benefits until 1938). There was a real power shift occurring, and though its ripples were gentle at Highclere, everyone felt them.

Those attending the July house party, meanwhile, spent a very happy week enjoying new amusements as well as old ones. A gramophone had been purchased, for the playing of records by the American bands that were becoming as popular in Britain as they were in the States. The modern world, with its increased freedom of social mobility and relaxation of old customs, was creating its first soundtrack. Isham Jones and his Orchestra, who toured the UK in 1924, or Paul Whiteman, the 'King of Jazz', who commissioned Gershwin to compose 'Rhapsody in Blue' in the same year, made music that fused early jazz with classically inspired popular song. There was an 'anything goes' spirit creeping in, and fun to be had. Highclere wasn't yet quite swapping dinner and conversation for cocktails and dancing, but now the sounds of

Miss Catherine Wendell on her engagement.

Catherine's father, Jacob Wendell.

Catherine's mother, Marian Fendall Wendell.

Catherine with siblings. Left right: Jac, Regg Catherine, a Philip

Catherine and her sister Philippa were very close.

Catherine's birthplace – Willowbank, in Maine.

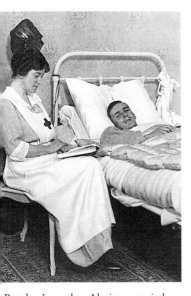

Porchey's mother Almina married the Earl in 1895. She is pictured here nursing a wounded soldier during World War One, when Highclere Castle was used as a hospital.

The Fifth Earl of Carnarvon, Egyptologist, discovered the tomb of Tutankhamun, November 1922.

Highclere Castle was designed by the architect Sir Charles Barry, who also designed and rebuilt the Houses of Parliament during the same decades. The first stone to mark the transformation from the Georgian house was laid in 1842.

Catherine was a renowned beauty.

The invitation
to the wedding
of Catherine
and Lord
Porchester.

Mrs Wendell

requests the pleasure of

Company at the marriage
of her daughter
Catherine
to
Lord Porchester,
7th (Queens Own) Hussars,
at St Margarets, Westminster,
on Monday, July 17th
at 12 o'clock,
and afterwards at
31, Grosvenor Square.

R.S.V.P to

Sandridgebury,
Sandridge,
Hertfordshire.

Catherine's bridesmaids, caught in a gust of wind.

Catherine arriving at St Margaret's Church, where Lady Almina was married 27 years earlier.

Catherine surrounded by her bridesmaids and, standing at the back left to right, her husband Lord Porchester, Mr Thomas Frost (best man) and HRH Prince George.

Lord Porchester having triumphed at polo in India, in 1923. The players are:
Moorhead, Porchester, Sheppard and Byass who played for the Ezra Cup (Calcutta
the Rajpipla Cup (Bombay) and for the Subaltern's Cup in Meerut.

Bronx Hall, their bungalow in Mhow.

Catherine and Porchey enjoyed the life of the British Raj as newlyweds in India, enjoying picnics and the round of the social life with their friends.

FINAL NIGHT EDN.

PALL MALL
GAZETTE AND GLOBE
London's Most Influential Evening Paper.

THURSDAY, APRIL 5, 1923.

ONE PENNY.

LORD CARNARVON'S FATE.

EXPERTS AND A LUXOR "POISON TRAP."

SUPERSTITIOUS BELIEFS RIDICULED BY WELL-KNOWN EGYPTOLOGISTS.

TRAGEDY OF HIS DEATH.

EARL WHO FOUND TUTANKHAMEN'S TOMB, BUT NEVER SAW THE MUMMY.

THE NEW LORD AND LADY CARNARVON

LORD CARNARVON'S LAST HOURS.

PEACEFUL END.

CHEAPER BEER

ACTION BY CHANCELLOR AND BREWERS.

2d. A PINT OFF.

NOVELIST AND CHILD.

PATHOS AT INQUEST ON FATHER.

"SHE WAS TAKEN AWAY."

THE GIRL'S CHOICE

NO THOUGHT OF "VENGEANCE."

Lord Carnarvon's tragic death so soon after discovering the tomb of Tutankhamun in 1923 shocked the world.

Lord and Lady Porchester walking through the Monks'
Garden at Highclere whilst on their honeymoon.

jazz drifted from the open doors of the Drawing Room on a summer evening, mingling with the smoke from the ladies' cigarettes as well as the gentlemen's.

To complete the happier mood, Eve announced in late August that she was planning to marry Sir Brograve Beauchamp, a great friend of hers who had been a constant visitor to Highclere over the previous couple of years. He was very much liked by the entire family, who were charmed equally by his evident adoration of Eve and his comically out-of-tune renditions of 'God Save the King'. The wedding was set for October.

Nineteen twenty-three was a year of transition at Highclere, and the summer was not without its dramas. Aubrey Herbert, on whom Porchey had been sent to keep an eye in Constantinople, had been prevented from travelling to attend his brother the 5th Earl of Carnarvon's funeral by chronically bad health. He had always been delicate, with severely restricted sight from his late teens. Now his eyesight was failing completely.

In July, he and his wife Mary made their way from their villa in Italy to Highclere to join the house party. Despite his sufferings he was excellent company, amusing everyone, as always, with his tales. Aubrey was inclined to dress as a tramp when he was travelling, and counted T. E. Lawrence as one of his friends. He had plenty of stories to tell.

Just two months later, Aubrey's eccentricities and strong propensity to follow his own path proved fatal. A disastrously ill-advised operation to remove his teeth, which a quack doctor promised would restore his sight, triggered a physical collapse. It transpired that Aubrey had a duodenal ulcer and, within days, poison flooded his weakened system. In late September he succumbed to septicaemia. Not even the combined nursing skills of his mother and Almina could save him. He was just forty-three when he died, and left behind his wife and four children. The Carnarvons lost two brothers within the space of four months, both to infections of the blood that today would be cured by a simple course of penicillin.

Eve's wedding, in October, was welcome indeed. She and Sir Brograve were married at St Margaret's Westminster, as Carnarvon family protocol demanded. Catherine was six months' pregnant as she watched her husband stand in the spot where she and he had stood the year before. The 6th Earl of Carnarvon gave his younger sister away, just as Jac had stood in for their father at Catherine's wedding. The child that Catherine was carrying would have no grandfather, but in all other respects, she must have felt that he or she would be fortunate indeed.

For Catherine, as for Almina before her, there was nothing so guaranteed to solidify her position, and her confidence, as bearing a child. A son, an heir, would be preferred. As an American, Catherine had been born into a system in which children of either sex could inherit; the system of male primogeniture was not a feature of North American law. Having lived in London for twelve years she had become familiar with the comparatively archaic practice of passing titles, land and estates exclusively through the male line. Since she had spent the previous six months observing the inevitable entanglements of what was in fact a straightforward succession, she must have been conscious that the whole thing would have been much worse in the absence of a clear heir.

Catherine's pregnancy lent extra urgency to the question of how to raise the money to settle the death duties. Almina, however, seemed to be distancing herself from Highclere and devoting herself to other people at a perilous time for her son and his heritage. Porchey was desperately upset but Eve managed to restrain him from saying anything too impetuous.

It wasn't just about the money, though. Porchey's resentment of his mother had crystallised over the previous few months in response to what he considered an enormous betrayal. Shortly after the 5th Earl's death, Almina had been introduced to Lieutenant Colonel Ian Dennistoun. The relationship progressed quickly. In November 1923, Lord Carnarvon learned that Almina intended to marry Dennistoun. Carnarvon made it plain that he regarded her remarriage as unwise and unseemly. The two of them were barely speaking.

Almina was sorry for the rupture with her son, especially as it formed the final upset in a long year of losses and emotional turbulence. She had never been minded to worry too much what other people thought, though, and she trusted that, with Catherine and Eve's soothing, he would eventually come round.

Almina, Countess of Carnarvon married Lieutenant Colonel Ian Dennistoun in December 1923 with a simple ceremony at a London register office; the only people in attendance were the loyal Eve and Brograve. Nowadays people might remark upon the alacrity, as her son did at the time—just eight months after her first husband's death—but those were different times. For many people who had lived through the Great War, when a few short weeks or even days or hours might be all the time that was left to you before some crushing loss, life was to be relished. Joys should not be postponed. Besides, Almina, for all her charisma and energy, was not equipped for self-sufficiency. She seems to have found in Ian Dennistoun both companionship and a focus for the next phase of her life.

Ian was kind, charming and a support to Almina in her

bereavement, but he was also chronically short of money and was not a well man: he had broken his hip in the war and was wheelchair-bound. For her, this was very probably all part of the appeal. Nursing him reconnected Almina to her wartime experience of running a hospital, which had been the most fulfilling work of her life. Almina was a woman who thrived when she had a project, a woman who needed to be needed, and now here was a kind man whose needs she delighted in trying to meet.

Ironically, given everything that would happen later, Almina and Ian were introduced by Dorothy, Ian's ex-wife, who was a great friend of Almina's. The women had met on 29 November 1920, having rushed to the bedside of a grievously sick mutual friend. Lieutenant General Sir John Cowans had been Quartermaster-General to the Forces throughout the Great War and was a lifelong visitor to Highclere. When he died, in April 1921, he was given a military funeral funded by the state, in recognition of his exceptional service. But, as would subsequently become clear, the war hero had been having numerous affairs, and one of his mistresses had been Dorothy.

Not that Almina had any inkling of this when she and Dorothy struck up a friendship. As far as she was concerned, her friend had been separated from her husband for years, though they remained on speaking terms, and lived a quiet and blame-free life. Before long the two women were inseparable. Dorothy, who was living in very reduced circumstances, was always at Highclere, keen to enjoy the Carnarvons' hospitality. Long before Almina became embroiled in Ian's financial woes, she had become very familiar with Dorothy's.

The Dennistouns divorced in March 1921. Dorothy was persuaded to accept that Ian was in no position to pay her back for various loans, or to pay out for her ongoing upkeep.

He simply didn't have the funds. But an informal agreement was apparently made that, should his financial circumstances alter for the better, he would compensate Dorothy. They seem to have been one of those couples that, having finally resolved the crisis of their failed marriage, were able to behave far more civilly towards one another. They began to see each other socially. In 1923, Dorothy introduced him to her friend and benefactor.

Eight months later, Ian's circumstances did indeed alter, very much for the better, when he married Almina. Dorothy, who had spent so much time at Highclere, was in the perfect position to gauge the implications for her ex-husband's finances, and her own. The fact was, neither Dennistoun had a penny. Almina never cared about such things: she was in a position to be generous to a fault, first to her friend and later to her new husband. But it would turn out to be a serious problem when the emotional dynamics shifted.

Almina's second wedding was sandwiched between Ian's divorce and his ex-wife's subsequent claim for alimony. It was hardly a propitious beginning. The couple—and by extension all the new inhabitants of Highclere—would shortly have to endure their names and reputations being dragged through the law courts in one of the most notorious high-society scandals of the 1920s. The saga would seal the freeze on relations between Almina and Porchey for several years.

That Christmas, as Eve and Brograve joined a party at Highclere, Almina and Ian spent a quiet holiday at their new home in Scotland. Ultimately, it wasn't Porchey's disapproval they needed to worry about; it was Dorothy's determination to extract her dues.

For Catherine and Porchey, the Christmas and New Year of 1923 were their first as Lord and Lady Carnarvon. They had the imminent birth of their first child to celebrate, and were looking forward to marking the festivities in their new home. There was a great deal to feel thankful for, but it had also been an exhausting year of extremes and Catherine especially was feeling tired. They invited a small group of old friends and family and were just ten for Christmas.

It was to be Streatfield's last hurrah. He had worked for the Carnarvons at Highclere for nearly forty years, during which time he had served three generations of the family. When he began his service as House Steward, in 1887, the 4th Earl was Secretary of State for the Colonies in Lord Salisbury's government and Queen Victoria had another fourteen years to reign. Streatfield had devoted his life to ensuring the prestige of Highclere Castle and the wellbeing of the family that lived there. He had outlasted a great many of them but now it was time to step down and let George Fearnside, formerly the 5th Earl's valet, take over. His last task before he went was to help the new Lady Carnarvon allocate rooms, plan menus and decorations and organise the traditional local children's tea party on New Year's Eve.

The house looked and smelt beautiful. The Drawing Room, Dining Room, Library and Catherine's sitting room were decked with holly and ivy that the gardeners had cut from Highclere's woods. Catherine had arranged it on mantelpieces and directed housemaids to use it to festoon mirrors and bookshelves. There were pine cones to burn in the fireplaces for their fresh scent and, down in the kitchens, the cook and the kitchen maids had been baking and preserving, mulling wine and potting game. The days running up to Christmas Eve were flavoured with tempting aromas of cloves and cinnamon, sage and juniper drifting from the back staircase used by the servants.

The centrepiece was the Christmas tree. Workers from the estate's forestry department had felled a pine tree and brought it to stand, well over eighteen feet tall, in the Saloon, festooned with glass baubles and piled round about with presents for the local children.

Catherine had felt a moment's doubt about maintaining Almina's tradition of the children's party. With her pregnancy so advanced and the intention being to have a quiet family Christmas, she wasn't sure she was up to hosting an event for 500 children. In the end, she resolved to lean on Streatfield for assistance with logistics and Porchey for help on the afternoon itself. He was enthusiastic. Continuity of tradition was important to him and he knew that it was essential to Highclere's position as the centre of a community that such occasions be upheld. It would involve clamour and chaos, but it would be good fun.

Arthur Portman, a friend of Porchey's from the racing world, arrived with his wife on the 22nd of December, but neither they nor anyone else from the upstairs world were invited to the social occasion that took place on the following night. Every year one of the houses in the local area took their turn to host a dance for all the staff of the nearby establishments. There was beer and food and dancing, and a chance to meet with friends or make new ones. The parties tended to go on late—so late, in fact, that the housemaids, who got up before anyone else to light the fires in the kitchen and bedrooms, often went without sleep altogether. That year the party was being held at one of the neighbouring houses. The maids set out a cold buffet and some tureens of soup in the Dining Room, and then the entire household staff left the Carnarvons to their own devices and headed off to enjoy their Christmas.

On Christmas Eve, the house party assembled. There

might have been just eight house guests, but that also meant an additional quota of servants. The household had effectively doubled in size overnight. On Christmas Day, once a leisurely breakfast was completed, Porchey helped his wife into the Rolls-Royce Silver Ghost to make the short trip to attend church. Their guests either piled into their own motorcars or walked through the park, past the cricket pitch and into Highclere village. Practically the entire congregation depended upon the Castle to some degree. Catherine and Porchey received endless congratulations and well-wishes before making their way home. After an excellent lunch of turkey and all the trimmings, there was coffee in the Drawing Room and a walk or a rest, before charades in the Library in the evening, in front of the Christmas tree. On Boxing Day, Porchey, Tommy and various others went out for a day's shooting and then the following day their guests took their leave, full of praise for the wonderfully relaxing visit they had enjoyed. It had all gone just as Catherine had hoped. Now, not even the prospect of the children's party could faze her. She was marking time, waiting for her baby to be born. She prayed that 1924, in contrast to 1923, would be a peaceful and joyous year.

5

The Heir Is Christened

On 19 January 1924 Catherine was safely delivered of a healthy baby boy. He was named Henry (for his father) George (for both his late grandfather and his godfather) Reginald (for his uncle, Catherine's beloved brother and Porchey's great friend) Molyneux (a family surname).

An ecstatic Porchey declared he had won the champagne stakes and telephoned the news to Eve and Brograve, Almina at Seamore Place and to Fearnside, newly installed as house steward, so that he could inform all the staff at Highclere. All trace of rancour between Porchey and Almina was temporarily set aside amidst the general rejoicing.

Catherine and Porchey had been in town since the beginning of January, staying in a house in Mayfair they had taken for the duration of Catherine's confinement. Dr Johnnie, Almina's friend and colleague, spent Christmas at

Highclere in order to be on the spot just in case. Once the New Year's celebrations were concluded, Catherine was anxious to travel while she still could, conscious that her baby might arrive at any moment. She had asked her mother to come to stay with her.

Porchey consulted Dr Johnnie, whom he had known all his life, on the engagement of nurses and doctors to attend Catherine. He also asked his mother and sister for their thoughts. Both Almina and Eve suggested Dr William Gilliatt, a renowned gynaecologist and obstetrician whom Almina had met as a result of her nursing work. Dr Johnnie concurred. Catherine had experienced no problems during pregnancy but, naturally, both she and Porchey were apprehensive.

Quite aside from the nerves common to all first-time parents, the fact was that childbirth in the 1920s was almost as risky for the mother (though not for the child) as it had been when Queen Victoria had ascended the throne in 1837. It wasn't until the mid-1930s that maternal mortality began to decline dramatically, due principally to the rigorous use of antiseptics, which massively reduced the risk of puerperal fever, the greatest cause of death in childbirth.

Counter-intuitively, an upper-class woman in Britain in the 1920s and 1930s was more at risk of dying during childbirth than a working-class one. She was typically attended by a physician, who tended to advocate more interventionist methods that carried greater risk of infection, rather than a midwife, who from the 1920s onwards had increasingly received excellent specialist training in obstetrics, and favoured natural birth.

Fortunately, the birth went smoothly, and she and Porchey were jubilant over the arrival of their son. Two days later, Catherine began to receive visits from family and close friends. She had been advised by her doctor to take at least ten days of complete bed rest, so Doll ushered the visitors into Catherine's bedroom. Doll was kept very busy bringing in the endless flowers and messages of congratulation, and liaising with nurses and the temporary household staff. Philippa and Eve were constantly at the house, enchanted with the baby and eager to help. Porchey, one suspects, probably availed himself of the opportunity to slip away to his favourite club, the Portland, to celebrate with friends over brandy, cigars and a game of bridge.

After the customary period of lying-in, Catherine was eager to return to Highclere. The bustle of well-wishers was joyous but also tiring, and she was longing for the peace of what she now thought of as home. All her married life, Catherine preferred to be at Highclere rather than in town.

At the end of February, Lord and Lady Carnarvon set off with the new Lord Porchester. They arrived at Highclere to a repetition of the chorus of delight they had left behind, from friends, neighbours, tenants and employees alike. For the many staff who had given years of service, this birth was an occasion for sincere happiness. For everyone, downstairs as well as up, the significance of His Lordship's arrival was clear. The world was changing at a pace, but even so, the birth of a healthy baby boy was hugely significant when a complex succession could still feel as tortuous as a medieval saga.

Highclere and its inhabitants were far more modern than, say, the fabulously wealthy Earls Fitzwilliam at Wentworth House in south Yorkshire, who cultivated the lifestyle of a feudal clan. It was the Fitzwilliams' custom to celebrate the arrival of an heir with a spectacular party for their tens of thousands of tenants and employees. They spurned such luxuries as electricity and sanitation well into the twentieth century and were still squabbling over the 1902 succession of the 7th Earl seventy years after the event. Such lavish melodrama was quite alien to Porchey and Catherine, but there was still a whiff of the seigneurial about the summoning of the staff to the Library to receive at Lord Carnarvon's hand a drawstring purse containing a gold sovereign, in honour of his son and heir. One maid recalled that 'we all had to have spotlessly clean aprons. We were to say, "thank you my lord," curtsey and go.'

Porchey was very much in favour of maintaining such traditions. In many ways he was a moderniser in his social circle and his personal habits, a man who all his life enjoyed the company of fun-loving, easy-going people, be they duchesses or actors, but he also took his responsibilities seriously. Some aspects of communal life at Highclere were just the same as they had been for generations, and this was a moment heavy with the symbolism of many centuries. For the outside staff, it was the first time they had been in the house, and for the kitchen and scullery maids, it was the first time they had been upstairs. Old-fashioned the gesture might have been, but doubtless the generosity was very welcome.

Lord Porchester was christened on Easter Sunday, 20 April, in Highclere Church, which sits just outside the gates to the western side of the estate. It is a beautiful Victorian Gothic building of flint and brick. The 4th Earl of Carnarvon commissioned Sir Gilbert Scott to design it as the rather larger replacement for the succession of churches that had stood next to the mansion at Highclere since medieval times. Sir Charles Barry and later Thomas Allom had already created the soaring castle but were both undecided on how to redesign the church to complement the new style of architecture. Barry died in 1860 and the 4th Earl then took the simpler option of constructing a wholly separate Highclere Church.

Spring sunlight filtered through the stained-glass windows and the building smelled of narcissi and apple blossom. It was already filled to overflowing with the congregation, a sea of neat hats and happy chatter.

The first car to leave for the church contained Lady Evelyn and Sir Brograve Beauchamp, Reggie and Philippa Wendell and Dr Johnnie. Catherine followed in the Rolls-Royce, with her mother and husband. The ubiquitous press reports tell us that she was wearing a 'crepe marocain in a delicate shade of fuschia' while her mother wore a 'smart black and white charmeuse'.

Following tradition, Lord Porchester was to travel in the arms of his nanny, Mrs Sambell, driven by the coachman in the gleaming phaeton. The baby was dressed in the ivory satin christening gown that had been used for both his father and grandfather; the garment had lain carefully wrapped in tissue paper in a trunk since its last outing, a generation previously, at Eve's christening.

The happy parents stepped out of the car to waiting photographers from the London papers and the local *Newbury Weekly News*. There was no sign of the phaeton. They waited for a few minutes and then, slightly worried, had just asked Trotman the chauffeur to return with the car to look for it when they arrived, the pony trotting smartly through the church gates. 'Sergeant Cass, the gallant police officer from Kingsclere' assisted Mrs Sambell and Lord Porchester's safe descent from the little carriage.

The service was conducted by the Reverend Isaac James. HRH Prince George had delighted Porchey and Catherine by agreeing to stand as godfather, though Reggie Wendell had to deputise for him when he was held up at a function at Windsor Castle and arrived just as the ceremony was finishing. Marian Wendell acted as proxy for Almina, in her role as godmother. Ian was too unwell to be left alone so she did not attend the ceremony, though she sent a very warm telegram of congratulations. Afterwards a large part of the congregation made for the house and drank Lord

Porchester's health in some of the finest vintages that Highclere's cellars could provide.

The focus of the event, meanwhile, was laid in the elaborate cradle in which his father and grandfather had slept before him. The nursery was on the second floor, a comfortable series of rooms comprising day and night nurseries, and a bed-sitting room for Mrs Sambell. Catherine had undertaken refurbishments between shooting weekends and house parties during the autumn of the previous year, so the wallpaper was fresh, as were the blankets and quilts and piles of baby clothes. Maud Stratford, the night watchman's daughter, was taken on as nursemaid.

Catherine's album contains a series of photos of her and the infant Lord Porchester, taken to celebrate his birth and published, as was now customary for any significant event in her life, by the press on both sides of the Atlantic. In one, she is shot in profile, gazing down at her child, who lies on what appears to be a white rug. They almost fill the photo frame. She is wearing a white fur stole and pearls and a white satin evening gown and looks impossibly glamorous, like the 1920s equivalent of today's Hollywood goddesses, back in slinky shape just weeks after the birth of their children.

January 1924 was momentous for the country as a whole, as well as for the Carnarvons. There had been a general election in December of 1923, called by Stanley Baldwin, the Conservative Prime Minister, who was effectively seeking a referendum for his controversial protectionist policy. He had assumed the position of PM after the sudden death in May 1923 of the sitting Prime Minister, Andrew Bonar Law, who, though also a Conservative, had held the opposite view on the vexed question of whether or not to reform Britain's trade laws. Stanley Baldwin felt it was essential to ask the electorate for its support rather than plunge into a policy for which he had no mandate. The result was the loss of its majority of seats for the Conservative Party, and a collapse among the Liberal vote from which the political descendants of the venerable Whigs never recovered.

The precursor of the modern Labour Party had been founded in 1900 at a conference in Farringdon Street, London, which brought together left-wing organisations to sponsor Parliamentary candidates. It was now the second-largest presence in the House of Commons. When it became clear that there would be a hung parliament, and since Baldwin had suffered a comprehensive defeat and could not therefore credibly continue as Prime Minister, the King sent for the leader of the new opposition. In January, Ramsay MacDonald became the first Labour Prime Minister of Great Britain.

The political scene in the early and mid-1920s very probably struck anxiety into the hearts of Porchey, Catherine and most of the people they knew. As well as the moves towards limited independence for India, the jewel of the British Empire, the Irish Free State Constitution Act had been passed in 1922, granting independence to a dominion that would become, in 1949, the Republic of Ireland. The long and increasingly bloody struggle for Irish Home Rule, independence and full nationhood had taken its crucial turn. For the strong Unionist element in the Conservative Party, it was a betrayal of principle, and a buckling under to terrorism.

Domestic politics was also undergoing a period of significant change. The interests of the landed classes had traditionally been allied with the Conservative Party, whilst commerce had found its representatives among the Liberals. Those distinctions, both between social classes and allegiance to political parties, had in practice been breaking down since the end of the nineteenth century. During the first three decades of the new century there had been periods of considerable fluidity between the Conservatives and Liberals, who at least viewed each other as known quantities. For six years from 1916, there was a coalition government, formed by the centrist wings of the two parties. But the emergence of the Labour Party, which sought to represent the interests of newly enfranchised working men, was a wholly new phenomenon. Some segments of the media and the people regarded the Labour Party as little better than a front for Soviet Russia but there were many, even among the party's political opponents, who could see that its existence was both inevitable and necessary.

Duff Cooper reflected on the emotional mood of the electorate in 1923 in his memoir, written some thirty-five years later. He observed that it was a time not of poverty but of plenty, but only for a very few. He was referring at least as much to those new men who entered the House of Commons on the back of the money they had made during the war, as to the aristocracy. There was a sense in political circles that, in the circumstances, the Labour Party deserved to earn its spurs, despite the fear of revolution that was very real in the wake of events in Russia in 1917. Duff Cooper expressed some slight disappointment that the Labour victory demonstration struck a note of 'respectable middle-class non-conformity' rather than anything more violent. As he says, he ought to have been relieved, and presumably, despite the rhetorical flourish, he was.

On 14 October 1924, Philippa Wendell, Catherine's little sister, married Randolph Algernon Ronald Stewart, 12th Earl of Galloway, at St Margaret's Westminster. The bride and groom had met at Porchey and Catherine's wedding. He was thirteen years older than her. If Jac Wendell had felt a twinge of misgiving about Porchey as a prospective brother-in-law, it was nothing to the outright suspicion with which he regarded Lord Galloway.

The reasons for Jac's unease are not obscure. Quite apart from the age gap, there was the fact that Lord Galloway spent a lot of time in London, where he enjoyed a great many women's company. Jac saw no sign of him giving up the habit. In addition, although the Earls of Galloway are an ancient Scottish family, they had fallen on hard times. They lost their ancestral seat, Galloway House, in 1908, and relocated to what had once been a shooting lodge, Cumloden House, just outside the small market town of Newton Stewart. Of all the Wendell siblings, it had been Jac, as the eldest, who had seen most closely the effect that losing his wealth had on their father. Jacob Wendell's self-reinvention after his bankruptcy was a brave act, but it had come out of a profound crisis. Perhaps Jac had an instinctive older brother's fear that Philippa was exposing herself to a burden she did not really understand.

In any case, the wedding went ahead. Catherine kept a photo taken some months later, of the newly married couple sitting on a garden bench. Philippa is in a striking embroidered blouse that looks like the sort of thing the artist Frida Kahlo would wear. Her strong features and the artful curls on her forehead contribute to the impression of Bohemianism. Her expression is intense, almost smouldering. Lord Galloway is far more conventionally dressed, in a three-piece suit. He looks distinctly pleased with himself, as well he might, given the presence of his beautiful young wife by his side.

By the time her sister married, Catherine was pregnant again and Porchey's debt to the Exchequer now urgently needed to be paid. The trustees had been accurate in their predictions of the sum required. The moment had arrived to take some difficult decisions about what to sell.

There was one particularly tangible and valuable asset, though he was loath to part with it: the famous Carnarvon pearl necklace. It had passed from generation to generation and can be seen adorning the neck of the 1st Lady Carnarvon in her 1638 portrait by Anthony Van Dyck, which still hangs in the Dining Room at Highclere. It pained Porchey greatly to lose the pearls and he felt badly for Catherine, who had worn them only once and would never wear them again. But she was brisk. 'Don't be silly, darling. I don't mind at all and it's so much better than the alternative.' So Porchey's first strategy was to head to Paris. He decided to negotiate in person with Jacques Cartier. In the end he received £55,000 for the necklace, a fantastic sum. Next he sold two farms bordering Highclere and some of the household's better silver; then Bingham, a smaller estate in Nottinghamshire. It was not enough.

Almost in despair, Porchey went to his mother. To his immense relief, she was quite breezy about everything. 'We are in a far more fortunate position than many families, darling. It is simply a matter of deciding which pieces to sell. Of course I am happy to help.' Good as her word, Almina began by gifting Porchey most of the 5th Earl's collection of race-horses. Highclere Stud had been another of the 5th Earl's expensive projects but, unlike Egyptology, was an interest that his son shared. Porchey was already something of an expert and was excited about building up the stud as a source of income. He was consequently very reluctant to sell the horses.

Then Almina announced that she was arranging the sale of her husband's beloved Egyptian collection. Howard Carter would help her catalogue it and it would probably raise the most money if sold to America. The next step would be to hold a sale of works from her father's outstanding collection of paintings and antique furniture. Almina stipulated that Porchey also had to do his bit and should draw up a list of pieces to sell from Highclere. 'Why don't you start by asking Mr Duveen down to give you his opinion?'

6

Saving Highclere

Mr Joseph Duveen was the leading art dealer of the age. He arrived at Highclere on an unseasonably warm day in early November 1924 and was shown into the Library. It was all part of his job to notice that the room was elegantly proportioned, grand but not too imposing, furnished with an exquisite Agra carpet; several magnificent desks, one of which, he knew, was believed to have been Napoleon's, and a pair of exceedingly comfortable-looking red sofas. He suspected that there would be treasures indeed for him to acquire.

Bright autumn sunshine streamed in through the double-height French windows that gave onto one of the finest landscaped parks in England. Mr Duveen admired the prospect of Capability Brown's gently rolling lawns, neo-classical temples, and the stately cedars of Lebanon.

These days Mr Duveen was a businessman before he was an aesthete, but he had a fine feeling and genuine passion for rare books, antiquities and, above all, paintings by the Old Masters. He could not have become as wildly successful as he had without excellent taste as well as sharp instincts.

'A most beautiful room, Lord Carnarvon. A library such as this is the work of generations.'

'Quite so,' responded Porchey. He was sitting, not entirely at his ease, on the matching sofa on the other side of the splendid fireplace, facing his guest. Lord Carnarvon did not particularly relish making small talk with the man who had come to value his family's assets.

The art dealer took the cup of coffee offered to him by Fearnside. 'Will you require anything else, my lord?' the house steward enquired of his employer.

'What do you think, Mr Duveen?' said Lord Carnarvon. 'Do you need anything in particular?'

Mr Duveen returned the delicate bone-china cup to its saucer and placed it on the fine walnut table to his left. His expression had become focused, and he spoke plainly.

'I need a stepladder, a footman to hold it, and a torch.'

Lord Carnarvon looked at Fearnside, who nodded and removed himself to fulfil the request.

'Right,' said Porchey, relieved to be getting to the matter in hand. 'I suggest we start in the Drawing Room.'

By the time of his meeting with Lord Carnarvon, Joseph Duveen had already made a fortune on the back of a simple but powerful observation: 'Europe has a great deal of art and America has a great deal of money.' That had been true even before the First World War; by the mid-Twenties it was infinitely more so. Duveen cultivated the friendship of men like J. P. Morgan, William Randolph Hearst, John D.

Rockefeller and Henry Clay Frick and inspired them with his taste for great art and beautiful things. These magnates might not be dukes or earls, but no matter: the portraits they acquired from the hard-up aristocrats of England had titles aplenty.

In the green silk Drawing Room, Mr Duveen performed another expert initial assessment. Several exceptional portraits, presumably of family, and other paintings by eighteenth-century British artists of the first order that were sure to be of interest to his clients. He congratulated himself on the infallibility of his instincts. He was not above compensating the staff for specific information relating to the quality of artworks and the desperation of their owners to sell, but no such information had been required in this case. Highclere's reputation as a treasure house preceded it, as did the reasonable assumption that its heir was still struggling to raise money to pay death duties. Mr Duveen had observed his host's air of despondency as they drank their coffee.

Eyeglass screwed in firmly, the better to inspect the brush-work in front of him, Mr Duveen wobbled atop the ladder. He squinted closely at the canvas. *The Wood Gatherers* by Sir Joshua Reynolds. 'Shocking state. Needs to be cleaned,' he announced. The art dealer restored and polished his clients' acquisitions in his own studios before he despatched them. The new owners liked to be able to see themselves reflected in the varnished surfaces of the gleaming paintings, and he was happy to oblige.

Charles, the footman holding the ladder, repositioned it for Mr Duveen's next ascent. He had only recently joined the household and his real name was in fact George Widdowes, but by custom (baffling to our minds), all footmen were dubbed Charles, for the convenience of their employers. Widdowes was following the afternoon's events with keen interest. He was also wondering whether he would still have a job in six months' time.

As Fearnside glided into the room to observe the comportment of his new member of staff, Mr Duveen inspected two very large portraits of eighteenth-century Carnarvon ancestors, by Gainsborough. 'Twenty-five thousand pounds for the lady and seventeen thousand for the gentleman,' declared the art dealer. 'Men are never as valuable as ladies, you see.'

Porchey turned away and looked out over the lawns.

'What do you say?' came the dealer's insistent voice from behind him.

'Thank you for coming, Mr Duveen,' he replied. Turning around to shake hands, Porchey was relieved to see that the man had at least descended to floor level to receive his answer. 'I shall leave Fearnside to look after you as you finish up. I'll have to consult my mother to discover her views, but doubtless we will speak very soon.'

Porchey took refuge in the Smoking Room. He could not face Catherine until he had recovered a semblance of his good mood. Mr Duveen's prices were not as high as he had hoped, or as he needed them to be. The dealer clearly had the instincts of a bloodhound, sniffing out a fallen man. His mother had suggested that if Joe Duveen proved unsatisfactory, they should try an auction house; he would have to telephone to Christie's to ask them to send someone down as soon as possible to offer an alternative valuation.

In the event, Mr Duveen didn't directly acquire any of Highclere's artworks. He did, however, negotiate with Almina Lady Carnarvon to purchase three superb full-length Gainsboroughs, two fine Holbein miniatures, a group portrait by Sir Thomas Lawrence and various other works of art from her father's collections.

Christie's, the august Mayfair auction house, was given the greater responsibility for gaining the best results for the Carnarvon family. Almina, who had a gift for what in modern parlance might be called 'creating a buzz', set about generating curiosity and excitement. She also extended a personal invitation to Mr Duveen to attend the auction, which he accepted with alacrity. This was no moment to bewail the fact he had lost out to a rival: the Carnarvon sale was set to be one of the most important of the decade. It included works by da Vinci, Botticelli, Van Dyck, Greuze, Guardi and outstanding paintings by François Boucher, Aelbert Cuyp, Philips Wouwerman and David Teniers. When Duveen, along with thousands of others, crowded into the auction rooms at Christie's in May 1925, he also spotted the works by Gainsborough that he had inspected at Highclere six months previously.

According to *The Times*, the auction house resembled nothing so much as a private view at the Royal Academy; the great press of visitors meant it was nearly impossible to see the treasures. International dealers competed for Sèvres porcelain and fine French furniture. On the third day of the sale, an illuminated Italian missal made for Claude, Queen of France in the early sixteenth century, caused a frenzy of bidding. Alfred de Rothschild had spent his life building up the exquisite collection; now it was being dispersed in order to save Highclere. On 22 May alone, a total of 110 lots raised more than £54,000 (about £16 million in today's money). *The Times* summed up its article by observing that 'the sale has had no parallel in London for many years.'

At the end of it all, when the debt was paid, Porchey and Catherine set about rehanging paintings to replace the ones sold. They brought some dusty relatives out of the attics and redecorated. To their young friends who gathered at Highclere in the years to come, the gaps on the walls would not even be noticeable, though after the 5th Earl's death the house was never again the collection of museum-worthy pieces that it had been. The greater losses were at what was once Alfred de Rothschild's home Seamore Place, though: it was Almina and her Rothschild inheritance that had saved the Carnarvons.

Highclere was safe, but Porchey's relationship with his mother, which had not been easy for some time, was really fraying. So were his nerves. In the aftermath of the sale of the bulk of the Egyptian collection to the Metropolitan Museum in New York, Porchey came across a few pieces that Howard Carter had judged could be left at Highclere. Irritated by this reminder of the 5th Earl's decision to settle so many assets on his wife rather than his heir, Porchey asked Fearnside to have them bundled up and put away at the back of cupboards.

In his more rational moments Porchey knew that his mother had sacrificed a great deal on the family's behalf, but, nevertheless, he struggled with feelings of hurt and disappointment that his father had not left him more secure.

Almina was quick to point out that it had not been deliberate. 'Your father had already begun to implement savings, Porchey, but he couldn't possibly have known how little time he had left to economise.'

Though it was Almina's money that ultimately made the difference between losing the house and not, her son tended throughout his life to lose sight of that fact. Nor had he understood her hasty marriage to Ian Dennistoun. Catherine had none of her husband's prejudices, and in fact remained firm friends with Almina throughout their lives, but she knew she would have to bide her time before she attempted to steer them towards any kind of rapprochement.

As far as Almina was concerned, between them they had secured the future of Highclere: not without sacrifices, but the house was safe and so was the core of the community of people who worked there. True enough, the staff was reduced to a skeleton. Fearnside would only have two footmen, a hall boy and an usher; a chef, two kitchen maids and a scullery maid; five housemaids; an electrician; a night watchman; two chauffeurs; a head groom, two assistant grooms and a stables cook. It would not be as it had been in Almina's day, at least not for a while. But the Carnarvon legacy was more or less intact and, really, Porchey needed to look forward. He had a wife and would soon have two children; he had his whole life ahead of him.

If Almina had been a different sort of woman, she might have observed to her son that the voguish remedy for a British aristocrat who even suspected the state of his finances was to marry a wealthy American girl. Her own marriage had been a love match, but she was not a fool and she knew that her husband had also weighed the value of her vast independent wealth. Porchey, though, had married an American girl with no money to speak of. But quite apart from the fact that Almina loved Catherine, she had supported her son at the time and was not about to change her tune, though neither was she about to absolve Porchey for what she perceived as his lack of gratitude.

7

Life and Death in the Roaring Twenties

Duff Cooper, who was a prolific diary keeper, noted in March 1925 that Porchey had written to tell him that 'the adorable Catherine had presented the new heir with a sister.' Lady Anne Penelope Marian Herbert was born in London on 3 March 1925.

There is a photo taken at Penelope's christening, which was, like her brother's, held at Highclere. A family group stands on the drive that sweeps around the house, as if they have all just stepped out of the French windows to the Library. Catherine holds her daughter, who is dressed in a long white christening gown. Lord Porchester is a bonny baby of fourteen months, also dressed in white and held firmly on the nurse Mrs Sambell's knee. The mood is quite different from the highly staged and glamorous shots of Catherine and her son that were published in the press.

This is a family snapshot. Catherine's hair is immaculately curled in a fashionable Marcel wave, but she is wearing sensible day clothes, and has the proud but slightly harried look of a mother of two children under eighteen months old. By today's standards, Catherine had a huge amount of help in the care of her children, but even so, 1924 and 1925 had been exceptionally busy years.

Once again, Almina did not attend, though she was thrilled at the arrival of her first granddaughter, but Eve and Bro were at Highclere for the service. Eve was five months' pregnant at the time and they were living by then in a small house on Deanery Street next to the Dorchester Hotel, which Almina had gifted them on their marriage. Everyone was hugely excited, especially Eve's mother-in-law Lady Beauchamp, who was thrilled at the prospect of an heir to carry on her husband's name and title.

In July, when the time came for Eve to have her baby, she had no hesitation in engaging William Gilliatt to be in attendance. Almina would be with her, too, a calm, practical presence. But Eve did not have the happy experience that Catherine had. She was eventually delivered of a healthy baby girl, but she had such a difficult labour that she very nearly died. Even Almina's fortitude was stretched to its limit by the long, traumatic birth and the rising sense of panic in the room that Gilliatt could not conceal. When baby Patricia arrived, Almina was euphoric, Eve barely conscious. She rallied at the sight of her daughter, but her recovery was difficult and at the end of it all, Dr Gilliatt told her that she would not be able to have any more children. It was a bitter blow for Eve and Bro, who comforted themselves by lavishing Patricia with love, but even more so for Lady Beauchamp. The baronetcy would end with Brograve.

Porchey was just massively relieved that his beloved sister

had come through her ordeal. He and Catherine, and indeed Eve and Bro, were delighted that Patricia had been born soon after Penelope so that the two girls could grow up more like sisters than cousins. His happiness over the births of his daughter and niece was also a welcome distraction from the tension with his mother. If Almina had hoped that his resentment would quickly die away, subsequent events only conspired to make it worse.

After they were married, Almina and Ian had agreed to pay a number of small sums to Dorothy, Ian's ex-wife and Almina's former friend. But before long she was asking for more and threatening to go public with allegations that Almina had begun a relationship with Ian before the 5th Earl's death. Almina was convinced that Dorothy was black-mailing them, and that the only way to deal with this was to refuse to pay her anything at all. This provoked Dorothy to a rage. In March 1925, she issued a writ for £13,000 and back payment of the support she claimed she had been promised for her quiet compliance with the divorce. The Dennistoun v Dennistoun case exploded in a gory mess of allegation and counter-allegation. Nobody came out of it looking good. Public interest in this sensational 'high-society behaving badly' drama was heightened by the fact that Almina was still particularly in the public eye, thanks to the 5th Earl's discoveries in Egypt, and his subsequent 'mysterious' death. At the first whiff of scandal, the media were in raptures.

Dorothy's claim to Ian's newly acquired assets rested on her assertion that she had played a material part in his promotion through the army to the rank of Lieutenant Colonel. A particularly intimate part, in fact. Dorothy alleged that Ian had insisted she begin an affair with Sir John Cowans, in return for which Sir John would engineer

Ian's ascent. Her husband had, in effect, pimped her out in order to get on.

Naturally Ian denied this, claiming that Dorothy was only looking for a convenient cover-up for her own sexual promiscuity. It was well known that she had numerous lovers all over Europe, he claimed. In exasperation, the trial judge told Ian's lawyer that he would not be allowed to read out a list of the names of these alleged lovers. But it was too late to contain the scandal. Allegations of blackmail and intimidation were made. Several reputations, most notably that of the late great Sir John Cowans, were in tatters. Almina was called as a witness and gave a spirited defence of her husband. It wasn't enough to dispel the lingering suspicion that the Dennistouns were probably both culpable, and that Almina had got mixed up in highly distasteful matters. The 6th Earl was horrified that his mother had gone to court and dragged their names through the papers. The Christie's sale was being promoted at the same time and the publicity was desperately tawdry.

The case took thirteen days to arrive at its conclusion, and once the press realised what it had to work with, they covered it in excruciating detail. *Punch* magazine nicknamed it the Dustbin Case. King George V was sufficiently disgusted by the washing of so much dirty laundry in public that he wrote to the Lord Chamberlain to express his dismay that the case had ever come to court. He wasn't the only one who thought a new low had been reached. In 1926 Parliament passed the Judicial Proceedings (Regulation of Reports) Act, which curtailed the detailed reporting of divorce cases in the press.

In the end, Dorothy was awarded just £472, the sum of a loan she had made to her ex-husband. Ian's lawyer argued that the assurance he had made to pay her maintenance in due course if circumstances allowed, was not binding. The jury agreed with him. The suspicion that Dorothy was targeting the couple out of greed and a desire for revenge had evidently lodged in the jurors' minds.

The outcome was ghastly for everyone, though. The legal fees cost Almina approximately £400,000 in today's money. Her standing in society took a tumble and her relationship with her son, already faltering, was dealt a terrible blow. Whatever the truth, mud sticks, and her husband had been labelled a scoundrel; Ian lost his army commission and retired without rank. But the decision to fight the case was typical of Almina's bravado. She believed that her former friend had betrayed her, flinging her generosity back in her face and setting out to blackmail her with scurrilous lies. Dorothy had also attacked the man whom Almina had pledged to look after. Almina was not the sort to take such behaviour lying down. If she and Ian had settled with Dorothy out of court, they probably would have saved themselves an enormous amount of money and escaped a vast amount of embarrassment, but Almina would not hear of it. She insisted that they fight. In point of fact they had won, though the reality was infinitely less positive.

It cost them dear but the court case did not sink them. Before long Almina had found suitable premises at which to open a new hospital. She named it Alfred House, after her father, and it became the choice of society ladies when it came to giving birth, setting standards for excellence in nursing care. The cynics were confounded about the marriage, too: Almina and Ian remained happily together until his death, in 1938.

From the mid-Twenties, Porchey began to focus his energies on building up the Highclere stud, which his father had started in 1902 on 250 acres of chalky grassland below

Siddown Hill, next to the golf course. Porchey had been devoted to the sport of horseracing since he was a young boy. He knew his horses well, was a skilled horseman and came to be considered one of the best amateur jockeys in England. He also had a good memory for horses' race pedigree and breeding, which he put to use enthusiastically when he was placing bets. Like many before and since, Porchey felt that his passion could become his life's work. He knew it was imperative that Highclere begin to generate an income, and this was by far the most pleasant way he could imagine for that to happen.

The stud was already a going concern, but had always been run as a pastime rather than an enterprise. Now Porchey persuaded Marcus Wickham Boynton, a well-known figure in the horse-breeding world, to help him to expand activities. Porchey already had an excellent stud groom in Charlie Whincup, who had worked for his father. Charlie was a spare man, slightly too tall to be a jockey, a fountain of knowledge who appreciated the enthusiasm and expertise of the new young Lord Carnarvon.

One of Porchey's first decisions was to build up his brood mares and then send his youngsters to be trained by Dick Dawson at Whatcombe, who trained the Aga Khan's horses. He also sent horses to Harry Cottrill and Fred Darling; the latter trained seven English Derby winners and is commemorated by the Fred Darling Stakes, run at Newbury racecourse.

The horseracing, breeding and training world is full of dreamers and eccentrics, driven men (it usually is men, and certainly was in Porchey's day) whose existence has been overtaken by the hope that one day, one of their horses may win a Grand National, or an Epsom Derby, and become a household name. The sport is full of great individualists from all walks of life: thrill-seekers and gamblers, canny businessmen and sportsmen devoted to the turf.

Porchey loved to bet, and intended to augment his income from the stud with some well-chosen punts. When Sir Marcus arrived to help run the stud, the two of them pooled knowledge and placed some sizeable bets. Porchey was a good gambler. He wagered only as much as he could afford to lose and always kept a cool head, noting meticulously all the details of his wins and losses.

Catherine had not previously experienced the racing world, but since her husband spent a great deal of time at race meetings, now so did she. She quickly discovered that as well as the thrill of the race itself, which she loved, there was a diverting social side. The Highclere guestbook shows that she and Porchey hosted numerous parties for friends during race meetings at Newbury, when the days were spent at the track and the evenings in revelry at the house. Catherine accompanied Porchey on his trips to Newmarket and Epsom, Aintree and Ascot. Often Eve, who was almost as much of a fanatic as her brother, would join them, the somewhat less enthusiastic Brograve in her wake. Reggie was frequently with them, spending the morning with Porchey talking horses and the afternoon with Catherine. She lunched or took tea with her girlfriends, all dressed for the occasion in the latest fashions and charming hats. She appeared regularly on the newspapers' best-dressed lists, which then as now loved to discuss women's fashion choices. She also started to place bets herself and had quite a streak of beginners' luck.

Porchey was delighted that Catherine was having fun, since it meant that he was able to get on with the business of his own analyses of different horses, with competing in races and with socialising. He took it upon himself to teach her how to understand the basics of racing form, but seems to have been considerably less meticulous about monitoring her gambling than he was about his own. Presumably, as someone who had no urge to recklessness, he didn't consider the possibility that Catherine might not be quite as self-controlled.

One day, one of the bookies approached him and said that he thought Lady Carnarvon's bet needed hedging. 'She's laid £5,000 to £2,000 on Saucy Sue.' 'Heaven help us, thank god you told me,' said Porchey, rushing off to find his wife and dissuade her. Catherine was duly persuaded both to hedge and reduce her bet but, perhaps unfortunately, Saucy Sue won. Catherine continued to place bets for several years after that. She had a few more notable wins but many more losses and, in the end, Porchey learnt that the tiara given to her by his father on their wedding day had gone to Ladbrokes. He urged Catherine to give it up, which she did manage to do, and thereafter she contented herself with being a spectator, joining in with Eve, who was famous for her noisy displays as she cheered a horse home.

Catherine wasn't the only one who sometimes lost her head over the amount of money to be made from the horses. Porchey very nearly landed himself in serious trouble when he asked a friend to do him the favour of 'bidding up' on a particularly good colt that he was selling at auction. The horse was named Blenheim, by the stallion Blanford out of Porchey's mare Malva, and Porchey was convinced that the Aga Khan would snap him up.

Blenheim was duly despatched to the renowned Tattersall's sale ring in Newmarket, without a reserve price. Determined that he should fetch the right price, Porchey asked his old friend Jock Delves Broughton to bid on him in order to drive up the price that any interested party would have to pay. Sure enough, the Aga Khan did want him and, thanks to Jock's efforts, he ended up paying 4,200 guineas for him.

Porchey was in Newmarket a few weeks later, only to be brought up short by a bark of fury aimed at him from across the paddock. Captain Gerald Deane, a partner in Tattersall's, tore him to shreds for breaking the rules so flagrantly. He threatened that any repeat performance would mean that Tattersall's would no longer accept horses from Highclere. Porchey backed away, apologising sincerely. He never made that mistake again.

1926 and 1927 were glorious years for Catherine and Porchey. They had two children they adored and had made Highclere their family home. The house was financially secure; the stud was flourishing. They were young and wealthy and the Roaring Twenties were in full swing around them. London was only an hour away by train and there was a huge amount of fun to be had there. Porchey in particular took full advantage.

In her memoir of a deb's life in 1920s London, Loelia the Duchess of Westminster made an astute comment about the self-mythologising that characterised the decade. 'The glamorous twenties have long been a legend. Even in 1932 the present Lord Kinross was writing about them as though they were a remote Golden Age . . . the nightclub age. The majority of Londoners never saw the inside of a nightclub, of course . . . On the other hand you couldn't help hearing them talked about.'

Much like the Swinging Sixties forty years later, another era that invented its own myths on the hoof and in the morning-after haze, the Roaring Twenties probably only happened to a tiny number of people. But those people enjoyed themselves a great deal and were well positioned to tell the rest of the world about their fun.

If the Carnarvons were in town together, going to the theatre or a dinner party or a ball, they stayed at the Ritz. London was dancing mad, and Catherine in particular loved to dance. As well as nightclubs and balls there were tea dances in the afternoons, so one could dance from four in the afternoon to four the following morning, if one wished. Nightclubs were more the preserve of Porchey's outings with friends, but the couple attended endless balls together during the season. Fancy dress was a mania and people flitted from one great house to another, changing their costumes for each party, running into different groups of friends en route.

When Porchey was in London without Catherine, he stayed at one of his clubs. Porchey frequently joined the Prince of Wales and Prince George, who took their carousing very seriously indeed. They all loved the theatre and would often start their evening at the Windmill Theatre for one of Noël Coward's plays, or the Pavilion on Piccadilly Circus where C. B. Cochrane produced his famous revues. Then the party would head off to the Embassy Club on Old Bond Street for dinner. Various pretty girls accompanied them, champagne flowed, and Luigi the head waiter provided cold quails in aspic. The Embassy was always full of their friends, from Lord and Lady Mountbatten to Alfred Duff Cooper and Lady Diana Cooper, the Duke of Westminster with Coco Chanel, and Fruity Metcalfe, a chum of the Prince of Wales. There would be cabaret acts or a jazz band with dancing until the early hours, when the guests tumbled out amidst noise and laughter onto the streets. London had never been this gay: previously one had to go to Paris to have anything like as much fun.

The Prince of Wales was exceptionally charming with perfect manners, and was unsurprisingly very popular. An early girlfriend was Miss Poppy Baring; very pretty with large dark eyes and short dark hair: the classic flapper. Like many of her contemporaries she was less closely chaperoned than would have been the case before the war. Prince George was also rather keen on Poppy, whom he had met when on leave from the naval duties that occupied him throughout the 1920s. The Highclere Castle visitor books record several weekend racing or shooting parties when both PG and Poppy were staying with Catherine and Porchey. The interconnecting bedroom doors meant that it was hardly even necessary to creep along the corridors.

Highclere was full of life again. Or at least it was until the night of 16 July 1928, when Reggie Wendell wandered out of the Library after supper to take some air and suffered a massive brain haemorrhage. His prone form was found by Porchey, who came to look for him when he didn't return. Doctors were sent for as Reggie was carried upstairs and laid in his bed. Catherine was beside herself with grief and panic, and refused to leave her brother's side that night. Reggie never regained consciousness. He was two weeks older than Porchey: just thirty-two years old.

Porchey telephoned Jac and his wife Eileen who, late that night, left their children with their nanny and drove to be with Catherine and Gar, who was also staying at Highclere.

One can hardly imagine Gar's anguish. Her beloved husband had sickened and died in a matter of days when he was in his prime; now her second son had been snatched away in a moment. It was senseless and heartbreaking. One of the most affected of the family was Catherine. She was devastated, and began to turn not merely to a sherry before lunch but to several rather strong gins.

The funeral service took place a week later at Highclere Church. The mood was of desperate sadness. A stunned congregation of young friends as well as relatives could scarcely believe what had happened. There were more than fifty wreaths and floral tributes even before Catherine and Porchey, Jac and Eileen and Gar placed the family tributes on Reggie's coffin.

Following the service, the Carnarvons and Wendells left the church to drive slowly back through the sunny park to the chapel and cemetery, where Reggie was to be buried. The gothic chapel is a flint and stone Gothic structure, built by Henrietta, the 3rd Countess, 'to comfort those in sorrow'. Reggie had died ten years younger than his father, and that had seemed unbearably young. Now he would lie in the graveyard beneath a redwood tree and shaded by a spreading beech. Catherine would be able to walk down to pray or leave some flowers on his grave as often as she wanted. It wasn't a lot of comfort in her sorrow, but it was something.

If Catherine was utterly inconsolable, Porchey was also devastated. Reggie had been a great friend, a co-conspirator at the races—more a brother than a brother-in-law. In years to come Catherine always said that the loss of Reggie was a bitter blow to her marriage as well as to her. Reggie had mediated between Porchey and Catherine in subtle ways, had given them an additional way to understand each other. He was also, being his sister's natural ally, a check on some of Porchey's more unthinking behaviour. With him gone, the grief that she had learned to weather after her father's death turned into a permanent sadness. The consequences would be grave indeed for the Carnarvons.

8

Highclere in All Its Glory

On 24 December 1928, Catherine climbed into the Rolls-Royce, which Trotman the chauffeur had drawn up outside the main door to the castle. She and Porchey were spending Christmas at Blenheim Palace, one of the greatest of all British country houses. Catherine could summon hardly any festive spirit. It had been just a few short months since Reggie's death and she still felt low. The thought of the traditional family Christmas at Highclere had been weighing upon her for weeks. It could not possibly be the same without her brother, who had always spent it with them. In the end, Porchey had resolved that a change was required. Better to do something different than to struggle to replicate the beloved routines with heavy hearts. He accepted an invitation for him and Catherine to spend three days with the Duke and Duchess of Marlborough and their son and heir, his old friend the Marquess of Blandford. The children would spend Christmas with their aunt and uncle, Eve and Brograve, and their cousin Patricia, in a household where all the jolliness of the season was in full swing.

Porchey tucked a blanket around his wife's legs and sat beside her. It was a short journey to Blenheim but the afternoon was cold. Behind them his valet Van Celst was helping Charles the footman to load their bags into a shooting brake, which would transport both staff and luggage. Doll was supervising, to ensure that nothing was forgotten.

Despite her gloomy mood, Catherine could not help feeling curious and even slightly excited. The Palace was a draw in itself, and then there were the inhabitants, whose notoriety preceded them. She knew the Marquess of Blandford well since he was probably her husband's closest friend, and was acquainted with the Duke and Duchess of Marlborough, but she and Porchey had never before stayed at Blenheim. It is one of the largest houses in England, and the only non-royal or episcopal residence to be designated a palace. It was built on a monumental scale between 1704 and 1724 for the first Duke of Marlborough, the war hero who triumphed over the French at the battle that lent its name to his house. Catherine adored Highclere, which is both magnificent and beautiful, but she knew that Blenheim was a homage to glories on a different scale.

In the years after the First World War, it also had something of a reputation for being a hotbed of sin. Before her marriage, Lady Diana Cooper, who was later a frequent visitor to Highclere on account of her husband Duff Cooper's friendship with Porchey, had been prevented by her mother from attending house parties at Blenheim. The Duchess of Rutland was most reluctant to allow her beloved daughter, who was reckoned to be the most beautiful and brilliant girl of her generation, even to set foot inside the palace. Her Grace considered it an unsuitable environment for an unmarried lady, especially one with Diana's famously wild tastes in stimulants and capacity to arouse passions.

The Duchess of Rutland was perhaps rather suspicious of the tone set by the 9th Duke, who had turned around the sagging fortunes of the once-great house by marrying Consuelo Vanderbilt, the American railroad heiress, in New York in 1895. Marriages to wealthy Americans had become de rigueur by that point, but there was something almost distasteful about Sunny Marlborough's total disregard for his wife's feelings and openness about his motivation. He told Consuelo on their honeymoon that he was in love with another woman, and kept a string of mistresses throughout their marriage.

Having spent millions of pounds of the Vanderbilt dowry on restoring the palace to its former magnificence, he settled down to an affair with Gladys Deacon. Gladys was also American but was born in Paris and her childhood was shaped by melodrama. When she was six years old, her father shot her mother's French lover in the bedroom next to her own. Gladys and her siblings were sent to a convent, from which their mother abducted them on the eve of their father's release from jail. Gladys grew up with her father in New York but, following his death in a mental hospital when she was twenty, she returned from the States to Paris in 1901. She promptly became the toast of Europe, pursued by princes and aristocrats of all nations, famed for her startling beauty, turquoise eyes and eccentricity. Marcel Proust said of her, 'I never saw a girl with such beauty, such magnificent intelligence, such goodness and charm.' Despite countless proposals of marriage, Gladys nurtured an old infatuation for the 9th Duke that she had developed as a young girl, on the strength of press coverage of his marriage to Consuelo. When she and Sunny finally married in June 1921, after his divorce, they had been lovers for fifteen years, a relationship that was considerably more successful then their marriage proved to be.

Gladys, the new Duchess of Marlborough, arrived at Blenheim in 1921 and was comprehensively disliked by the staff and refused acceptance by Oxfordshire society. The Duchess of Rutland wasn't the only one who found her beyond the pale. It wasn't so much the long-standing affair that rankled. Such relationships were in fact widespread among the aristocracy. Even the disapproving Duchess had never denied the widely held belief that her daughter, Diana, was the child of her lover rather than the Duke of Rutland. It was rather Gladys's flagrant disregard for the rules of discretion and the good opinion of her peers that won her enemies and her house a reputation for louche living. Society may have been awash with extramarital liaisons (and even premarital ones as the 1920s drew on), but care must be taken to draw a veil over the consequences, even if it meant hiding a child's true parentage in the plain sight of a husband's name and acceptance. Gladys was indifferent to such niceties. She was prone to advise young girls who were worried about getting into trouble, 'If you have any problems, go to the vet. That's what I always do!'

By 1928, when Catherine and Porchey visited, the Duke and Duchess's marriage had descended into hostility. Gladys was reported to have once led the ladies into dinner before producing a pistol as she sat down, laying it on the table beside her. Asked why it was there by an alarmed guest, she responded breezily, 'Oh, perhaps I'll shoot Marlborough.'

Judging by Catherine's memories of her visit, both Gladys and Blenheim's reputation might have been exaggerated for effect. Lord and Lady Carnarvon cannot have had too many qualms about accepting the invitation to visit, as they invited the Marlboroughs to Highclere in return, the following year. Perhaps the Duchess of Rutland had been over-cautious in her concern for her daughter's virtue, or perhaps Porchey and Catherine were simply rather more sensible than Lady Diana, whose extravagances included not just a serious champagne habit but also (briefly) a fondness for morphine and chloroform.

In any case, the entertainments on offer that Christmas were quite without scandal. It was more snowball fights in the park and games of sardines played all over the house than opium in the drawing room, pistols in the dining room and assassinated lovers upstairs. Once Catherine had got over her initial awe at the extravagant English Baroque architecture, the vast scale of the house and the splendour of the state rooms, she was grateful for the distractions of her surroundings. She remembered having fun at Blenheim but recalled it as a cold house, the wood fires burning in the bedrooms not equal to their task. She missed Highclere's hot water radiators and other modern comforts.

In fact, neither Blenheim's palatial proportions nor the infamy of its current chatelaine were quite as alarming as the mannerisms of one of the Carnarvons' fellow guests. Winston Churchill had been born at Blenheim in 1875 and was a nephew to the 9th Duke and cousin and lifelong friend to the Marquess of Blandford, who became the 10th Duke in 1934. Though he never lived there as an adult, Churchill regarded Blenheim as his second home and, naturally, he and his wife Clementine would sometimes spend Christmas there. He was the best part of a generation older than both Porchey and Lord Blandford, and already had an eventful and distinguished political career behind him, not to mention a reputation for fierce intelligence, hard drinking and pugnacious manners.

On Christmas Eve 1928, Churchill was fifty-three years old and at the height of his powers. He had served as Chancellor of the Exchequer since 1924, under Stanley Baldwin's premiership, which made him effectively the second most powerful man in British political life. Churchill had both the habit and the knack of dominating conversation and loved to talk politics, a subject that held little interest for Porchey, and about which he was at that point in his life largely ignorant. During a pre-dinner discussion of the relative merits of prospective prime ministers, Porchey offered a small contribution. Eddie Stanley, who had held various minor offices and was then Deputy Chairman of the Conservative Party, would, he thought, make a good PM. Churchill, who was by far the most conspicuous candidate for the office the next time it became vacant, stopped puffing on his cigar and, leaning over, said, 'My dear Porchey, I can scarcely think of anybody who would make a worse Prime Minister.' Snubbed, Porchey thought he had better stick to occasional remarks about racing.

Porchey was certainly not alone in feeling rather frightened of Churchill, but the great man carried all before him with an endless stream of fascinating stories. During the course of their stay at Blenheim, Catherine realised that above all he should not be interrupted, although she was wise enough to spot that he granted more indulgences to his audience when it was made up of pretty women.

Perhaps Churchill's reaction to Porchey's opinion could have been foreseen, for this wasn't their first run-in over political matters. At the end of a dinner in 1926, hosted by the Aga Khan, Winston had leant back, brandy and cigar in hand and, turning to Porchey, asked him what he, as a racing man, thought about the Exchequer's betting tax. The measure, the first of its kind, had been introduced in April of that year, levying a 5 per cent tax on all bets placed. Many in the Conservative Party were opposed and there was uproar among the racing community; bookies in Windsor had even gone on strike in protest. In July Churchill had moved to reduce the 5 per cent flat rate to a tax of 2 per cent on transactions at racecourses and 3.5 per cent at bookmakers'. This fudge was in the process of proving itself unworkable at the time of the dinner.

Porchey responded promptly, 'I'm sure there are more beneficial ways to raise revenue.' 'Well, I should be very interested in your suggestions,' remarked Churchill, much to the younger man's surprise and delight.

It took Porchey six months and careful discussion with all parties to produce his proposal, which he personally delivered to Downing Street. Winston later told him that he hadn't read it but his advisers thought it wasn't a realistic plan and he had decided that the only thing to do was to scrap the tax entirely. It was in fact abolished by the Labour government that was returned to Parliament the following year. Porchey felt utterly put down, a sensation that was repeated, albeit on a smaller scale, during their discussion of Eddie Stanley's prime-ministerial qualities.

Despite – or perhaps even partly because of—the bracing effect of being at a house party alongside Winston Churchill, the Blenheim trip was a success. It had taken both Porchey and Catherine's minds off the tragedy of Reggie's absence. They began 1929 determined to be as happy as possible and spent a whirlwind of a year at Highclere, building up the stud and giving parties and shooting weekends, throwing open the house to their many friends.

The autumn of 1929 had been unusually wet and there

was no let-up as the year turned towards Christmas. Tremendous gales battered the cedars of Lebanon around the Castle lawns and brought down large branches from the beeches and oaks up on Siddown Hill, as a shooting party collected at Highclere for the first few days of December. The Duke and Duchess of Marlborough came, on one of the last social occasions they ever attended as a couple. Weeks later, when the Duke had finally tired of Gladys's odd ways and her troops of Blenheim spaniels that messed all over the house, he would evict her and all her dogs.

Despite the weather, the shooting party was a tremendous success, in large part thanks to Charles Maber, the head gamekeeper. Maber had inherited his position from his father, who had worked for the 5th Earl, and had spent years acquiring a deep familiarity with the land and honing his skills. He was determined to maintain Highclere's reputation for being one of the best shoots in England, and the castle's game book records that, on 4 December, the guns were shooting at the Beeches and the bag amounted to 672 game. Lord Carnarvon's guests were delighted: that was excellent sport in strong winds.

As well as Porchey and the Duke of Marlborough, there was Harry Brown, a close friend of Porchey's and a superb shot and first-class rider. He was very debonair and marvellously handsome; every girl was head over heels in love with him, despite the fact he was married. Sir Hugo Cunliffe-Owen, Chairman of British American Tobacco, was another of the guns. He was a keen racing man; his horse, Felstead, had won the Derby the previous year and he was a frequent visitor to Highclere, while Porchey and Catherine often stayed with him at Newmarket. Sir Victor Mackenzie, who had been wounded and decorated for bravery in the First World War, was also staying. Sir Victor was something of a professional courtier; he went on to serve three successive monarchs—George V, Edward VIII and George VI—as a groom-in-waiting.

Ladies did not shoot, though they sometimes accompanied their husbands, to enjoy the fresh air and exercise and to assist with collecting the game. On a similar occasion, Catherine was photographed out in the park with her great friend Lady Diana Mabey. They are giggling at one another, both in ankle-skimming tweedy skirts and feathered caps, the game birds dangling from their hands. One rather imagines that, between the bad weather and the bitterness that was finally sinking the Marlboroughs' marriage, the ladies elected to remain indoors on this particular weekend.

It is a mark of Catherine's confidence that she was no longer daunted by welcoming a most eclectic mixture of guests to Highclere. Gladys might have been the wife to one of the grandest and richest dukes in the realm, but her reputation for idiosyncrasy meant she had not been received in Oxfordshire society for years. Socially, Lady Carnarvon was unassailable, her reputation beyond reproach.

It's impossible to know how Catherine regarded Gladys on a personal level. They were very different people. Gladys was one of life's adventurers with a taste for being the centre of attention and a proclivity for drama at whatever cost. Catherine, despite her light-hearted love of dancing and fun, was wholesome and straightforward by comparison. But they were both intelligent American women who had married the English aristocrat they loved and settled into a world very far from the one in which they had been born. It's possible that Catherine thought Gladys's decline was predictable but more likely that she felt sorry for her.

There was yet another shooting party before the Christmas celebrations of 1929 finally got under way. This year the

Carnarvons were at home with their children and a group of friends and family. They had not forgotten Reggie, but it was time to move on.

The 1930s had until recently promised more of the steady success of the past few years, at least for Highclere's owner. After six years of careful economising, in which Porchey was greatly assisted not only by Fearnside but also by Marcus Wickham Boynton, who continued to act as his agent and adviser for the estate and stud, Highclere was in much more stable financial shape than it had been when Porchey had inherited.

He had looked for ways to generate income as well as cut costs. A particular success was the golf course, which he turned into a subscription course in order to make it pay for itself. Golf was an increasingly popular pastime, and no longer just for Porchey's guests. Local people and Highclere staff could enjoy a game. In fact Fearnside the butler and Van Celst the valet exasperated their employer by consistently achieving better handicaps than him. Lord Carnarvon would get his revenge by turning up to play in shorts, which infuriated the other players as they were forbidden to wear informal garb.

The 1920s were boom years for many, particularly financiers and industrialists. Lord Carnarvon's situation was, if not booming, certainly not desperate. There was a general sense among the asset-owning classes that the stock market couldn't fall and the threat of international conflict was receding. It was a decade that saw the consolidation of great fortunes alongside the continuing exposure of millions to poverty. There was a steady unrolling of rights and a gradual shifting of power, as witnessed by the rise of the Labour movement, but events such as the failure of the 1926 General Strike demonstrated that though the times were volatile and unemployment was rising, the country was a long way from revolution.

For years afterwards, Porchey loved to tell a story about his contribution to the settling of the strike. The government was unsure of the scale of the threat but had been making preparations for some time and had drafted the Army to assist the police in the preservation of order. Porchey had maintained links with his regiment ever since his succession to the title, and now found himself in Liverpool, in command of a platoon of 7th Hussars. They erected a sandbag barricade close to Union Street and each man was then issued with five rounds of ammunition, which Porchey was adamant should not be loaded without his express command. At the approach of 'a mob of men and women', and fearing escalating tension, he jumped up to speak and the crowd halted. 'I firmly believe that my horse, Gracious Gift, ridden by Tommy Hulme, will win the Novices' Chase at Manchester at three o'clock,' proffered Porchey. He was loudly applauded and the crowd dispersed. Sure enough, Gracious Gift, which had started at odds of 11–8 against, did indeed win. The following day a steady stream of eager punters filed past the barricade in expectation of another winning tip. As Porchey wrote in his memoirs, 'I replied sadly that I did not know any more but the best winner for all would be for them to go back to work so we could return to barracks.' The strike was duly broken (only in small part, one suspects, thanks to Porchey's generosity with his hunches) and many, especially among the establishment, heaved a huge sigh of relief.

Thirty years later, when Duff Cooper came to write in his memoirs about the election of May 1929, he reflected on politicians' inevitable difficulties in assessing the mood of the moment. The country had felt itself secure, he wrote, there were no storm clouds yet on the horizon, either financially from the west or from war in Europe. The country was bored with the government, who were perceived as old and tired, but the Conservative Party campaigned on 'Safety First'. As Duff Cooper put it, 'No greater psychological mistake could have been made than to promise safety to a people pining for excitement.'

The Conservatives lost their majority, Labour formed a minority government with the balance of power held by the Liberals (campaign slogan 'We can conquer unemployment') and, just five months later, things started to get very exciting indeed, in spectacularly challenging ways.

In October of 1929 the Wall Street crash profoundly destabilised the world's economy. The effects did not immediately take a toll on Highclere but it was nonetheless a shock to the Carnarvons, as it was to the country at large. Nationally, unemployment remained high at 10 per cent, with the likelihood of much more to come, and the new administration seemed to have no robust response to the signs of worsening gloom.

In the event it was Labour leader Ramsay MacDonald who became the next Prime Minister after Stanley Baldwin's departure, not Churchill, who in 1930 was entering his so-called 'wilderness years' in opposition. If MacDonald's name had cropped up at all during that conversation at Blenheim, it seems safe to assume that Churchill would have applied some withering epithet. On other occasions he famously referred to MacDonald as 'the Boneless Wonder' and remarked that he possessed a great skill for 'compressing the largest amount of words into the smallest amount of thought.'

In fact, MacDonald and his Chancellor of the Exchequer, Philip Snowden, were not so much thoughtless as overly committed to the conventional wisdom of the day. Lloyd

George and John Maynard Keynes were among the many from outside as well as inside the Labour Party who were already urging a spending programme to stimulate growth. MacDonald and Snowden were far more cautious, being staunch supporters of an orthodox approach to finances that regarded borrowing to fund state-sponsored growth as little more than Bolshevism run mad. As the two opposing blocs of opinion squabbled, a sort of paralysis set in.

The 1929 election, nicknamed 'the Flapper election', was the first in which women were able to vote on the same terms as men. The franchise had been extended to all women over the age of twenty-one in the Representation of the People Act of 1928 and, thanks to the abolition of the requirement that a woman voter should be a householder or the wife of one, it also had a huge impact in terms of social class. Without the 1928 legislation, Catherine would not have been able to vote in the 1929 election, since she did not meet the age requirement of thirty. Most of her female staff, who had previously been both too young and most definitely not of the property-owning classes, were in a sense doubly enfranchised. Young working-class women who had never given politics a second thought, on the understandable grounds that it was literally no business of theirs, now had the vote. Upstairs and downstairs, the world was changing for women, but within the microcosm of Highclere, the relationship between Catherine and her employees remained the same as it ever had been.

In 1932 an eighteen-year-old local girl named Gladys joined the household as a junior housemaid. More than forty years later, having read the 6th Earl's memoirs, she wrote to him with recollections of her time at Highclere. She remembered that during the course of her work she often saw and admired Lady Carnarvon, but that they never spoke. There was simply no need for conversation within the terms of their relationship. Gladys recalled that the Countess was always in a hurry to see Lord Porchester and Lady Penelope first thing in the morning, and since she was frequently still blacking the grate and relaying the fire in the nursery, she often saw her there. Lady Carnarvon wore the most beautiful negligees and robes made of light-coloured silk, Gladys remembered, and would come running up the Red Staircase in her haste to see her children. 'She seemed to float,' said Gladys, 'she was that beautiful.'

Catherine might not have spoken to her housemaids but she had a much more direct relationship both with the cook, Mrs Mackie, and with the housekeeper, who from 1932 was Mrs Lloyd. With Mrs Mackie she planned menus for the family and in particular for the house parties that were such a feature of Highclere's life.

Even when the shockwaves of the Great Depression finally did reach them, Porchey's love of doing things properly meant that splendid hospitality was still one of the very first priorities. 'In 1931 I suddenly woke up to the fact that my securities and properties were worth about one quarter of what they had been valued at a year previously.' This didn't stop him from spending a great deal on food, wine and the talents of the kitchen staff. In July 1933, a couple of years later, when, admittedly, the slump had eased up a little, the monthly total for Highclere's expenses, including staff wages, provisions, coal, the telephone bill—everything required to keep the great house in peak form—was £909 7s. 8d. This sum included £265 on provisions alone, which dwarfed the combined wages bill for more than twenty-five people, of £157. Extra money was spent on fruit and vegetables.

Porchey and Catherine cut some costs when they were alone but not when they entertained. Novelist Evelyn Waugh, who spent the inter-war years flitting from country-house party to country-house party, remarked approvingly of any establishment that met his exacting standards for lavish comfort that it was 'very Highclere'.

Waugh was an occasional visitor during the mid-1920s, but didn't return after the failure of his brief and acrimonious first marriage to Porchey's cousin, also called Evelyn, daughter of his aunt Winifred, Lady Burghclere. The engagement had been met with considerable opposition from Lady Burghclere on the grounds that Waugh was not just a penniless and unsuccessful writer but also a dissolute drunk. The marriage went ahead, nonetheless, in June 1928, in the presence of just three friends of the couple. A year later Waugh's wife announced she had begun an affair with a mutual friend and he sued for divorce. Nothing daunted, eight years later he was to marry another of Porchey's cousins, Laura, the youngest daughter of his uncle Aubrey. The family was even less impressed than it had been on the previous occasion, despite Waugh's attainment of considerable success as a novelist and travel writer in the interim.

Evelyn Waugh was not the only Highclere guest to appreciate its blend of laid-back atmosphere, appetite for fun and unstinting attention to detail. Such a combination was made possible by Catherine and Porchey's youthful spirits, wealth and, above all, their staff's professionalism. House parties were a particular test of the smooth running of a household. They entailed a huge amount of additional work, on top of the already demanding everyday schedules.

The housemaids and kitchen maids were the castle's earliest risers. Gladys's first job after she woke, typically at six in the morning, was to clean and black-lead the Wyverns—the heraldic mythical creatures, which feature in the Carnarvons' coat of arms and stand guard by the front door—before scrubbing the marble of the entrance hall and cleaning out the grate in the Saloon.

Meanwhile, down in the kitchens, the second kitchen maid, Gwendolen, who shared a room with Gladys in the servants' quarters right at the top of the castle's turrets, was making a start on breakfast as the kitchen porter shovelled coal into the great Carron stoves. Mrs Mackie bustled in to oversee preparation of eggs and cold meats for the Dining Room and breakfast trays laden with fresh fruit, tea, toast and marmalade for the footmen to take up to the ladies.

Gwendolen had started as a scullery maid when she was sixteen years old and she rose to be the vegetable maid before being promoted to second kitchen maid under Mrs Mackie. Once breakfast was out of the way, her first task was to clean the copper pans with soft soap, salt and lemon skins so that they shone like burnished gold. Mrs Mackie took a particular pride in her coppers and had exacting standards.

Two footmen would hurry up the staff stairs so that nothing became cold, push carefully though the green baize door onto the quiet Gallery and deliver the trays. Meanwhile the nursery footman would take up the children's breakfast to the very top floor.

When all the dirtiest jobs in the house had been done, safely out of sight of the family and visitors, and breakfast had been provided, all the servants would sit down to their own meal. It was always an abundant and delicious breakfast; there was no stinting at Highclere. Having checked that the family had everything they required, Fearnside would join Mrs Lloyd and Van Celst in their dining room, where they took their meals together, waited on by one of the junior footmen.

Once breakfast had been cleared, kitchen maids had to get straight on with lunch. Housemaids set off to the upper reaches of the house, but discretion was required. Bedrooms could be tidied and cleaned only once their inhabitants were safely downstairs. Since the family moved from Morning Room to Dining Room to Library throughout the day, the footmen and maids who served and cleaned would follow in their wake, always just out of sight unless specifically summoned.

Housemaids and footmen could rest for a couple of hours during the afternoon, until tea was served in the Library, but then it was time to prepare for dinner, which might be a relaxed or a formal occasion depending on the number of visitors. The family always dressed for dinner in white tie if they had guests, but by the end of the 1920s, Porchey and Catherine had adopted the more informal dinner jacket if they were dining alone, which was considered sufficient in the privacy of one's own home or club.

Tea-time was the housemaids' opportunity to prepare the bedrooms so that the company could take some rest, write letters or read a little in private and then dress for the evening. Highclere had had some en-suite bathrooms with running water from the end of the nineteenth century, and Porchey's renovations on his succession to the title had installed more. It was nonetheless customary to provide jugs of hot water with fresh white towels. There were no radiators on the first floor, so fires had to be lit and beds turned down so they could air. Footmen came on duty again to serve drinks in the Saloon, and at dinner. The kitchen was working at full pelt. Even a simple meal consisted of three courses. There were five courses when Lord and Lady Carnarvon had company.

When guests were staying there were more trays to prepare,

more courses to cook and more fires to light. In exceptional circumstances, Mrs Mackie might petition Mrs Lloyd for temporary staff, but often the maids were simply required to pitch in and help out. This was sometimes a welcome change of routine. Gladys remembered that after a few months she was allowed to assist the footmen as they took the early morning cups of tea to guests. On one occasion, when both the Prince of Wales and Prince George were staying, she was thrilled to take them their morning tea. She had only ever seen their photos in the newspapers and was almost overwhelmed. She never forgot, that same weekend, that she collided with Prince George on the Gallery as she rushed to finish her duties. This was a terrific faux pas, since the art of being an effective housemaid was to be an invisible presence, not a physically tangible one. But he gave her such a lovely smile that, even as she blushed and apologised profusely, she couldn't help thinking how good looking he was.

Prince George was a particular favourite with the Highclere staff. He was a frequent visitor throughout the 1920s and early 1930s, and endeared himself to everyone by being polite, appreciative and cheerful. Gladys remembered that the housemaids jostled with one another to be the one to air his room and turn his bed sheets down, hoping they might catch a glimpse of him. In accordance with the strict seniority of rank that governed life below stairs just as it did upstairs, it should have been the head housemaid's privilege. One day, junior housemaid Betty couldn't resist and, in a fit of bravery, sneaked ahead of the senior maid to turn down his bed and lay out his pyjamas.

These encounters could all be a bit much for some, though, especially the younger staff. Gladys remembered that when her friend Gwen was a newly arrived scullery maid, she was once petrified into timid silence by the sound of Prince George striding through the kitchens late in the evening and calling out for Mrs Mackie. He often came downstairs after dinner to pass on his appreciation for her excellent cooking, but Gwen, who was the only one still present, didn't know this. She hid in the patisserie room, far too shy to answer his call. Mrs Mackie was furious when she found out.

Gladys remembered that the house party weekends were hard work, but for a young woman like her who loved to look at magazine pictures of movie stars in their gowns, they had their dreamy romantic qualities as well. Visiting royalty, handsome young sportsmen, ladies in beautiful fashions: she enjoyed it all, and sometimes tucked herself behind a pillar on the Gallery to listen as the guests assembled down in the Saloon, complimenting each other on their dresses or laughing as they chatted about some mutual acquaintance.

The two footmen, George Widdowes, or Charles as he was known to the family, and George Rand (whose name really was George), would stand tall and straight in full evening dress with their silver trays of cocktails. The custom of assigning conventional, typically 'smarter', names to staff seems totally archaic now and was dying out by the late Twenties. Traditionally, valets were always George, first footmen, Charles, but in the time between George Widdowes' and Van Celst's arrival at Highclere, the practice had slipped from favour. His Lordship's valet was known as Mr van Celst to staff and simply Van Celst to the family.

Lady Carnarvon would have made a careful study of her guests' interests and planned the most appropriate placement for dinner, one that took account of precedent and tastes. Fearnside, who had worked for the family for nearly thirty years, was a useful ally, since he knew everyone and could advise Catherine on who might prefer not to sit next to whom. It was his task to write out the cards with guests' names. On his signal that all was ready, Catherine took everyone through for dinner. Lady Carnarvon and Lord Carnarvon sat opposite each other in the middle of the long table and, if Prince George were there, he would always be seated on her right.

Gladys remembered that if Widdowes or Rand came down to the kitchens with the report that the word 'dancing' had been mentioned, it was all hands on deck. The men would set about rolling up the carpet in the Saloon and Mrs Mackie would heat up a mixture of beeswax and turpentine for the girls to apply to the wooden floor. One of the footmen would assist Lord Carnarvon to set up the gramophone. Lady Carnarvon was such a good dancer and loved nothing more than to encourage her guests to dance; on these evenings the fun would go on late into the night. The footmen had to ensure the cigarette boxes were refilled and drinks were offered in fresh glasses to those guests catching their breath in the Drawing Room. While Lord Carnarvon enjoyed the occasional cigar, Lady Carnarvon smoked cigarettes that she fitted into beautiful slim holders.

Only once the party had everything it needed could Gladys and the other housemaids and footmen go back downstairs for their supper. The visiting valets and lady's maids, were seated depending on their consequence (or rather, their employer's). Footmen, guests' valets, kitchen boys and all other male employees sat on one side of the table in the main staff dining room, in order of seniority, with female staff down the other. Once the meal was finished, Mrs Mackie carried out the final checks on her kitchen maids' cleaning, Widdowes made one last trip to see that there was nothing else the family required, and to clear empty glasses from the side tables in the Saloon and Drawing Room. Mr Fearnside checked that the front door was locked, as was his wine cellar, and then everyone trudged upstairs to their rooms and fell into bed, while the scullery maid finished off the last bits of washing up.

If the work was demanding for Highclere's downstairs inhabitants, their positions in a large and well-run household were nonetheless highly desirable. There was a community that provided a social life, and food and lodgings were excellent. There were possibilities for advancement, and ladies' maids and valets enjoyed travel and variety. Domestic service in smaller or more chaotic establishments could be a far tougher proposition. If a servant worked alone or with just one other member of staff, they were vulnerable to the whims of their employers. At Highclere, the hierarchy was strict, but in the words of Matilda Hart, who joined as the fourth housemaid, the place functioned as 'a well-oiled machine'.

In 1979, Mrs Hart wrote to Lord Carnarvon, having read his first volume of memoirs, to share her reminiscences of Highclere. She remembered how, the moment they'd finished in the bedrooms, she and her fellow housemaids had 'chased through the state rooms, plumping cushions and emptying ashtrays.' They were always in a terrible hurry before the family and their guests came down to dinner. Their task was rendered more difficult by the fact that they had to 'wipe their footprints from the carpets' as they went. No indication of how such an operation might be performed is given, but it must have slowed them down considerably.

Leisure time was great fun. Mrs Hart had learned to dance in the servants' hall. The house must have fairly shaken with dancing, downstairs as well as upstairs. Matilda shared a room with Betty, who was flighty, and the two of them used to get into trouble with Nanny for playing their gramophone records loudly in their bedroom. When the girls were separated one night, Matilda awoke to a knocking on her window, an alarming occurrence since her room was right at the top of the castle's turret. It was Betty, who had walked along the lead guttering just for the fun of it. Matilda was persuaded to do likewise in the opposite direction.

Like Matilda, Gladys had mostly very happy memories of the house. She worked hard but enjoyed her weekly trip to the cinema or to a dance in Newbury with Gwen. There was one recollection, though, that still made her shiver, years later. One night, as she and Gwen arrived at the back door, having walked across the park after a dance in town, they were startled by the night watchman's dog, which was snarling at thin air. Stratford, a typically stolid man, looked shaken. He claimed that the castle ghost had just processed along the downstairs corridor and ascended the back stairs towards the staff bedrooms. Gladys and Gwen were inconsolable and had to be persuaded that it was hardly practical to spend the night in the staff dining room. Hanging on to each other for dear life, and accompanied at their insistence by Stratford, they climbed gingerly to the foot of the stairs that ascended from the first floor to the second and performed the ritual knocking and calling out of a request for the ghost's permission to enter that was taught to all newly arrived Highclere staff by their colleagues. It must have pacified the spirit, for the girls had a quiet night and woke the following morning to radiant sunshine and the blessedly familiar start of another long day's work.

9

There May Be Trouble Ahead

Gladys was not in a position to see much apart from sunshine and glitter in her employers' lives; for her, the evident joy in Lady Carnarvon's early morning visits to the nursery, or the glimpses of her silk dresses and her enjoying cocktails with Prince George, seemed proof enough that Her Ladyship's life was charmed.

Other members of the household knew that, in reality, tensions were building between Lord and Lady Carnarvon. From 1932 onwards Lord Carnarvon was often away from Highclere, without his wife. In previous years they had made many trips together to race meetings, a couple of times to Scotland to visit Catherine's sister Philippa, Countess of Galloway, and of course they were often in London.

Now Lord Carnarvon spent more and more time in town, alone. Van Celst would be informed that they were off to stay at His Lordship's club, and would have to pack quickly. It would be left to Doll to console Lady Carnarvon, to look for ways to distract her beloved mistress from fretting, smoking too much and drinking.

Catherine had suspected for some time that Porchey was not the sort of man who could live his life without intrigue. He sincerely loved his wife, but in common with other men of his era and social position, he did not believe that extra-marital liaisons need compromise that love. Within a few years of his marriage, he was delighting in his reputation as a ladies' man. He didn't deliberately bring it to Catherine's attention, but neither did he go out of his way to conceal his activities.

Love affairs are of course a constant of human beings' interactions, in all times and in all places, but they had some interesting particularities among the upper classes in Britain at the end of the nineteenth century and in the early decades of the twentieth. For a start, a great deal of licence was extended to those who observed the conventions that demanded discretion. Secondly, women were granted almost as much leeway as men, so long as they followed the rules: first of all, get married so you have a husband's protection; then, stick to your own class, don't cause a fuss with the wife and never, ever make a spectacle of yourself.

The ultimate example of this sort of arrangement working out well was the Duff Coopers' marriage. Lady Diana almost certainly confined her love affairs to the platonic realm but they could be passionate and emotionally intimate nonethe-less, and frequently lasted years. Alfred Duff Cooper was quite open about his several long-standing love affairs, most notably with Daisy Fellowes, whom his wife knew and would meet at social events. Daisy was famously witty, caustic and fashionable and came to stay at Highclere several times, though with her husband rather than her lover. When Duff Cooper was later serving as British Ambassador in Paris, at the end of the Second World War, he and Diana even contrived to be in love with the same woman at the same time. Louise de Vilmorin was a bewitching figure, a novelist, poet and femme fatale. Diana gave full rein to her passionate admiration, Duff became absolutely infatuated and launched into a sexual relationship. Such arrangements might seem risky or at least unusual to some minds, but there is no doubt that Diana and Duff adored one another and though Diana sometimes suffered, despite her husband's habitual discretion, she never doubted that he loved her above all other women.

The success of this arrangement was surely exceptional, and yet such behaviours were not at all uncommon. Lady Diana came from a world in which her own discovery that she was not her father's legitimate daughter, at the age of nineteen, had not seriously ruffled any feathers. She was glad to be a duke's daughter in name since it conferred status and privilege, and also quite glad to be the product of an intense amour. The Duke and Duchess of Rutland were equally phlegmatic. Diana, her siblings and her mother spent summers at her mother's ex-lover's country house. The sexual relationship seems to have been well and truly over by then, but everyone was on the best of terms. No scandal had been caused and no rules broken.

Catherine did not experience her husband's infidelities in anything like the same way. She had none of Lady Diana's racy charm, her taste for pushing the limits, or her uncompromising sense that she was unique and therefore could not be seriously rivalled. Catherine had spent her early childhood among the East Coast American upper classes, where quite different codes operated. In addition, she was personally unsuited to decadence. Porchey knew that, and it was one of the things he loved about her. She was an innocent, quite unlike the new class of sexually adventurous young women who began to emerge during the 1920s and 1930s among the society set. Premarital sex had always been taboo for such women, but as female emancipation took off in the post-war years and sexual mores shifted, there was a new type of worldly debutante, one who cultivated night-club stars and dancers such as Tallulah Bankhead. Even Diana was slightly taken aback by her friend Polly Cunard's frank appetite for sexual adventures. Where Diana loved to experiment, to flirt and to be adored, she considered Polly's sybaritic enjoyment of sex, drugs and parties at her house in Bloomsbury distasteful. Diana cultivated an aura of 'anything might happen' daring, but she had her limits.

Catherine was the total opposite of this high-Bohemian, liberated spirit. She was flirtatious but she adored her husband and their children and hoped that her devotion to their family life would be enough to make him curb his behaviour. It was not. Porchey's liaisons continued, and grew more numerous as he started to spend more time in London. They were a torment for her, though when she discovered them she forgave him, more than once. Catherine had absorbed at least one element of the code: don't make a scandal. Rather than challenge Porchey, she seems to have preferred to hope against the odds for him to reform himself. In the meantime, the sadness that had settled in her since Reggie's death grew and grew. So too did her dependence on drinking as a means to muffle and control it.

Catherine seems to have had a compulsive streak, judging from her propensity to place ever bigger bets and drink ever larger gins at lunchtime. By 1933 she was spending more and more time alone at the castle, often with not enough

christening of Henry, the new
d Porchester, Easter 1924.

Catherine's family left to
right: Her brother Jac,
Dr Johnnie, Jac's wife
Eileen, and their mother
Gar, Marian Wendell.

Henry's nanny,
Mrs Sambell, in the
carriage on the way
to the christening.

Mother and son in January 1926.

enelope's christening in 1925. From left: Sir Brograve Beauchamp; Reggie Wendell; Lady Carnarvon holding Penelope; Lord Carnarvon; Lady Evelyn; Arthur Portman; Mrs Portman holding little Lord Porchester and Catherine's mother Marian (Gar).

Catherine and Henry at Penelope's christening.

Catherine with her mother and Penelope in the pram.

Catherine with her children.

SISTER OF THE COUNTESS OF CARNARVON: MISS PHIL-IPPA WENDELL of New York as She Appeared at the Spanish Shawl Ball at Clar-idge's in London.

Philippa married Randolph Algernon Ronald Stewart, 12th Earl of Galloway, on 14 October 1924. The bride an groom had met at Porchey and Catherine's wedding.

Catherine's sister Philippa was a striking beauty.

Philippa with her husband the 12th Earl of Galloway.

The Sketch announcing the birth of the Countess of Galloway's son and heir in 1928.

Alfred Duff Cooper and his bride,
Lady Diana Manners, in 1919.

Lady Diana Cooper in 1923

Catherine's brother Jac married Miss Eileen Carr in 1923.

Both Catherine and Porchey enjoyed spending time at the races with friends. They are pictured here at Epsom racecourse in 1928.

Catherine with her sister-in-law Lady Evelyn.

Evelyn Waugh was an occasional visitor to Highclere. He married consecutively two of Porchey's cousins. The first, short-lived, marriage was to Evelyn Gardner in 1928 and he later married Laura Herbert (right) in 1937.

Christmas Card 1936. HRH the Duke of Kent, with Princess Marina and their son Edward, remained friends with Catherine as well as Porchey for many years.

Lord and Lady Carnarvon
attending various race meetings.

Lord and Lady Carnarvon outside the front door of Highclere Castle.

to do. Once she had visited her children, discussed the planning of the day's meals with Mrs Mackie and had her meeting with Mrs Lloyd the housekeeper, she might take coffee in her sitting room and catch up on any correspondence, but that done, it was far too easy to drift into the Drawing Room and pour herself a drink. For those with untroubled minds there is something tranquil about its beautiful pale green silk walls, but this most feminine of all the state rooms at Highclere can also feel a little melancholy on an overcast day if one is not in the best of spirits and there is no prospect of them being lifted. Catherine discovered that one sure-fire way to dull her sadness, if not disperse it entirely, was to drink gin before lunch and afterwards retire to her bed for the afternoon. There was always sherry before dinner, wine with dinner and a later nightcap.

Eve came down to cheer her up. She loved and supported her brother but could see that his actions were causing Catherine huge distress. Divorce had become a fact of life by the mid-Thirties but, even so, nobody looked forward to such a prospect and Eve was convinced that the Carnarvons could still make their marriage work.

Catherine was grateful for the company but found it difficult to confide in Eve, out of loyalty to Porchey. She tried to be discreet about her problems but her misery and its causes were quite obvious to the whole family. Jac had always had his suspicions about Porchey and frequently remonstrated with his brother-in-law, which did little good. Philippa was a long way off in Scotland, which meant that though she had similar difficulties of her own, both sisters struggled alone rather than together. Gar was the obvious candidate for confidences, but Catherine had no desire to compromise her mother's comfortable opinion of Porchey. It was often Doll she turned to, when no one else was there.

If Catherine's big problem was feeling lonely in her marriage, her great consolation was her children, Lord Porchester and Lady Penelope. Patricia, her niece, who grew up with the Carnarvon children, remembers that Catherine adored them but was careful not to mollycoddle them, especially Henry. She clearly enjoyed having them both with her at home. She and Porchey had decided to educate both children at Highclere until young Lord Porchester was eight years old, at which point he would be sent to board at Heatherdown Preparatory School in Berkshire, which would lead to Eton.

The children saw their mother every day, but only at certain times. She made early morning and late afternoon visits to the nursery but didn't stay for long. On Sundays Henry and Penelope would spend the afternoon downstairs with their parents. It was often the only time in the week that they saw their father, whom they adored but who was a far more remote figure than their mother. Porchey wrote in his memoirs that he had always dreaded the emotionally glacial tone of his own parents' weekly visits to the nursery, and he was a far more jovial and relaxed parent with his own children, but there was simply no cultural expectation that he should be a hands-on father. He loved his children and relished spending time with them, but in very particular circumstances. He was insistent that both Henry and Penelope should ride well, and there is a lovely photo of Lord and Lady Carnarvon with a broadly smiling Penelope, aged about five or six, on her pony. One imagines that these were the moments that Catherine must have lived for.

When the children were small, most of their day was spent in the care of Mrs Sambell, their nanny, who was their principal carer. Her place was later taken by Doll. Porchey was particularly keen that Henry and Penelope speak good

French. His French was really outstanding, so much so that the Frenchmen he met were incredulous that an Englishman could speak their language so well. Doll, Catherine's beloved lady's maid, whom the children had grown up with, was consequently taken on as governess and was henceforth known to the household as Mademoiselle Huc. It seems to have suited everyone. The children had been apprehensive about a stranger coming to impose a new and potentially disciplinarian existence. Doll was a far brighter prospect.

A schoolroom was installed on the top floor of the castle, complete with chalkboard, books, globes and desks for both Lord Porchester and his little sister, who joined him in due course. They took classes in the morning, which left them plenty of time to roam all over the house and its grounds, to play and to get into mischief. Gladys the housemaid recalled that the children were so friendly that she once got drawn into playing railways with them in the nursery rather than carrying out her duties, and was reprimanded by Nanny when the three of them were discovered. Gwendolen, the second kitchen maid, remembered that Lord Porchester, Lady Penelope and Miss Patricia were forever fetching up in the kitchens, where the staff made a fuss over them. Mademoiselle Huc knew that if she had failed to locate her charges in any other spot, she might very well find them there and would bustle in, demanding in French that they return to the schoolroom. Gwendolen grew very fond of the children and considered applying to be a nursemaid, but was told somewhat sharply by Mrs Mackie that she was more use in the kitchen.

During the first few years of the 1930s, Highclere was still outwardly a happy house, loud with the noise of children playing and frequent social gatherings, but it was shot through with an inner seam of uncertainty and melancholy. Catherine's sadness increased after her son left for prep school. Her mother came often to stay at Highclere, as did Eve and Bro with Patricia, but she missed Henry terribly and also her brother Reggie—she was sure he would have steered her husband back towards her. She created a rose garden near the castle where she could go to sit and think. Its quiet setting soothed her. It was such a charming refuge that the staff would ask to be allowed to take their mending work out there on sunny days.

Catherine discovered during those lonely hours in her rose garden or the Drawing Room, nursing her gin and tonic, that—though she loved Highclere—it was far more her husband's home than hers. Her place in it was contingent on their marriage. He could come and go, choose to live his life elsewhere, at his club or on the racecourse, but Highclere would still be his ancestral home until the day he died. And if Porchey chose to shift the centre of his world away from Highclere, and away from her, there was nothing she could do about it.

There was a potential ally who was ideally placed to understand this particular aspect of Catherine's difficulties, of course. Almina's tenure at Highclere lasted twenty-eight years. Her money saved it over and over again, and funded the expeditions to Egypt on which her late husband's fame rested; but when he died, she had to leave. Streatfield, the long-serving house steward, lived there longer than she did. She felt a certain degree of ambivalence about both her former home and her son for years afterwards.

So Almina might in theory have been the perfect person to talk to about the challenges of being Countess of Carnarvon, despite the fact that Catherine, disinclined even to talk to her own family about her marriage, would surely not have confided in her mother-in-law about the specifics of her woes with Porchey. She might also have worried that Almina, who, partly through temperament, partly through the power of her money, had found it much easier to stamp her own personality on Highclere, would not understand her. It's true that Almina was tougher and more pragmatic, but she would probably have sympathised with her daughter-in-law, whom she liked very much. As the illegitimate daughter of Alfred de Rothschild, who married into the aristocracy, she had once known a great deal about not quite feeling at home.

The biggest obstacle to the flourishing of Catherine and Almina's relationship was that the two women rarely saw one another. There had been a considerable warmth between them in the early years, when Almina championed Catherine's cause with her late husband and hosted parties for her. Almina's subsequent involvement with Ian Dennistoun froze her relationship with her son and, by extension, her daughter-in-law. They had always corresponded and saw each other occasionally in town, when Catherine took the children to visit their grandmother, but in the ten years after her departure in 1923, Almina visited Highclere only once, in the October of 1931.

By that time things had started to thaw between Porchey and his mother, though the guestbook records that she came alone, without Ian. That weekend, two of Porchey's great friends were also staying: Jock Delves Broughton and the Marquess of Blandford, heir to the Duke of Marlborough. They were joined by various others including Dolly Wilde, niece of Oscar, who liked to dress up as her uncle and hold court. Dolly was a faintly scandalous figure, notorious for her heroin and alcohol addictions but, even in the star-studded literary salons of inter-war Paris, which was where she spent most of her time, she was also famed for her gifts as a conversationalist. She too came alone, without her long-term lover, American socialite Nathalie Barney.

The party must have been a boisterous one but it would take more than a cross-dressing heroin addict or the first visit to her old stomping ground in eight years to cow Almina. One imagines that as Dolly was in full swing, Almina took the opportunity to explain to Catherine in detail her latest project, the nursing home, at Alfred House. The home was named after her father and had been open since 1927 on a street just off Portland Place, close to the BBC's new headquarters, then under construction. It had built up a reputation for excellent nursing care, both for patients convalescing from surgery or illness and for mothers having their babies. Before long it was the choice for large numbers of society patients, including, in 1934, Lady Diana Cooper, who gave birth to her son at Alfred House. Almina's nurses still wore the strawberry pink uniforms she had insisted on at the military hospital she founded at Highclere in 1916 for wounded officers. The food they served was excellent and the standards of care they provided exceptional. Sir Berkeley Moyniham, who was President of the Royal College of Surgeons as well as a leading surgeon at Leeds General Infirmary, was the medical director whom Almina had worked closely with during the Great War.

Almina might have been busy with her own life and an infrequent visitor to Highclere, but she was concerned about Catherine and knew exactly what was going on. Eve was a constant source of information. In early 1934, Porchey absented himself from Highclere for two months' racing in Egypt, where he competed as a jockey and won several events. He returned, tanned and fit, at the beginning of April, in time to host some weekend parties with Catherine for the Newbury races. This was probably around the time when he began what would evolve into a more serious relationship, with Tanis Montagu. When, in October of that year, he contrived to include her in a house party at Highclere attended by their mutual friends, Poppy and Peter Thursby, Almina was furious with him. Catherine, by contrast, was in despair. She had known he'd met someone, and Catherine had been sitting it out at Highclere, hoping that it was again a casual fling and would not escalate. She was still tormented by doubts over what to do.

Porchey had in fact known Tanis for some time. She had been born into the influential and aristocratic Anglo-Irish Guinness family. Her father, Benjamin Seymour Guinness, was a very wealthy lawyer and philanthropist, and in 1931 Tanis had married the second son of the Earl of Sandwich, Drogo Montagu. By 1934 their divorce was almost complete. Tanis was Titian-haired, a soignée beauty, confident, worldly and a fixture in Hollywood circles. She was intensely exciting to Porchey and would soon prove to be the last straw for Catherine.

The wedding of Prince George might have clarified Catherine's thoughts somewhat, and prepared the way for her realisation that she would have to act. Prince George had been an admirer of hers for years and a staunch friend to both Carnarvons. It had been twelve years since he had stood as guest of honour at their wedding, and now, as they attended his, Catherine must have mused on the sad turn of events. The irony was that everyone admired Catherine except her husband, who, as Catherine was beginning to appreciate, simply didn't love her enough.

On 27 November 1934 she and Porchey attended the glittering reception for 2,000 people given at Buckingham Palace by King George V and Queen Mary, who were delighted that their son was marrying Princess Marina of

Greece and had created him Duke of Kent for the occasion. Catherine looked exquisite but Porchey, who was supposed to dance the first dance with his wife, refused on the grounds that he had already spent a lot of time with her. Catherine had so many friends and admirers that she nonetheless enjoyed a spectacular evening's dancing.

The new Duke and soon to be Duchess were already established as the celebrity royal couple of their age. They were handsome, glamorous, informal and very much in love, with an appeal to newspaper readers all over the world. That evening, moving among their guests in the crimson and gold state rooms lit by twinkling chandeliers, they were dazzling.

Prince George stopped to introduce his fiancée to his old friends, Porchey and Catherine. A few moments later, the Prince of Wales also paused. He was alone and Porchey thought he looked wistful. The two royal brothers had been so close, living together at York House in London, carousing in nightclubs in town and spending weekends at Fort Belvedere, the Prince of Wales' country retreat in Windsor Great Park.

This was the first occasion on which Catherine observed Mrs Simpson, whom the Prince of Wales had persuaded his reluctant parents to invite. They disapproved of their eldest son's relationship with the once divorced, and indeed still married Mrs Simpson, but they were desperately hoping, against all mounting evidence, that it would prove to be just another of the Prince of Wales' numerous infatuations.

Wallis Simpson arrived wearing exquisite jewels given to her by her royal lover. Her husband, Anglo-American shipping executive Ernest Simpson, stood awkwardly at the side of the rooms for much of the evening. The Prince of Wales managed to ensure Wallis was presented to King George and Queen Mary. Their indignation was cloaked by good manners, but this only stoked their anxiety that Mrs Simpson was of a different order to the Prince's previous dalliances.

Back at Highclere, Catherine forgave Porchey everything and tried to carry on in the hope that she could still save her marriage. She had no shortage of admiring visitors. The very well-known conductor Malcolm Sargent found Catherine quite entrancing. Impeccably dressed and nicknamed 'Flash Harry', he was good for her self-esteem. Porchey's old friend Jack Clayton, the racehorse trainer, was also devoted to Catherine and came down often towards the end of 1934 so that she was not on her own.

The first few months of 1935 were an intensely miserable period for Catherine. Christmas had felt like a charade. Henry, young Lord Porchester, returned from school and found his home an oppressive place of tension, in which his mother drifted and the staff were at a loss. Catherine was anxious to conceal the extent of the crisis from her children, but it was impossible to maintain the fiction that the cocktails and dancing, race meets and shooting weekends were still as they had been. Porchey's evident hurry to get back to London made Catherine's position impossible.

Porchey spent most of the spring of 1935 with Tanis, either in London (her family home in Carlton House Terrace) or in Paris, a city they both loved. Rumours circulated in society that the Carnarvon marriage was on the point of ending. Porchey began to plead with Catherine for a divorce. Perhaps it was this that finally allowed Catherine to act. For as long as there had been no direct threat to her position, she had trained herself to co-exist uneasily with Porchey's various flings and just about ignore the damage his sparse attention was doing to their marriage and her wellbeing. But Porchey had found another woman he wanted to marry. She saw that her position was completely untenable.

Catherine asked Gar to come to stay at Highclere for the first two weeks of May. On 3 May, elegantly dressed as ever and accompanied by her brother Jac, Catherine, Lady Carnarvon, travelled to the City of London offices of solicitors Broad and Son to enquire about divorce proceedings. She had spent years hoping that it would not come to this, but had allowed herself to be persuaded by Jac that she needed to take some control, to start looking for a way forward for her and the children. There were the mundane but necessary questions of maintenance, of where they would live. A plan was required.

In contrast to her personal disaster was the national celebration of King George V's Silver Jubilee, throughout the month of May. Catherine had taken a cab from Paddington Station and made her way along streets decked with Union Jack banners and bunting. The King was seventy years old and frail, but he undertook a programme of carriage rides to greet his subjects, accompanied by Queen Mary and their granddaughters, the Princesses Elizabeth and Margaret. The royal family could not have known it, but their own family scandal was just around the corner. For now, though, the mood of the nation and the Empire was buoyant.

Catherine, on the other hand, returned to Highclere full of the saddest sense that the life she and Porchey had made for themselves was at an end. Having resolved that she must leave as soon as possible, she took just a week to pack up her most important possessions and make arrangements to move out. Doll reverted completely to her former role of ·lady's maid and confidante. She and Gar took charge of practicalities and rallied the entire staff to help. The household was in shock. Though everyone had known this outcome was always a possibility, the staff now found themselves in the invidious position of having to wrestle with divided loyalties. Lord Carnarvon was their employer, but Lady Carnarvon was better known to them, and an object of sympathy.

On 12 May, Catherine, her mother and Lady Penelope left Highclere, driven by Trotman, the head chauffeur. In a demonstration of the extent to which individual members of staff had sided with Lady Carnarvon, Porchey's valet, Mr van Celst, left too. He became Catherine's butler in London. Mrs Gibbins, who had been head housemaid, became Catherine's housekeeper, leaving behind her husband who remained as second chauffeur. The ever-faithful Doll rode in the car with the family to provide comfort for both Penelope and Catherine.

Porchey knew that Catherine had resolved to leave him but she had said nothing to him about where she was going, or when. He returned to the castle from Paris one evening and, as he handed his hat and stick to Charles, enquired, 'Where is Her Ladyship?' 'I believe Her Ladyship is staying at the Ritz hotel, my lord. There is a letter on your desk, my lord,' the footman replied.

Porchey walked through to the study and sat down. He was almost overwhelmed by mixed feelings of guilt, relief and excitement. Unfolding the familiar notepaper, embossed with Highclere's address and his wife's crest, the words swam in front of him and he wondered in panic what on earth he had done. 'It is better we should part . . . I must have peace of mind . . . I am not really accustomed to this way of life.'

Tanis was still in Paris, and his wife had left him and taken their children, not to mention several of the staff. The full import of the new reality hit him. He at once telephoned Catherine at the Ritz, who insisted that they should not speak that night but that he would be welcome to come to see her at the hotel. She assured him that she didn't want any scandal and that Jac would handle everything for her. The effort of maintaining a dispassionate tone nearly resulted in her collapse.

Porchey did go to see Catherine, and walked out of the Ritz hotel afterwards feeling nearly as intolerably sad as she did. As he remarked in his memoirs, they had lived in harmony together for many years and he had forced the demise of their marriage. Now, despite his sadness, he wanted to play the game to the end. On 29 May he booked a room at the Charing Cross hotel with one Lucy Nugent, remaining there with her for an hour. He then passed this information to Jac so that he could in turn send it to Catherine's solicitors. During the course of their conversation at the Ritz, Porchey had tried to persuade Catherine that the best thing for everyone was now a speedy resolution. He hoped that Catherine would file a petition as soon as possible.

By the time the news reached Catherine, though, she had suffered a complete nervous collapse and been taken by her mother and brother to a convent-run nursing home in Surrey. The strain had finally proved too much. She had adored her husband constantly; he had adored her, but with far less constancy. Theirs had been a love match that simply ran out of steam, exacerbated by his affairs, her sadness and turning to drink, and a gradual emotional retreat from one another. For Catherine, the suspicion that he would emerge practically unscathed from the wreckage was too much to bear. She would not return to Highclere for ten years.

10

Bitter Sweet

Highclere was a forlorn place in the summer of 1935. Porchey spent a great deal of time there, more than he had in many months, and invited friends to stay, but the *joie de vivre* had gone out of the house. The staff were as lacklustre as their employer, wondering what on earth might happen next. Porchey urgently needed something to do, a project in which to lose his mixed feelings of sadness, remorse and nervous excitement about the future. The problem was that there was little to command his attention. Lord Carnarvon's devotion to the stud was passionate but, now he had the enterprise well run and the estate well managed, there was no pressing need to be there unless he wanted to be.

The more one knows about Porchey, the more one suspects that his adult life was defined by the need to be a character, without having the advantage of actually possessing either definite talent or vocation. His role, of course, was to be the Earl of Carnarvon, but it was starting to become clear that it was no longer enough to play the lord of the manor without a little more substance to back up the feudal froth. Porchey was a great raconteur, a superb mimic, an entertainer. He was a serious sportsman, he was a very loyal friend—but none of these things were enough.

He fell back on traditions, his own and those of his class and generation. Porchey was, as always, concerned to maintain stability, but he was also aware that his children needed things to stay as close as possible to the way they always had been. Catherine had taken the responsibility for running a happy household, but he was determined to keep Highclere going as normal, despite the fact that he was desperate to be with Tanis, who was out of the country. He asked Eve if she would be able to host certain occasions along with him, to which she readily agreed, bringing Patricia and Bro with her as much as possible. There were racing weekends, and some new friends from the theatrical world came to stay. Henry and Penelope visited their father regularly over the summer, in the care of Lord Porchester's tutor, Mr Bosanquet, and Doll respectively. Eve was conscious that her niece and nephew were dealing with the separation of their parents, and needed extra attention. She took all the children to play tennis, or out in the shooting brakes for picnics up in the woods above the park and on the downs.

Henry was now eleven years old, Penelope ten. They wrote to their mother while they were away, telling their 'darling mama' that 'people missed her', enclosing drawings, signing off as her 'two little Ps'. From the recollections of Patricia, their cousin, who continued to play with them that summer at Highclere, it would seem that they were filled with the common desire of children of divorcing parents to see a reconciliation. To their credit, neither Porchey nor Catherine ever encouraged these desires, and neither did they speak badly of each other. Old-fashioned English decorum was, on occasion, extremely useful. Nevertheless, it was a huge sadness for the children, made worse by the fact that the collapse of the Carnarvon marriage was fodder for speculation in the press and chatter in society drawing rooms. The newspapers gleefully seized on this fresh opportunity to wheel out their beloved fantasy, the Curse of Tutankhamun, as explanation for the latest misfortune to overtake the house of Carnarvon.

The more prosaic reality was that the marriage had simply broken down irrevocably. In the immediate aftermath there was a sense of being in limbo for both parties. For a number of weeks after she left Highclere, Catherine was too unwell to push on with the divorce. Her family ensured that she was well looked after and visited her at the nursing home, but her doctors had made it clear that what she required was total rest. That meant giving up alcohol and getting lots of fresh air, good food, gentle exercise and early nights. She was to have only close family to visit and absolutely no contact with her solicitors until she was better.

Catherine was at the convent for nearly three weeks. The choice of a Catholic sanatorium was surprising to her friends. The Wendells were Protestants through and through and Catherine had worshipped in the Church of England ever since her arrival in the United Kingdom. But as she grew unhappier she had started to seek out possible sources of meaning and guidance, and had become interested in the Roman Catholic Church. In the depths of her crisis she found herself desperately in need of spiritual comfort for the sickness she felt in her soul as well as her mind. She asked her mother and brother to look for a Catholic refuge that might allow her to explore her interest in the faith as part of her recovery and, despite the Wendells' slight bemusement, they readily complied. Catherine needed to get better; it hardly seemed the moment to dip into the establishment's traditional suspicion of the Roman Catholic Church.

Almina was extremely anxious about her daughter-in-law's welfare. Porchey had told her about the meeting he'd had with Catherine at the Ritz, at which she had appeared to him to be desperately sad, but coping. Almina deduced that Catherine had acted with great bravery and managed to convince her husband that she was calm, but her worries were confirmed when she discovered that Catherine had entered a nursing home. She immediately wrote to her to invite her to stay at Alfred House whenever she liked. Just over two weeks later, on 5 June, Catherine Carnarvon checked in.

By the time she was well enough to consider her next steps, her brother Jac had done his research. He introduced her to Lewis and Lewis of Ely Place and thence to Sir Reginald Poole. Sir Reginald was a highly distinguished specialist in divorce cases and a great support to Catherine, softly spoken and calming. He informed Lord Carnarvon's lawyers that Lady Carnarvon had been too unwell when the original admission of her husband's adultery was obtained and that he would build the case for her anew, from scratch. Lord Carnarvon was once again followed round London and down to Bognor Regis, where the necessary evidence was procured to allow Lady Carnarvon to file for divorce and custody of her children. It was a start. Catherine, though still terribly sad, began to feel that she would come through.

Jac helped her to find a house. Number 30 Hertford Street was a late eighteenth-century London town house just off Piccadilly, in Mayfair. Catherine set about establishing it as a temporary home for her and the children, with the help of the staff who had come with her from Highclere. She was intensely touched by the loyalty of her employees, several others of whom moved into town to her establishment during the autumn of 1935 and spring of 1936.

The greatest loss to Porchey was George Fearnside, who had served as his butler for twelve years. Fearnside did not join Catherine; instead he took the opportunity presented by change at Highclere to retire from service. He was nearly sixty, so this was entirely reasonable. Nevertheless, Porchey might have hoped that his old retainer would stay a year or so and help him to maintain some continuity at a time of upheaval. The timing suggests that Fearnside, like so many others at Highclere, had feelings of fierce and divided loyalty to the separating Lord and Lady Carnarvon. Porchey's domestic arrangements were rescued by Almina's swift offer of her footman, Frederick Smith, who became butler at Highclere in the early autumn of 1935. As for Catherine, she was never a vindictive person, but she might have been forgiven for feeling a touch of *Schadenfreude* when contemplating Porchey's situation at the castle.

Having set up house, the next thing was to find a school for Pen. Henry would continue at Heatherdown preparatory school, but it was no longer appropriate to school Penelope at home. Mademoiselle Huc would continue to provide extra tuition in French, as well as companionship for both Pen and Catherine, but Penelope was with her cousin Patricia enrolled in Miss Faunce's day school in Bayswater.

As Catherine slowly pieced her life back together, Porchey found himself trapped in a maddening long-distance relationship with Tanis. Between May 1935 when Catherine left him, and November 1936 when his relationship with Tanis had run its course, he saw her for a total of just eight weeks.

Part of this was surely due to Porchey's sense of his obligations at home, but most of it was due to Tanis's preference for spending the summer at her brother's in the south of France and the autumn and spring in New York—without him. If Porchey had been looking for warning signs, they might quickly have been apparent.

There is no doubt, though, that he sincerely believed himself to be in love. He relished the time they spent together in France that summer, thought of her constantly, pressed her to come to visit him at Highclere. She did not, perhaps partly out of a sense that it would be inappropriate, but she did write him many long letters assuring him that she was missing him terribly and sent him even more sweetness and sympathy than before. Tanis had been divorced herself; she understood the state of melancholy and shock that had engulfed her lover. 'I know that everything is crumbling around you at present . . . just exactly as it once crumbled around me.'

After they had seen each other in Paris, she wrote again to say that her friends had started to talk about his divorce in her presence, and to speculate about their marriage. 'I know little about it but haven't even seriously considered it yet,' she commented, before going on to regale him with tales of dashing about France in her new Ford car, thanking him profusely for the exquisite jewellery he had given her and hoping that all manner of lovely things would happen for him, since he thoroughly deserved them.

In August they met up in Deauville and played golf, but were together only a couple of weeks before Tanis set off on her travels again. She spent the next month in Austria and then headed to Venice with Poppy Thursby (previously Poppy Baring, the former girlfriend of both King Edward VIII and the Duke of Kent) 'to see how we like that.' Tanis never stinted in sending fulsome letters, though they often contained explanations for why she really couldn't speak to him on the telephone early in the morning or in the evening when she was rushing to a dinner appointment. Letters from Porchey followed her around Europe.

He consoled himself for her absence by throwing himself into racing, which always cheered him up. He had some notable successes with his horses, and as a jockey. The sporting press reported that 'he smiles a lot and looks as if life is worth living.' He had won the Welter Plate at Ripon in early May, beating an odds-on favourite, and his latest fancied colt was tipped by a journalist to win the Derby the following year. There was nothing better to look forward to in racing. Porchey also rode in several races on various occasions. He was feeling so positive that he offered a bet of £1,000 on 10 August that no amateur jockey could concede a 10-lb handicap and beat him, though it isn't clear that anyone actually took him up on it. In September he rode his last race. His doctor had told him that, after his latest back injury, he was no longer fit enough to take part. It was a huge blow to Porchey to lose one of his great passions, especially at a time when he needed to feel busy to keep his mind off the collapse of his relationship with Catherine—and off Tanis, too.

He found sanctuary from this disappointment and the sad memories at Highclere at his mother's house. She made no attempt to hide her disapproval of his behaviour and what she saw as his infatuation with Tanis, but she nevertheless wanted to help him get back on his feet. Porchey described her as 'a grand old lady' and though he refused to listen to her over Tanis, subsequent events demonstrated to him that he would do well to pay heed to her judgement. Above all, he knew that she could be relied upon to help in a crisis, with her characteristic blend of pragmatism and brisk warmth. They squabbled frequently, usually over money, and even fell out for long periods, but they valued each other enormously and saw more of each other in the five years after Porchey's divorce than they had in the previous ten. Almina always coped well with adversity and enjoyed being needed by the people she loved. She liked to help, and Porchey was in need of help.

Even so, she found his inveterate philandering intensely exasperating. In the September after he retired from racing, when Tanis was making plans to leave Europe for the States and resisting his pleas to spend some time in the UK en route, he attended one of Almina's parties at Seamore Place. Porchey found himself dancing with a gorgeous woman dressed in white satin whose husband, so she told him, was away in Ireland. Almina spotted them slipping off upstairs, and when they reappeared half an hour later, she sidelined her son to administer a very pointed remark. Porchey was somewhat chastened, but not nearly so much as he was ten minutes later when the woman's husband appeared. He had returned a day earlier than expected and rushed straight over to join his wife. Porchey downed a large Scotch to steady his nerves, and beat a retreat.

Such escapades were temporarily diverting, but Porchey was still pining for Tanis. His responsibilities to Highclere and his children did not keep him busy enough to stop him from moping and obsessing. Henry and Penelope continued to stay with him for the occasional weekend, but these visits were made stilted by everyone's distress, and Porchey struggled to know how to behave. The business of the stud was now arranged, if anything, rather too well. He had come up with a new strategy that would yield more certain returns, and done a deal with the Aga Khan whereby he leased him 96 acres and 40 boxes, and took over the management of the horses. It was a clever piece of business but, since he had built up such a good staff, there was little for him to do except keep a general eye on things. Perhaps Porchey was hoping that some of his 'tenant's' success might rub off on him. Of the previous seven years' Derby winners, three had been owned by the Aga Khan, a remarkable achievement. Porchey's record was good, but not on anything like that scale.

He was occasionally racked with guilt over the end of his marriage, but he fell back on the fact that he would make Catherine a very generous settlement by way of consolation. He might have felt more certain about the rightness of his actions had he been happier now, or had he had the prospect of certain happiness to come, but that was not the case. He spent the autumn of 1935 waiting for Tanis to send him word that she was moved by his argument that they were meant to be together, and for his divorce to grind through the legal system.

In December, he could bear it no longer. He wrote to Catherine to suggest that since Christmas was likely to cause them all pain, the best course of action this year might be for him to go away. He then booked on to the *Aquitania*, Cunard's venerable and luxurious cruise liner, and set off for the States with his old friend Harry Brown. Porchey felt more and more that America was key to this next phase of his life. He was always something of a sensation seeker, and had become increasingly fascinated with theatrical and film people. He wanted a dash of Hollywood glamour in his life. This was surely a large part of Tanis's appeal for him. She had aspirations to write a screenplay and connections with the Hollywood set.

Porchey had hoped to see Tanis but, though he sent her gifts, including a gramophone player, they didn't meet up.

He was disappointed, since he'd half convinced himself that she had already accepted his proposal of marriage, but he knew she could be flighty and, in truth, he still felt sure of eventual success. She wrote him more effusive letters from New York, and Porchey and Harry spent two happy months enjoying the sunshine, playing golf and hosting dinners at the Everglades Club in Palm Beach. As with so many Europeans before him, there was something of the desire for a fresh start in Porchey's love for all things American.

Porchey was out of the country for an event that had been expected but, when it came, proved to be the starting gun for the greatest crisis ever to engulf the British royal family. The old King had been increasingly frail for some time. He complained that his poor health was made worse by the strain of his relationship with his heir, the Prince of Wales, whom he (and indeed most other observers, including the Prime Minister, Stanley Baldwin) considered dissolute and lazy. When his beloved sister died on 3 December, the King was so distressed that he cancelled the state opening of Parliament. He sickened in the New Year and died on 20 January 1936 at Sandringham, surrounded by three of his four surviving sons. (The Duke of Gloucester was confined to bed with laryngitis in London.) Queen Mary, composed and regal, kissed the hand of the new King, Edward VIII, after which he rushed to phone Mrs Simpson, apparently hysterical with grief.

By the time Porchey got back to London on 19 February, it seemed the whole of society was in thrall to the question of the new King's relationship with Wallis Simpson. With the succession, King Edward's single status had also become legitimate subject for speculation in the British media, as it had long been for the American and European newspapers. The tone, in Britain at least, was curious rather than scurrilous thus far, and there was no particular focus on Mrs Simpson, but the establishment knew that such punctiliousness could not last. As one headline from America's United Press put it, 'Will New King Marry Noble English Girl? Friendly With Many Attractive Americans'. Edward had indeed been linked with numerous different women, popular musicians such as Edythe Baker and married women such as Lady Furness, rather than the eligible European princesses that his parents and the political and social establishment were so keen to see him marry.

Porchey had met Wallis on a couple of occasions and never warmed to her, which meant that of late he had seen a great deal less of his old friend. The couple tended to cut people who didn't side with them in what had developed into a pitched battle between them and the rest of their social circle.

King Edward VIII continued to live with Mrs Simpson at his country home, Fort Belvedere, and the affair became more and more intense even as the storm blew up around them. Queen Mary still hoped her son could be persuaded to do the job he had been born and trained for, but few in government shared her optimism: the new King's government papers were more likely to come back with wine stains than signatures. As Alan Lascelles, his private secretary for eight years, memorably put it, 'For some hereditary or physiological reason his normal mental development stopped dead when he reached adolescence.' When Mrs Simpson voiced her approval of Count von Ribbentrop, the Nazi Ambassador, there was even greater mistrust of the King's political judgement.

On his return from the States, Porchey stopped off in London to see Almina and his daughter. He also wanted to check with his solicitor on the progress of the divorce proceedings. He confided in his mother that the household was still somewhat short-staffed. It was Catherine who had always taken care of that side of things and he was at a bit of a loss. This was precisely the sort of problem Almina was good at fixing. She came up with the plan to reroute Robert Taylor—the twenty-two-year-old she had just taken on as first footman for Seamore Place—to Highclere, to serve under Smith the butler. Robert had been due to leave his small Welsh village in a week's time for London. Now, he would travel instead to Highclere.

Robert had worked for a hunting family in north Wales, first as a hall boy, then a footman, and finally as acting butler. It was a remarkably rapid ascent for such a young man, even in a small household. On 29 February he bid his tearful mother goodbye and set off on a long cross-country train journey to Highclere. His new position was a huge promotion, and the first step in a career in Lord Carnarvon's household that spanned nearly five decades. Forty-five years later, Porchey wrote in his memoirs that it was an accepted fact that Robert had long since attained the platonic ideal of perfect butler. Their relationship was based on deep mutual respect. By 1979 Porchey knew that in some fundamental way it was totally anachronistic, a last link to feudalism, as he put it, but he described Robert and the other five members of his staff as 'unique people, irreplaceable'. One senses that he means not just to him personally but in a more literal sense of being the last representatives of an almost vanished type of social and economic relationship between people.

When he arrived at Highclere village station on that day in 1936, Robert stepped from the train to the platform, retrieved his luggage with the help of a porter and steadied his nerves. He caught sight of a gleaming Rolls-Royce, just pulling away from the station, in which sat a little girl of about ten and her governess. The following day he would identify them as Lady Penelope and Mlle Huc. Now he looked around him and was relieved to see that there was another car pulling up, a small Vauxhall, and its smartly dressed driver was waving as if he had been sent to collect him.

Donald Alder, the second chauffeur, turned out to be an amusing man with a good line in jokes and wicked stories. As they turned off the main road, Alder turned to him and shouted over the noise of the car engine, 'On no account should the likes of you and me be using the main entrance!' as they swept past London Lodge. Robert's mild alarm was dispelled by Alder's infectious laughter. 'Come on, man, what do you think will happen? Anyway, you should see the length of the drive. Bit different from what you're used to, I imagine.'

They swung into the courtyard at the back of the house where Alder helped him down with his bags and waved him off. Robert stepped into the cool of the basement and was ushered the length of the corridor and into the presence of Mr Smith.

Frederick Smith was just ten years older than Robert, extremely young for such a prestigious job. He had only been in his post for six months. As far as Robert was concerned, though, Mr Smith was cloaked in all the dignity and authority conferred by his position and the grandeur of the establishment. He felt apprehensive. Would he be out of his depth? Robert knew nothing at all about his new employer, or his household. He had accepted the post on the basis of Almina's letter informing him of the change of plans. Neither side had seen any references. Robert was grateful when Mr Smith told him, 'Once you have had your tea I shall show you the house. There is no need for you

to come on duty tonight; be ready to start in the morning.'
He breathed a little more easily as the second footman
showed him to his room to leave his things.

After tea, Robert accompanied Mr Smith on his tour of
the state rooms and principal bedrooms. Emerging from the
back stairs, they first looked into Lord Carnarvon's study
and then a small and pretty pink room. 'This is Lady
Carnarvon's sitting room though, of course, as you know,
her ladyship is no longer living at Highclere.' Robert nodded,
and the subject of recent tumultuous events in the household
was not mentioned again.

The two men stepped into the Saloon and from there
passed through the top door of the Library into the small,
ornate Music Room with the beautifully painted ceiling
and priceless embroideries. Smith took Robert through the
tall gilded double doors into the elegant Drawing Room
hung with green silks. Robert thought he had never seen
such beautiful rooms and was particularly taken with the
transition from one to another through a sequence of hidden
or linen-fold panelled doors.

The following morning, work began in earnest when Mr
Smith showed him the series of rooms downstairs where
Robert would spend a great deal of his working days. Smith
took him to the strong room and swung open the heavy
steel door to the safe. He produced a long list and handed
it to Robert. 'This is the Bretby service, that's the Chesterfield
one. This one here is used for luncheon, that for breakfast.
I will let you know if the silver is to be required of an
evening. This is entirely your responsibility, so please take
good care of all of it.' 'Yes, Mr Smith,' replied Robert.

Several days elapsed before Robert had occasion even to
see his employer. Lord Carnarvon was only just back from
his trip to the States. The return from the sunshine and

distractions of Florida to the reality of his life without Catherine at Highclere, and the absence of Tanis, was taking its toll. The pattern of his days at this time of the year did not vary. He rose every morning at six and breakfasted on fruit and a cup of tea before climbing into the Rolls-Royce and setting off to Harry Cottril's yard in Lambourn to ride work. Donald Alder, the chauffeur, had to go to collect the post and would hand it to Lord Carnarvon as he climbed into the car. Porchey developed a habit of skimming through the correspondence looking for the letters he wanted, most particularly those from Tanis, and dropping anything that looked like a bill or something similarly dull through the car window onto the gravel as he sped off. Robert Taylor would then have to scrabble around collecting up the discarded letters and deposit them on His Lordship's secretary's desk.

Robert weathered his first mornings with Lord Carnarvon but ran into trouble a couple of days later when he answered the telephone downstairs. The lady explained that she was calling for Lord Carnarvon about plans for the weekend, and rattled off a long list of names of people coming to stay including a Mrs Saunderson. Robert desperately tried to keep up as he scribbled them all down but, before he knew it, she cheerily hung up. Robert went to consult Mr Smith who thought that, since Mrs Saunderson was in fact the name of the housekeeper, it would be wise to confirm the list with His Lordship. When Smith broached the subject with Lord Carnarvon later that afternoon, his employer's response was, 'If this new chap can't take a message, sack him.'

Smith made no comment, merely withdrew and, having put two and two together, deduced that the lady must have been Lady Evelyn, whom he telephoned to clarify arrangements. He was highly amused by the whole thing and did his best to reassure Robert, who nonetheless was quaking in fear that he would be sent back to his mother in Wales. But as he subsequently observed, Smith knew how to handle Lord Carnarvon and there was no more said about the matter.

Lady Evelyn, Sir Brograve, Miss Patricia, her nanny and Patricia's beloved dog Tom Thumb duly turned up for the weekend, followed by several more guests, all of whom were settled by Smith and Mrs Saunderson into the rooms that had been prepared for them. Robert encountered His Lordship again that weekend, when he rang the Red Staircase bell to alert the staff to the fact that he was retiring for the night. Whoever was on duty would run to bid him good-night and see if there was anything he required.

On the Saturday, His Lordship, who had taken to retiring earlier than he used to, rang at half past ten. Robert attended and exchanged his first words with his employer.

'Please ensure my guests have everything they need.' Porchey might have been feeling somewhat less the soul of the party these days, but he was still anxious that everyone have fun.

'Yes, my lord,' replied Robert, thankful that His Lordship seemed to have overlooked the telephone message incident.

As Lord Carnarvon climbed the stairs to his bedroom, Robert headed for the Drawing Room that he so loved, to clear glasses and return with more drinks. Every drink was still served in a fresh glass. Standards would be maintained. Once the last guests had gone upstairs he could clear and tidy and head for his own bed. He retired to sleep exhausted but happy in his new life, which was more than could be said for Lord Carnarvon.

II

Two Divorces and a Wedding

On 22 April 1936, Lady Carnarvon was granted a divorce and custody of her children on the grounds of her husband's adultery. Catherine was just thirty-five years old and had spent almost all her adult life with Porchey. Now that period was practically over, though it would take another few months for the divorce to be declared final.

Porchey was relieved that progress was being made and telephoned Tanis to tell her the news. She was pleased for him, but still evasive about what would happen next in their relationship. The only concrete thing she said was that she was heading for Hollywood, leaving New York in a few weeks' time.

If Porchey fretted over his love's steady progress away from him, he tried not to let her know it. Besides, he was also genuinely pleased for her and delighted to be able to ask her to give his regards to Bing Crosby, with whom he'd recently played golf at Everglades. The flat-racing season was about to start and he had high hopes of a Derby winner. Life was looking up.

That summer Tanis sent letters full of detail about her charming Hollywood house and how much she loved the beautiful roses that Porchey had been clever enough to send her, but very little in response to his suggestion that he come out to join her. She signed off, 'You sound awfully sure of yourself and of your own mind. I wish I could say the same for myself.' She was tossing and turning but sent 'as ever masses of love'.

Months passed with little shift in relations. In July Porchey went to Baden-Baden to take a cure for his back injury. Tanis's letters referred to the furious reaction of her father, Mr Benjamin Guinness, to certain rumours that had started to circulate about her lifestyle in Hollywood. Tanis was at pains to stress to Porchey that, though she might once or twice have stayed up all night hosting her parties, she was otherwise living a model existence. She had finally succeeded in getting her script to Mervyn LeRoy, a director at MGM, and was on tenterhooks waiting to know what would happen next. She mentioned in the same letter that she was distressed by the news she'd had from her brother, Loel Guinness, about their friend, Hugh Lygon. Apparently Hugh had been killed in a freak accident on a motoring trip to Germany. After everything that had befallen the unfortunate family, it was a terrible loss, and Tanis commented to Porchey that they must both write to poor Sibell immediately.

Sibell Lygon, Hugh's sister, had spent a lot of time with Catherine and Porchey at Highclere in 1931. She was one of four clever and rather racy Lygon girls who delighted in throwing decadent parties at Madresfield Court, the ancient family seat, much to their starchy eldest brother's disgust. The Lygons had become the subject of a huge society scandal when their father, William Lygon, the 7th Earl Beauchamp, had been 'outed' by his brother-in-law as a homosexual; a criminal offence at the time. Lord Beauchamp had to flee Britain to avoid prison. His children were devastated. Although some society hostesses refused afterwards to receive his daughters, Highclere proved a sanctuary. Now Sibell was suffering once again. Porchey wrote immediately to offer his condolences and invite her to stay, but it was to be another year before Sibell returned to Highclere.

Porchey's cousin by marriage, Evelyn Waugh, was devastated by Hugh Lygon's death. The two had been great friends and possibly lovers at Oxford, and afterwards Waugh spent a great deal of time at Madresfield. Of all Waugh's many adopted country houses and aristocratic families, it was the Lygons of Madresfield Court that came closest to capturing his heart. Hugh's death planted the seed of anguish that led to his great novel *Brideshead Revisited*, about a scandal-hit family of Anglo-Catholic aristocrats in desperate self-destructive decline.

Perhaps the news of sudden death made Tanis reflective. Towards the end of the month she wrote to thank Porchey for his recent letter, seemingly a rather serious declaration of love and purpose. It had made her cry, she said. Why didn't he come out to New York in early November and they could discuss things? She, meanwhile, had tired of waiting in Hollywood for a signal from Mervyn LeRoy and was embarking on a trip through Mexico to Havana and thence back to New York.

It was precisely the news that Porchey had been waiting almost a year for. He was jubilant and set off to London at once, to buy a ring. He spent the next six weeks at Highclere entertaining on a lavish scale, all gloom forgotten. On one particular weekend in October he invited a collection of close friends to celebrate his absolute belief that the woman he loved would soon be his wife, and a new phase of his life was beginning. He was joined by Prince Ali Khan, by his old chum Blandford, who had succeeded his father to become the 10th Duke of Marlborough two years previously, by Alfred Duff Cooper, and Prince George, Duke of Kent, among others. It is safe to say that for the duration of their visit, Porchey did not ring the bell to inform the staff that he was retiring to bed until a great deal later than half past ten.

Robert was by this time familiar with Highclere's code of spectacular hospitality, but he had never seen anything like this. The house was merry again and packed to the rafters with guests, their wives, their valets and ladies' maids. When it came to dress for dinner, the Gallery thronged with hovering valets waiting to be called in to assist with ties, coats or shoelaces. The ladies' maids fluttered around their mistresses and between their rooms, begging extra hair clips from one another en route. That weekend the kitchen had to provide dinner for ninety-five: twenty-five upstairs, seventy below. At Highclere, every courtesy was extended to visiting staff as well as to their employers.

Over cigars in the dining room, the Duke of Kent leant in to Porchey to ask him whether he could rely on his support should matters come to a head with David, as his brother the King was called by intimates. Startled, Porchey replied that he could indeed. The Prince said no more about it on that occasion, but his evident worry confirmed what Porchey had heard from Duff Cooper and Lady Diana on a previous occasion. The Duff Coopers had, somewhat to their surprise, been invited to join the King and Mrs Simpson on what became a notorious cruise around the

Adriatic aboard the yacht *Nahlin*, over the summer. They had both found it rather trying. The King and his mistress were crabby and tense with each other by day, and caroused by night. Duff Cooper, who was himself an inveterate drinker and bon viveur, was nonetheless irritated by the King's preference for lunchtime cocktails and card games over visits to any of the treasures of the ancient world that surrounded them. Diana found Mrs Simpson's lack of courtesy, both to the assembled company and the dignitaries they encountered along the way, hard to stomach. It had been a spiteful, drunken, claustrophobic catastrophe, and they had been relieved to leave.

It had also become perfectly clear to them that David intended to marry Wallis. Rumours to the same effect had been circling for months by the time the Prince spoke to Porchey at Highclere. If the King's indifference to matters of state was a worry for his government, his lack of interest in the traditional rituals of court also generated friction. The coveted presentation at court, whereby young girls made their official entrance into society by being presented to the monarch at the debutantes' ball at Buckingham Palace, was that summer brushed aside. Edward VIII decided to use a garden party for the occasion. Halfway through he got bored and told those debutantes who had not yet performed their curtsey to consider themselves officially presented. He then took off to play golf with Mrs Simpson. On one hand it might seem understandable to prefer the direction of one's own time to the stuffiness of ancient ritual, but it was also a dismissal of the dreams and aspirations of a great many people. Society was not impressed.

A week after PG's quiet word, Porchey set off for New York. On 2 November his divorce from Catherine became absolute. That very day he steamed past Staten Island amid a flurry of newspaper reports on both sides of the Atlantic announcing that he had sailed to America to marry the Hon. Mrs Tanis Montagu. Porchey had not been at all circumspect about his conviction that his happiness was almost a settled thing, and consequently British society had been speculating about a new Countess of Carnarvon for weeks. He would come to rue his lack of discretion, bitterly.

Porchey made straight for Tanis's hotel. It had been six months since he'd seen her and he could barely contain himself in the cab. Tanis's maid, Serena, opened the door of the suite to Lord Carnarvon and curtseyed. Porchey bustled in, all smiles, only to be told by an embarrassed Serena that, yes, Madam was indeed returned from Havana, but that she was not currently at home. Porchey was somewhat deflated but even more so when Serena admitted, at some prompting from him, that Madam was out with another gentleman. Porchey was astounded, and left without a word.

An hour later he received a call at his hotel. Tanis was desperate to see him, could he come over? He was thrilled at the sound of her voice and rushed round, all anger momentarily forgotten. Tanis admitted that she had been feeling doubtful, but they spent a wonderful evening together and she seemed to be swept away by Porchey's enthusiasm and charm. 'So you're feeling sure now?' Porchey asked her. 'I'm fairly sure now,' came her answer. 'Fairly?' Porchey exploded.

They talked long into the night, getting more and more exasperated, and each claiming that the other was quite impossible. Finally they agreed, and toasted their decision in champagne. This was more like it, but still hardly what Porchey had been hoping for. They retired for bed that night feeling exhausted rather than romantic.

Porchey spent the following day making arrangements. He acquired a special licence for them to be married in

Baltimore, from the British consulate. He and Tanis had agreed that getting married there rather than in New York might minimise the number of journalists. Porchey also booked a suite at the Lord Baltimore hotel for the night before, and their wedding night. That evening they gave a small drinks party for their New York friends. Though the couple had hoped to keep them secret, the press reported details of the wedding plans.

When Tanis arrived at the hotel in Baltimore on the eve of their wedding day, she appeared to be in a bad mood. Having dined with Porchey, she insisted on sleeping on a different floor of the hotel, with Serena, and left him to his own devices. Disgruntled, he took himself off to bed. Barely had he fallen asleep than the door opened and there was Tanis, fully dressed and brandishing a torch.

'I can't do it, Porchey. I'm sorry, but I can't marry you.'

He sat up in bed as she flung the ring he had just given her and various other pieces of jewellery, pearls, brooches, in his general direction. They whistled past his head and landed on the counterpane. 'I'm going now. Don't look for me, just go back to England and forget all about me.'

With that, she turned on her heel and left an astonished Porchey reeling. He felt desperate. His reception in America had been less satisfactory than he'd wished for, it was true, but he felt that if only they could marry, everything would be resolved. He called the night porter for coffee and set about gathering the jewellery together. What now? Feeling dreadful, he called his sister.

It was breakfast time in London. Porchey was cheered a little the moment he heard Eve's familiar tones, full of affection and sympathy. She listened to his account of events and then announced, 'Well, it's really too early here but I shall do it nevertheless: I'm going to open a bottle of champagne and toast your good fortune with a full glass. You don't know how lucky you are!'

'How can you say such a thing when you know I love her?' asked a plaintive Porchey.

'Nonsense,' said Eve, who was on occasion very like their mother, Almina. 'Tanis was right about one thing: you've got to forget her. Now, get on a train to New York and come home.'

Unfortunately for Porchey, he didn't follow either his ex-lover's or his sister's advice. He made it back to New York and booked himself into the Ritz-Carlton for a night, planning to buy a passage back to Southampton the following day. He took the precaution of informing the concierge that he would accept no calls, but hadn't banked on the 'plumber' who came to repair a basin turning out to be a journalist interested in his side of the story. The press were in full cry, of course; it was a wonderful story. Overwrought and tired, Porchey lost his temper. 'Everyone's very sympathetic,' insisted the reporter. 'Besides, I can tell you where she is.'

When Porchey rang a certain hotel in Washington looking for Tanis, he discovered that the reporter hadn't lied. Tanis sounded contrite about her behaviour but was adamant that she would not change her mind. 'Could we talk about it in a civilised way,' she asked, 'over lunch? I'd like to say goodbye properly.'

Porchey met her at what is now LaGuardia Airport. She looked a million dollars as she got off the plane. They headed for the St Regis hotel and Tanis apologised for behaving in a beastly manner, in between eating an excellent lunch. 'I shall always love you,' she told him. 'I shall never love anyone as much as I have loved you. It's hopeless, though; I'm just not cut out for being chatelaine at Highclere.'

Porchey remained glum and could only pick at his food.

'I'm not going to say a word to anyone, especially the press,' she assured him, before adding, 'My father and brother will be livid with rage with me because they like you tremendously.'

That night Porchey boarded the *Europa*, bound for England. A swarm of newspaper reporters and photographers awaited him on board, insisting that he give them an interview. The ship's purser took him into his office, where Porchey explained that he would have nothing to do with them, since he and Mrs Montagu had agreed not to talk to the press. The purser pulled out the evening papers. There was Tanis, looking lovely in a new frock, holding court at the St Regis. 'Earl jilted at last moment. Said to have savage temper' ran the headline. Porchey could hardly read the words. He sat down, heavily.

Porchey decided that he would after all grant an interview and sent some champagne to the pressmen, asking them to come to his cabin in an hour. They found him in the deluxe bridal suite, a picture of dejection. In front of an audience and with a stiff drink to hand, he began to feel fractionally better. 'I shall just have to enjoy shooting, as much as possible,' he remarked. 'I'm going to shoot a lot of pheasants. How would you feel in my position, though?' he asked rhetorically. 'Pretty tough on a chap, having to go off alone on his honeymoon.'

The *Daily Sketch*'s headline the following day was: 'Pa Found Tut's Tomb, Earl Can't Find Bride'. Utterly crushed, Porchey spent most of the crossing in his suite. Fortunately he'd bumped into an old friend, who kept him in sight and told him emphatically, 'Porchey, it's the luckiest escape. Besides, never run after a woman or a bus: there'll be another one coming along behind.'

It was difficult to be quite so stoical. Porchey had sacrificed his marriage for Tanis, and had then spent the best part of a year pining for her. Now she had jilted him at the altar and the whole world was enjoying the story.

The *Europa* docked at Southampton on 12 November. Porchey was met by hordes of press, and his mother. He had telephoned her before he boarded the ship to let her know what had happened before she read about it. Typically of Almina, she didn't let the fact that she had never believed in Tanis, or Porchey's love, prevent her from rising to the challenge in a crisis. She swept down to the docks and, in a show of solidarity, scooped up her son and drove him back to Highclere. There is a press photo that shows her looking her very best 'grand old lady' self. Porchey is trying his hardest to bear all the attention; Almina seems simply to rise above it.

The next few weeks were a constant stream of humiliation for Porchey. He did indeed shoot pheasants every weekend and fill the castle with his closest friends to support him, but the story seemed to have a life of its own and his distress was considerable. Tanis wrote to him to say she wished she could have been more loyal to him but had to be loyal to herself. She wanted to write scripts in Hollywood, not live at Highclere, and had only weakened in the face of his persistence. She promised to return the money and presents he had given her, and only wished she could 'also return the very great affection and devotion you have unfortunately wasted on me.'

While Lord Carnarvon's marriage was definitely off, another one was looking increasingly likely. At the end of October, as Porchey sailed across the Atlantic on his doomed mission to marry Tanis, Mrs Simpson filed for divorce and the American press reported that her marriage to King Edward VIII was imminent. Alan Lascelles, the King's private secretary, wrote to him to inform him that 'the silence in the British press on the subject of Your Majesty's friendship with Mrs Simpson is not going to be maintained . . . Judging by the letters from British subjects living in foreign countries where the press has been outspoken, the effect will be calamitous.'

On 16 November, Prime Minister Stanley Baldwin was summoned to Buckingham Palace where the King told him that he intended to marry Mrs Simpson as soon as she was free to do so. Baldwin replied that such a marriage would not be acceptable to the people of Britain and her dominions. The King responded that if forced to choose, he would choose to abdicate the throne in order to be able to marry.

Various middle-ground options were considered by the King, the government and his advisers over the next few days, but nothing could be made to stick. Edward summoned several ministers to discuss the matter with him, including Duff Cooper, who was Minister for War at the time. Duff Cooper simply asked him to try to think about how his life would be if he pressed ahead with his resolution, and what he would do. The King was unmoved.

The royal family were appalled at the constitutional crisis that threatened the British monarchy, and Edward's refusal to do what they considered to be his duty. Appeals were made to numerous friends to intervene, to try to persuade him that he must choose the throne and give up Mrs Simpson. This was the helping hand that Prince George had requested of Porchey months ago, should the need arise.

On 23 November, the Duke of Kent was down at Highclere for the second shooting weekend in a row. Both men were in need of pleasurable distractions. Porchey might have been miserable, but he recognised that his problems were small in comparison with the crisis engulfing the royal family, and indeed the country.

The following week, Prince George telephoned Porchey to ask if he could come up to town as soon as possible. They wanted to leave no stone unturned in the effort to 'dissuade

David'. A plan was hatched. The Duke of Kent asked Porchey to contrive to meet his brother in the hammam on Jermyn Street in Mayfair, a Victorian Turkish Baths complex. Porchey would need to be there by 7.00 a.m. so that it seemed less of a put-up job, and could then have a quiet word.

Come the appointed day, Porchey was in situ as planned and making his way through the various steam rooms. Half an hour later the King arrived. With a grin he said, 'Morning, Porchey. Now, let me guess. George has put you up to this.'

Porchey decided it was better to own up immediately and then get straight to the point. 'Are you quite resolute, Your Majesty? Quite sure this is not an infatuation?'

'Of course I'm sure. That's what that bloody fool Baldwin asked me, too. No, no, Porchey, it's her brain. I can't tell you what a wonderful woman she is.'

Porchey reiterated his belief that the country would never accept a twice-divorced woman as queen and then, seeing that there was nothing more to be said, took his leave. He was very downcast at the thought of the certain crisis to come.

On 10 December 1936, Edward VIII of Great Britain, Ireland and the British Dominions beyond the Seas, King, Emperor of India, signed the papers to renounce his right, and that of his descendants, to the throne. His three brothers were with him in the drawing room at Fort Belvedere, to witness his signature. The following day, as the abdication was legally ratified by the British Parliament and that of the dominions, Prince Edward, as he now was, made a broadcast to the nation from Windsor Castle. His speech had been polished by Winston Churchill; he stressed that he did not feel he could do his job well without the support of the woman he loved. On the next day he left for Austria, to spend his life with Wallis Simpson.

Viewed from the great distance of eighty years, the fallout from the crisis was not as grave as the royal family and

Stanley Baldwin had feared. Baldwin was commended for having successfully resolved the situation; Prince Albert (Bertie), who became King George VI, was widely believed to be far more suited to the job than his elder brother, and Edward was allowed to head off and pursue what Canadian Prime Minister Mackenzie King called that 'jazz of life' of which he had always been so fond.

But the fact that the resolution was a success, and that public attitudes to many of the moral and legal arguments that underpinned the case are now very different, does not alter the fact that at the time it was deeply traumatic. Many members of the establishment never forgave Edward for putting his own personal happiness above the wishes and needs of his nation. Many of them never forgave Wallis for being Wallis. Prince George maintained a cordial but distant correspondence. Porchey played golf with HRH the Duke of Windsor, as Edward became, and dined with the Duke and Duchess from time to time, but he and Wallis never got on and gradually the friendship was allowed to decline.

The King's opponents were certainly wrong about one thing. The relationship was no mere infatuation. Edward married Wallis on 3 June 1937 in France and the marriage lasted until his death in 1972.

Thanks to the rumbling aftershocks of the abdication crisis, the British press largely forgot that they had been so excited about the Earl of Carnarvon's jilting only two months previously. Porchey must have been inordinately grateful for their distraction when he read in the *New York Post* on 16 January 1937 that the Guinness heiress, the Hon. Mrs Tanis Montagu, and vice-president of MGM studios, Howard Dietz, had eloped by plane from Newark to Juarez, Mexico.

The bridegroom had been divorced for three days and insisted that there was nothing at all impetuous about the marriage. Mrs Dietz had perhaps started to appreciate the value of circumspection. She confined her comments to, 'I am very happy.' The couple thought they would settle in Greenwich Village, New York.

12

Recovery

In January 1937 Catherine, Countess of Carnarvon, wrote to the Duchess of Kent, wife of her old friend, to congratulate her on the birth of her second child, a daughter. The infant Princess Alexandra had been born on Christmas Day 1936 at her parents' house, 3 Belgrave Square. Princess Marina replied, saying that she hoped to be able to show her the baby soon and wishing her 'dear Catherine every blessing for 1937'.

The Duke and Duchess of Kent had been excellent friends to Catherine since her separation from Porchey. She had until recently been living nearby, just the other side of Hyde Park, at Hertford Street, and Princess Marina had invited her to tea and to dine when they were having one of their quieter evenings. She and Prince George could see that Catherine was starting to feel better, but deduced that she was still in no mood for the Kents' typically boisterous evening parties, and probably would not enjoy seeing Porchey's old friends, who were such a fixture of their social circle.

The Kents, along with Catherine's numerous other friends and supporters, had reason to believe that she had turned a corner and was now really making an independent life for herself. At the end of 1936 she had bought a house on Wilton Crescent, a street of elegant late-Regency town houses just off Belgrave Square, in the heart of fashionable Belgravia. The Duke and Duchess of Kent were now even nearer neighbours, so it seems likely that she did indeed meet Princess Alexandra early in 1937.

Wilton Crescent was a new beginning. Catherine's excitement about it (and her longing for the divorce to reach its conclusion) is palpable in a letter she wrote to her aunt Edith, in New York, in the October of 1936. 'All this very sad affair of mine will be over on 2 November when I hope the divorce will be made absolute. I took [cousin] Mary over my new house yesterday and she thought it was lovely. So now I am very busy trying to get it all done up and settled for Xmas!'

Aside from being a beautiful house, 11 Wilton Crescent was the first significant asset that Catherine had ever owned herself. She bought it with part of the generous divorce settlement that her ex-husband made over to her, and it was hers and hers alone. Unlike Highclere, it truly was her home and no one could ask her to leave it.

There is something poignant about reading the inventory of furniture that was transported there by the removal company Messrs Camp, Hopson and Co., from Hertford Street on 11 November 1936. One realises how little Catherine had to call her own, despite the sixteen years she had spent as Lady Carnarvon. A double bed, a wardrobe, a settee and two easy chairs. A dressing mirror and some gramophone records, a silver teapot, sundry photographs. Her collection of dresses. The portrait of Catherine on the front cover of this book was painted by Simon Elwes in 1929, which now hangs again at Highclere in what was once her sitting room. The list of possessions, typed in fading purple ink, does not fill a single sheet of paper.

It was not that Catherine was left badly off. Porchey agreed to an income of £3,000 a year, for life and irrespective of any subsequent marriage. The Highclere Estate was charged as security, which meant that the settlement was cast-iron guaranteed. (An incidental, but fundamentally key consequence for Catherine's son, was that this would later provide a check on his father's sales of the remaining parts of the Highclere Estate. Because of the terms of the divorce, there would be something left for Henry to inherit.) The income was in addition to the money Porchey had provided for her to purchase the house, and his payment of most of their children's expenses (though Catherine, fair-minded, insisted that she contribute, too). By the time the final stage of settlement was concluded, as it was in April 1937, Catherine was a wealthy woman. She was able to buy beautiful new things of her own choosing with which to furnish her house. She might have decided to hang her self-portrait, which is a lovely likeness that captures her luminous prettiness and calm expression. Though perhaps she chose not to: having it displayed would mean being reminded that Porchey had not wished to keep it.

Catherine had left her childhood homes at the age of ten after her father's death, and then lived on the generosity of her mother's cousins, in their space. Highclere had been a happy home for years, but it was always her husband's family seat and her presence there was dependent on Porchey's say-so. As Almina had discovered before her, countesses come and go from Highclere, always having to make room for the next generation, or the next wife. Compared to the vulnerability of all these former homes, Wilton Crescent was a place of safety.

It would be her children's home, too, of course. Penelope was with her most of the time, except when she was visiting her father. Henry would return for the school holidays. Gar was frequently there, lending support. Jac and Eileen and their two children lived just a few doors away, at number 47, which was one reason that Catherine had decided on the house in the first place. Philippa was still far off in Scotland, wrestling with her own marital problems but, in other respects, it was like a return to the Wendells' old London days. They were still a close family who enjoyed each other's company as much as they relied on one another.

And of course, Catherine was still an attractive young woman with a love of dancing and music and conversation. She must at some point have realised that in some ways, she had never been this powerful before in her life. She had autonomy, money, and the sympathy of all who had wished her well during the past awful few years. She had battled her depression and her drinking problem, and the worst upset of her life was now behind her. She was free to do what she pleased. That was a challenging prospect in some ways for a woman unused to such liberty, but also an exciting one.

While 1937 began well for Catherine, for Porchey it was far more painful. Early in January he collapsed at Highclere and Almina swept down to collect him and take him back to Alfred House to nurse him better. Smith the butler was also ill and had to take some time off work; he had weak lungs and the damp winter was troubling him. It isn't clear what Porchey was suffering from—it might well have been at least partly physical – but judging from Almina's solicitude and the timing it seems likely that he was mostly at the end of his tether. His nerves were strung out after the separation and divorce from Catherine, worry over the impact on his children and then the whole ghastly Tanis affair that had culminated in his heartbreak and humiliation.

Porchey spent three weeks at his mother's nursing home, where he rested and ate well and where he could talk things through with Almina. Perhaps it was her idea that he take a holiday, somewhere warm away from the cold London winter. After all, her husband had been advised by his doctors to winter in Egypt, and though Almina had her misgivings about the place initially, she grew to love it.

Porchey spent a week or so in Egypt before travelling on to Kenya. He knew people out there, in particular Lord Delamere. The Delameres were the principal family in British Kenya. Tom Delamere's father had been so formative in building up the agricultural economy of colonial East Africa, encouraging the British upper classes to settle there and assuming unofficial social and political leadership when they did, that he was nicknamed the Rhodes of Kenya. By 1937 there were approximately 25,000 white settlers in the lush highlands of central Kenya and their presence had established the country as a holiday destination for wealthy safari-goers.

At the end of January, Porchey set off for Nairobi with a group of friends. He knew Myrtle and Flash Kellet from the racing set; Patty Hoyt was an attractive American friend of theirs whom he had met the previous year and taken a liking to, and with whom he had embarked on a love affair after his relationship with Tanis foundered. He was accompanied, as always on his travels, by his valet, George.

Nairobi in 1937 had a tiny central district of grand administrative buildings, built in a hurry by the British, a rapidly developing commercial sector and a railway line running out towards Uganda in one direction and Mombasa on the Indian Ocean in the other. Outside of the city were the country clubs of the white elite, complete with golf courses and airstrips for easy access to their vast farms. Porchey's party spent a night at the Norfolk hotel in central Nairobi and were then driven out to catch a flight that would transport them, complete with guns, cameras, tents and guides, to go on safari.

Porchey was away in Kenya for about seven weeks. As well as hunting in the Maasai Mara and the Serengeti, the group spent time in Happy Valley visiting the Delameres and other friends. It was evidently just what he needed: sunshine, relaxation, distance from his troublesome memories and time to reflect on them.

On his return to Highclere at the end of March, he carefully prepared photograph albums to give to the others as mementos of a wonderful trip. In due course Safariland Ltd, outfitters of safaris and scientific expeditions, despatched two cases of trophies packed for Lord Carnarvon but including items for Captain and Mrs Kellet and Mrs Hoyt. Porchey presented the stuffed head of a waterbuck he had shot in Tanganyika territory on 26 February to the Mayor of Newbury. It was probably well received at the time, but both the poor beast's head and the plaque that bears its details have long since been gracefully retired from the municipal offices.

When he was writing his cheerfully robust if somewhat unreliable memoirs, nearly half a century later, Porchey assured his readers that he was quite in agreement with the modern mindset that 'wild animals should only be shot with cameras', but one senses that he didn't quite mean it. He loved to shoot all his life and was proud of the quality of the shooting at Highclere. One suspects that Porchey probably continued to regard a waterbuck or two as fair game, much like the pheasants he shot at home.

Porchey loved Kenya, so it is tempting to wonder whether he sang its praises to his old friend Sir Henry 'Jock' Delves Broughton, and whether that conversation prompted the thought that would lead, eventually, to tragedy.

Sir Jock had been a prominent figure in the racing world for years, and had helped Porchey to build up the Highclere stud. He had always been a frequent visitor for race meetings, but by mid-1937 the baronet was in serious trouble with his gambling debts. He had already sold most of the family land and possessions and, being still in terrible debt, had started to look around for possible escape routes, should the need arise.

Unfortunately, Sir Jock's problems would only get worse. In 1939 he was suspected of insurance fraud after claiming for the theft of his wife's pearls and some of her valuable paintings. Shortly after that the couple divorced and, following a hasty second marriage, Jock decided it was time to get out of England for a while. He and his new wife, Diana, picked Kenya, and arrived in Happy Valley early in November 1940, where they threw themselves into the whirl of drugs, drink and wife-swapping that characterised the leisure time of the Happy Valley set. Less than three months later, Lord Erroll, with whom Diana had been having a highly visible affair, was found shot in the head in his car at a junction outside Nairobi. It didn't take long for the police—and indeed everyone else—to conclude that Jock Delves Broughton was the obvious suspect.

When Porchey heard the news, he defended Jock's

innocence to everyone who would listen, on the grounds that Jock was a lousy shot who could never have killed anyone. When Delves Broughton was acquitted for lack of evidence, Porchey sent him a telegram. 'Hearty congratulations understand you won a neck cleverly. Regards Porchey.' But Delves Broughton never got over the 'White Mischief' scandal. Abandoned by his bride, shunned in Kenya, he came back to Britain alone in December 1942 and committed suicide a few days later.

In 1937, though, Porchey had no reason to feel anything other than fondness towards Kenya. It had been the tonic his low spirits required. Not even the news that there had been a fire at Highclere in his absence could shake him. Fortunately, despite the fact that three bedrooms in the northeast corner of the castle were completely gutted, no one had been hurt. As Porchey reported to his sister, Eve, Penelope had been staying for a few nights and was sleeping upstairs when the fire broke out. Her room was on the opposite side of the castle, thank god, and Penelope was 'quite cool and not the least bit frightened'. Porchey set about the repairs and took the opportunity to completely overhaul the castle's electric lighting, at a cost of £130.

In this buoyant mood, Porchey allowed himself to be persuaded by his brother-in-law Brograve to buy stock in a technology company. The firm was French, based just outside Paris, and had developed a heat-resistant copper cable. Bro had recently acquired the licence to develop it in the UK and was planning to finance the patent and set up a factory in Newcastle to produce it. He just needed to secure a little more backing. Porchey invested £12,000. The British company was christened Pyrotenax and during the Second World War its product became an essential component of a great deal of military equipment. When it floated, in 1954, it netted Porchey £360,000 on his initial investment. Porchey was always a gambler but, not only did he know his limits, he also had good instincts.

This particular venture into industry would prove to be of a different order of return to most of Porchey's investments, which were designed to be solid earners. Throughout the 1930s he sold off assets such as the Carnarvon Arms pub and bought shares in basic industries and utilities. But the stock market was definitely considered the safest bet and it certainly far outstripped anything that could be achieved from farming on the estate. Marcus Wickham Boynton, Porchey's agent, concentrated on cutting costs by trimming the number of gardeners and letting the forestry workers go because increasing revenue was virtually impossible. By 1937 the larger farms that might have had the potential for redevelopment had been sold and there were only a few smallholdings left at Highclere. While the tenants continued to pay their rents and to farm for themselves, Porchey never seems to have regarded agriculture as a serious proposition. In this he was probably right. Britain was an import economy when it came to food (a fact that would cause enormous problems when war broke out two years later). It brought in three quarters of its wheat from abroad, virtually all its butter and the large majority of its meat and barley. Throughout the 1930s farmers found it harder and harder to make a profit, as global prices for wheat collapsed. Porchey was perhaps sensible to prefer that the old way of small-scale tenant farming should be allowed to continue.

The more positive outlook and the tranquillity that characterised both Porchey and Catherine's new, separate lives in the summer of 1937 could not have been in more stark contrast to the international situation. Barely had the financial crisis of 1929 blown its way through the already fragile post-war economies than the political situation in Italy, Germany and Spain began to shift in response.

The roots of European fascism lie in post-First World War disillusion with the nationalistic ambitions of democratic governments, ambitions that had led millions to slaughter. They lie in the horrified reaction to Russian Bolshevism and the resentment of the punitive demands imposed on the beaten nations, particularly Germany, under the Treaty of Versailles. But the sense of injustice and disappointment prevalent among ordinary Europeans was fuelled by a great economic depression. When this combustible mixture started to burn there was nothing to check it, or the many political leaders eager to fan the flames.

In Italy, Mussolini had been in power since 1922, following his staging of what was essentially a coup d'état with the March on Rome to oust the democratically elected Prime Minister. By 1927 he had established a one-party state. By 1929 he was ruling as 'Il Duce'. Right-wing dictatorship had arrived, and was showing an example to other European fascist parties, and their leaders.

Hitler was appointed Chancellor of Germany in January 1933 when his Nazi party won enough votes to be the largest party in a coalition government. From there, Hitler used emergency legislation passed in the wake of an arson attack on the seat of government to justify suspension of basic liberties and the brutal suppression of all political opponents. In March 1935, and in direct contravention of the Treaty of Versailles, he announced that a new Air Force was to be developed and the other armed forces were to be massively expanded. Almost exactly a year later, in another contravention of the terms of the post-war settlement, German troops reoccupied the demilitarised Rhineland, a buffer zone between Germany and Belgium. Three years before Nazi Germany began its programme of acquiring more *Lebensraum* (living space) through the invasion of neighbours, there was serious worry in some quarters in Britain and France about what seemed to be its vigorous preparations for war.

But another major current of thought, the dominant one throughout the mid-1930s, was that Germany had legitimate desires to reindustrialise and rearm, that she could not be punished indefinitely in the wake of the Great War, and that to try to do so would give more grist to the National Socialists' mill. With the benefit of hindsight, the policy that came to be known as appeasement seems tragically naïve and misguided, but the fact is that at the time it was supported by the vast majority of citizens across Europe and was based on a sincerely held belief that war was the evil that must be avoided at all costs. The other fatal mistake was in believing that Hitler's ambitions to expand German territory were limited and could be contained. The events of 1938 and 1939 would show that this was not the case.

In the October of 1937, at a moment when the new British Prime Minister Neville Chamberlain was adamant that Hitler was a man of his word and war a distant possibility that could be averted through diplomacy, Porchey hosted a weekend party that was, for him, unusually political in character. And the political mood was nowhere near as sanguine as Chamberlain's.

Brendan Bracken was born the son of an Irish Republican stonemason but moved to London via Australia and Cumbria, and reinvented himself en route as a magazine publisher and a Conservative MP. As was the case with his friend, Max Beaverbrook, his business and political interests overlapped continuously. He was a big man with tousled carrot-coloured hair who talked a million words a minute. He was also an accomplished autodidact of enormous charm who, aged nineteen, had passed himself off as a fifteen-year-old Australian orphan and talked his way into Sedbergh School, an ancient and prestigious independent school in Cumbria. Bracken was determined to acquire both the education and the trappings of English middle-class respectability. He had been an ardent supporter of Churchill from the 1920s and was invited to join the exclusive Other Club, Churchill's political dining society for the 'estimable and entertaining', which met once a fortnight at the Savoy hotel for drinks, dinner and ferocious debate. Bracken's loyalty to Churchill would be rewarded in due course with his appointment to the post of Minister of Information in 1941, but at the time of his visit to Highclere he was a mere backbench MP, albeit one with excellent business and political connections. Porchey had invited him primarily because he was amusing, which tended to be his main criterion for inviting anyone.

Porchey had known Max Beaverbrook, proprietor of the *Daily Express* and the *Evening Standard*—and consequently one of the most powerful men in the country—for years. Anyone who was anyone in Britain between the wars knew Beaverbrook, such was his political clout (it was said he could break anyone or anything) and his taste for socialising. He had certainly been regaled with stories by Porchey's friend Sibell Lygon on several occasions, and had in fact encouraged her to write a column for him. Sibell contributed a few pieces to *Harper's Bazaar* and the *Daily Express*, but it was eventually revealed that Beaverbrook had written most of her material himself. He was flexible like that: it was her aristocratic name that would sell his newspapers, the rest he could furnish himself. Lord Beaverbrook had never before been to Highclere, but now he thought he might make a foray into racing, and was keen to take Porchey's advice.

The other principal guest that weekend was Porchey's old friend Alfred Duff Cooper, who had frequently, during the course of his ten years as an MP and a government minister, had reason to be outraged by some stance or other taken by Lord Beaverbrook's newspapers.

Duff Cooper was at that point serving in the National Government—a coalition of Conservatives, Liberal Nationals and National Labour—as First Lord of the Admiralty. Like Bracken he was far more a Churchill man than a natural supporter of Chamberlain's. He had in fact spent most of the previous year pleading fruitlessly with Chamberlain, who was Chancellor of the Exchequer at the time, to allow him the budget to reform the Army and start recruiting. Consequently he expected to lose his cabinet post when Chamberlain took over from Stanley Baldwin as Prime Minister in May 1937 but, in the event, he was moved from the Ministry for War to the Admiralty. Duff Cooper's experience at these two military ministries meant he was in a good position to substantiate his long-held view that the British armed services were in a parlous state. Duff Cooper was convinced that it was folly to allow them to shrink in size when the Germans had spent the last five years aggressively rebuilding theirs. With Italy's invasion of Abyssinia, the virtual collapse of the League of Nations, the recent outbreak of civil war in Spain and Hitler's 1936 Anti-Comintern Pact with Japan, he and Churchill stepped up their calls for a programme of rearmament to meet the possibility of imminent war.

But Churchill was still regarded as a maverick and a pugnacious alarmist by many in the Conservative Party, the National Government, and in particular by the Prime Minister. In the course of a political career that had already spanned forty years, he had acquired as many detractors as friends. He had committed the ultimate political sin of switching parties, not once but twice. He had been condemned for the failure of the Gallipoli campaign during the First World War, and had alienated as well as impressed people by his capacity for brilliant speeches and equally brilliant insults. In 1937 he was still three years away from leadership and the country was in no mood to listen to his warnings that war was now inevitable.

The tone of the political conversation that weekend at Highclere must have been gloomy, but Porchey's guests were all by inclination convivial men, and Ernest Grimes, his excellent chef, could be relied upon to provide distractions from even the greatest cares of state. Porchey also had a very smart new toy to show his friends. He had decided to buy a new car and his great friend, Captain Kellet, had discovered a Rolls-Royce Phantom III in London. It was the last of the great classic-era motor cars, with a beautiful long chassis and a V12 engine that purred almost noiselessly. Resprayed in his colours with his silver jockey and horse on the front, it cheered him up whenever he so much as looked at it.

Nineteen thirty-eight brought no let-up in terms of worsening European politics. In March, Hitler's armies marched unopposed into Austria to unite the country with the German Third Reich. Though this action was expressly forbidden under the terms of the Treaty of Versailles, international reaction was muted. An editorial in *The Times* likened it to the union of Scotland with England three hundred years previously. Chamberlain told the House of Commons that the government 'could not regard the development with equanimity, that it was bound to lead to greater uncertainty in Europe.'

There was peace and quiet at Highclere, though. For much of the summer Lord Carnarvon was absent, travelling to the

States, spending time in New York and Florida with friends. Despite the mounting bad news abroad, there was still fun to be had. Years later, Porchey recalled in his memoirs that when he crossed the Atlantic in the summer of 1938, two of his friends, Randolph Churchill, son of Winston and occasional visitor to Highclere, and Noël Coward were on board. They didn't much like each other. One night, over a cocktail, Noël told Porchey he had just delivered a note to Randolph's cabin. 'Dear Randolph, if you are free I hope you will come to the first night of my new show in New York. I enclose a brace of tickets so that you may bring a friend, if you have one.' The following morning Porchey was treated to the other half of the correspondence by an indignant Randolph, who evidently lacked none of his father's gift for a witty put-down. Randolph replied, 'Dear Noël, unfortunately I am engaged on the opening night. Nevertheless I shall be delighted to come on another night, if you have one.'

Meanwhile Porchey had left Highclere in good hands. He had engaged a new secretary for the estate office, Miss Stubbings, in May 1937, and she noted that her employer left a great many things to his staff.

It was an attitude for which Robert Taylor had reason to be thankful. Despite Lord Carnarvon's telling him that he should be sacked if he couldn't manage a telephone message, and scarcely six months after arriving to work as a footman, Robert had proved his worth during Smith the butler's illness. In January 1937, just before his departure for his mother's nursing home, Lord Carnarvon had called Robert to his bedroom. 'Lady Evelyn tells me you have done a very good job, Robert. I hope you have been happy here, and if you have, I'd like to suggest that you stay another season, stand in for poor Smith.' Robert was thrilled that his work had been so appreciated and readily agreed. That was the first significant exchange between Porchey and Robert Taylor, the first of a lifetime's worth.

Robert was just twenty-three years old when he found himself appointed acting butler at Highclere. He managed the crisis of the house fire in Lord Carnarvon's absence and, when Smith returned to his post in late spring, made no fuss about resuming the duties of a first footman. His calm, competence and good humour meant he was well liked by everyone and marked him out as the up-coming man.

Robert's qualities recommended him to the local girls as well. On one of the Highclere staff's regular Saturday-night outings to a local servants' dance, a particular young lady caught his eye. Robert implored his friend, Ruby Benson, to introduce them. Ruby was a housemaid at Highclere and knew everyone for miles about, on account of her father running the Pheasant pub in the village. Ruby duly intro-duced Robert to Johanna, who was always known as Joan. She worked in one of the other local houses, and Robert put to use the foxtrots and waltzes that he'd been learning in the servants' hall. Joan was evidently sufficiently taken with him to agree to meet him at the next dance, in two weeks' time, and the one after that. They were officially an item.

In May 1938, Almina's second husband, Ian Dennistoun, died at Alfred House. They had been married for fourteen years and Almina had devoted herself to caring for him, moving house on a regular basis, always looking for a spot where Ian might be as comfortable as possible. They had tried Scotland (his family was Scottish), Somerset and the Isle of Wight (for its healthy sea air). With each new house, Almina had swept in, undertaken extravagant renovations and decorations with no idea of any sort of budget and then, bored or distracted, embarked on the next house that might be just the thing for Ian's health. One imagines that after a few of these moves, Ian might well have preferred to be left in peace.

Almina might have been flighty, but she also sincerely loved her husband and was grateful to Eve, who accompanied her to Ian's funeral, for the support. Porchey had never warmed to the man or really forgiven his mother for putting everyone through the very public court case that arose from Ian and Dorothy Dennistoun's divorce, so his reaction was much cooler. As so often before, they had also been at odds over money: Porchey thought she was spending most unnecessarily on these endless house moves.

Almina's response to sadness was, as always, to stay busy. She resolved to throw herself even more into work at Alfred House. She was now sixty-two years old, but still as energetic as she had been when she had been running her hospital at Highclere, twenty years before.

Catherine wrote to Almina to express her sympathy. She knew only too well the sense of being bereft, though perhaps she underestimated the therapeutic effect of Almina's vocation for nursing. Catherine had always been more introspective than her former mother-in-law, more inclined to analyse and less inclined to *do*.

There was certainly little time for introspection for Catherine during 1938. On the contrary: she was living the London life that she had never known during the Twenties when she was busy being a wife, a mother and the Countess of Carnarvon down at sleepy Highclere. Catherine had always had a gift for friendship. Now that she was free to take up her social life again, she accepted invitations to dinner, to the theatre, to dances. She was as in demand as she had been when she and Philippa used to arrive arm in arm at parties in the golden years of the post-war celebrations. The only difference was that, this time around, she was a little wiser and a little more confident, a little more sure of what she wanted out of life.

It seems likely that Catherine met Geoffrey Grenfell, a tall, handsome, highly amusing stockbroker with a slow smile that lit up his whole face, through his aunt, Lady Desborough. The Grenfell family was distinguished by a certain brand of upper-class Bohemianism, but also by incredibly bad fortune when it came to surviving into middle age. They had suffered more than their fair share of tragedy.

By 1938, Ettie, Lady Desborough, was no longer the glamorous society hostess that she had been in her heyday. In fin-de-siècle London society, she and her husband had been at the heart of a circle of wealthy and artistic types nicknamed 'the Souls', for their habit of discussing any and every subject so long as it wasn't politics, and their preference for dissecting each other's innermost beings. The Desboroughs had five children, three sons and two daughters. The first two boys were killed in action in France in 1915, within two months of one another. The third son was killed in a car accident in 1926, an event that caused his determinedly robust mother to retire to her bed for two months. Lady Desborough, who had lost both parents and her brother by the time she was six years old, never quite recovered from the onslaught that afflicted her family, but her grief made her kind rather than bitter, and she loved her nephew all the more. She continued to welcome guests to Taplow Court on the River Thames, and it was probably there that Catherine, invited through some mutual friend, encountered the man who was to become her second husband.

Geoffrey Grenfell was a gentleman broker who worked for the family firm of Grenfell and Co. and maintained houses in London, at Ovington Square in Knightsbridge, and in the Kent countryside. He was a couple of years older than Catherine and during the Great War had joined the navy at barely sixteen years old, in a fit of patriotic fervour that almost got him killed along with his cousins. He served on HMS *Warspite* and survived the ferocious Battle of Jutland that claimed Lord Kitchener, the Field Marshal and British icon.

Geoffrey, like Catherine, had been married before and had a child, a daughter, whom he adored. He was the antithesis of Porchey in almost every regard, a man from a background much more like Catherine's own. He was connected to the aristocracy but, as the child of a younger son, had gone into the City and held down a job. Unlike Porchey, he had a clear sense of purpose and of who he was. There is a steadiness in the tone of the letters he would write to Catherine when he was away on service during the Second World War that broadcasts what must have been his chief attraction for her. Quite apart from his matinée-idol rugged good looks, Geoffrey was a reliable man, a man who offered her straight-forward devotion and no funny business on the side. If Catherine had married Porchey in part because his quickness with an anecdote and boisterous charm reminded her of her father, she married Geoffrey because he was the opposite of flighty. It proved to be a supremely happy match.

In September 1938 the court circulars carried the news that Catherine, Countess of Carnarvon, was to marry again. The *New York Times* picked up on the story and reported the latest twist in the tale of one of its favourite descendants of 'two of the oldest families of the United States of America'.

Catherine married Geoffrey on 21 September at Kensington Register Office. Porchey wrote to congratulate her. Her immediate family, Jac and Eileen, Philippa and Gar all attended, as did her children. Henry was now fourteen years old and had recently started at Eton; Penelope was thirteen. They were both delighted with their 'Uncle Geoffrey'. So too was everyone who knew Catherine. How could they not be, when her happiness was so plain to see? By now 38, Catherine wore a smart coat and very chic little hat on her second, far quieter and more intimate wedding day.

It could not have been more different to her first, very public wedding to Lord Porchester as he had been then, sixteen years previously. Then the press had covered every detail of her wedding clothes, and crowds had gathered outside St Margaret's Westminster to watch her emerge on Porchey's arm. Now, after the brief ceremony, the ever-loyal Gertrude and Percival Griffiths hosted a small wedding breakfast at their home in Bryanston Square for family and close friends. But the mood of this second wedding day was every bit as happy as that first one had been. Geoffrey had restored the sunshine to Catherine's days. After all the turmoil and tears of the last years at Highclere, she was basking in the love of a man who adored her just as she was.

The terrible pity was that it was such an inauspicious time to be a newly-wed. Eight days after Catherine and Geoffrey married, Neville Chamberlain signed the Munich Agreement with Hitler and the world was set irrevocably on the path to war.

13

The Coming Disaster

On 30 September 1938, Neville Chamberlain returned from Munich to rapturous crowds of relieved Britons who were desperate to believe the Prime Minister when he assured them that he had secured 'peace for our time', having signed the Munich Agreement with Germany, France and Italy. On hearing the news, US President Franklin D. Roosevelt sent Chamberlain a two-word telegram: 'Good man'.

Those cheering crowds are a salient reminder that, though it seems extraordinary now, there were plenty besides Roosevelt who still believed that Hitler's ambitions had been satisfied and that a cataclysmic war had therefore been avoided. The irony of the Western powers' terrible misreading of the situation is inescapable for us, who know what happened next. But at the time, Alfred Duff Cooper, who resigned in protest the day after Chamberlain's now notorious declaration that Germany and England had agreed 'never to go to war again', was in a tiny minority. And even Duff Cooper had believed, right up to Chamberlain's return from Munich with what he saw as a disastrously conciliatory agreement, that the Prime Minister's conference would indeed succeed in averting war. It was Britain and France's failure to secure the means for holding Hitler to his pledge to go no further in Europe that drove Duff Cooper's decision, and not, strictly speaking, the abandonment of Czechoslovakia to its fate. The anti-war mood was again rampant, and Duff Cooper and Churchill were isolated in their belief that the agreement had made war more likely, not less. In his famous resignation speech, Duff Cooper concluded that he might have been persuaded to accept war with honour or peace with dishonour, but war with dishonour was too much.

Reaction to Duff Cooper's leaving was mixed, but MP Vyvyan Adams, who also opposed appeasement, described it as 'the first step back to national sanity'. Porchey, like many others, was stung into action by the resignation of his old friend. In October 1938 he wrote to Chamberlain expressing deep concern about the Nazi domination of Europe and urging that a programme of rearmament be adopted immediately.

The post-Munich relief lasted just a few short months. In November 1938, SA Nazi paramilitaries went on an anti-Jewish rampage across Germany and Austria in which thousands of civilians also participated. The pogrom claimed ninety-one lives, destroyed countless homes and businesses, displaced 30,000 people, and signalled to the world that Hitler's aggression was directed not just towards his neighbours, but also towards the resident Jewish population.

In March 1939, amid a mood of sickened realisation that all the concessions had seemingly been in vain, Britain pledged to support Poland in the event of invasion by Germany. On 27 April, Duff Cooper had the satisfaction of seeing that conscription had finally been introduced, as he had been urging for more than two years, though only for men aged twenty and twenty-one. Still, something had shifted. Britain was now gearing up to a war footing. Churchill was no longer the rebel, crying wolf on the sidelines; he was emerging as the most consistent opponent of Britain's past five years of foreign policy mistakes.

In April 1939, Porchey was informed by letter from the Ministry of Health that, in the event of war, he must make immediate preparations to receive the children and staff of Curzon Crescent nursery school, northwest London. Up to fifty children between the ages of two and five would be billeted in relative safety at Highclere. Porchey was relieved, both to be providing a useful service if the worst should indeed come to pass, and also that the house had not been requisitioned by the Ministry of Defence, whose activities would certainly have been more disruptive.

In between bad news, and despite the worsening outlook, life carried on. The Duke of Kent came to Highclere for a few days' shooting in December 1938, and charmed the entire household, as usual. He brought reports of Catherine, who was apparently looking radiant, and her new husband Geoffrey, whom he had recently met and thought an excellent fellow.

Porchey seems to have been sincerely delighted at his ex-wife's new happiness. Catherine had not, like Tanis, got the upper hand at the last, nor had she ever behaved badly or exposed him to ridicule—quite the opposite. This meant that Porchey's feelings were the far more straightforward ones of fondness and gratitude, rather than the lingering interest he felt towards Tanis Montagu.

In June 1937, six months after he had collapsed in distress at Tanis's desertion, Porchey wrote to Douglas Williams, a friend in New York, asking him to bring him some gramophone records ('There's a Lull in My Life', 'This Year's Crop of Kisses') when he next came over to London. He also slipped in a rather transparently casual enquiry after his ex-lover. 'Naturally, I hear a considerable amount from mutual friends. It would be nice if you could make a point of seeing her prior to sailing, in order to give me the latest news of the whole situation.'

Porchey seems to have suffered from that very common human weakness of remaining hung up on the one that got away, while slightly overlooking the depth of love once felt for the more significant but less turbulent partner. Having said that, towards the end of his life, Porchey referred to Catherine as his 'beloved wife' when he wrote his second volume of memoirs. He had loved her deeply for many years, a fact that must have come home to him with all the greater force in the wake of more romantic disasters to come.

Catherine and Geoffrey were enjoying the bubble of newly-wed life. Geoffrey wanted to spoil her, and took her to the theatre and afterwards to supper and dancing at the Café de Paris or the 400 Club in a tiny cellar on Leicester Square, where London society could dance until dawn. These were Porchey's old haunts; now it was Catherine's turn to whirl with her love around the dance floor to the music of the resident jazz band.

She and Geoffrey had decided to live in his house at Ovington Square, but Catherine retained Wilton Crescent, of which she had grown immensely fond, and which had been her gateway to this new fulfilled and fun-filled existence. She trusted her beloved Geoffrey completely, but life had taught her that it was impossible to anticipate troubles, and she valued her new independence too much to give up her home completely. Gar continued to base herself there, so she was close to Jac and Eileen.

Porchey was just as keen as ever to find someone with whom he could share his life. He loved the company of women until his very last days and enjoyed love affairs immensely, but he continued to seek out the intimacy and comradeship of a potential wife. He was not a man who liked to live alone. In 1939 there were two candidates for the role of the next Countess of Carnarvon. Slightly predictably, given the track record demonstrated by his misadventures with Tanis, Porchey picked the wrong one.

Jeanne Stuart came to Highclere for the first time in June 1939. She and Porchey had met earlier in the year through mutual acquaintances in the London theatre world. Born Ivy Sweet, the pretty daughter of a north-London copperbeater, she changed her name and became one of the most popular and successful actresses on the London stage. (Jeanne, who had refused to tell Porchey her age and glossed over her change of name, was infuriated when he later tracked down her birth certificate, which revealed both.) By the time she met Porchey, she had also made twenty films, had a three-month marriage to a wealthy businessman whom she divorced in 1935, and then embarked on a three-year relationship with Hollywood actor James Stewart. Like Tanis, she embodied for Porchey a glamorous movie-star world but, unlike Tanis, she was a genuine if modest success, and was sincerely fond of Porchey.

Porchey's son, Henry, met her on several occasions as a teenager and always maintained that she was lovely to look at, intelligent and kind, with a practicality and easy-going charm that made her a pleasure to be around and a potential asset to his father and Highclere. Naturally, given all this, Porchey preferred her rival.

On Wednesday 26 July, Smith the butler took down a short list of names of those who would be arriving on Saturday to stay for two nights. Porchey aimed for casualness when he added, by way of afterthought, 'Oh, yes, of course there's also Miss Losch,' and Smith, ever the professional, merely raised one eyebrow. 'Very good, my lord, I will let Mrs Saunderson know.'

By the time he'd delivered the list of rooms to be prepared to the housekeeper, and retreated to the wine cellar to check his vintages, the news had blown around the house on a gale of housemaids' excited whispers. Tilly Losch was coming to stay. The famous Viennese ballet dancer turned legend of the London stage. The almond-eyed, exquisitely proportioned cover star of fashion and show-business magazines, who in her last interview had revealed a weakness for strong cigarettes and (improbably) Neopolitan ice cream. Tilly Losch, dancer, actress, singer, pianist, artist, would be here in just three days' time.

Porchey had known Tilly far longer than Jeanne. They had met for the first time at a party given by Jules Bache, financier and art collector, in New York in 1931. Porchey came across Tilly and Adele Astaire ministering to a guest who had passed out. On closer inspection, Porchey observed that it was Lord Charles Cavendish, younger son of the Duke of Devonshire. Tilly and Porchey went off to dance, leaving Adele to tend to the inebriated young aristocrat. (Adele Astaire must have made an impression on him because, the following year, she retired from her long-running dance act with her brother Fred and, as Lady Charles Cavendish, went to live at Lismore Castle in Ireland.) Porchey and Tilly, meanwhile, enjoyed themselves on the dance floor.

Tilly complimented him by saying that, unlike most English men, he could actually dance. Porchey was still happily married to Catherine at the time, but he never forgot his encounter with this ravishingly beautiful creature.

By that point Tilly was already a celebrity, feted in Vienna, Paris, London and New York for her performances and for her choreographies. At the time of Jules Bache's party, she was dancing with Fred and Adele Astaire in their Broadway show *The Bandwagon*, and had previously been acclaimed for her performances as a soloist with the Vienna Imperial Ballet and then with the company of Europe's most famous theatre director, Max Reinhardt. It was Reinhardt who told her he could make her a star if she would come to work for him, so in 1927 she had left Vienna and the Imperial Ballet and set out on tour. One of her early successes was with the choreography of the ballet in Reinhardt's production of *A Midsummer Night's Dream*. When she fretted that she had never choreographed before, Reinhardt told her not to worry. 'Talent is talent.' His faith was justified and Tilly went on to create two more pieces for him.

Tilly made her London debut in 1928 in Noël Coward's musical revue, *This Year of Grace*, and spent the next few years starring in revues staged by legendary impresario Charles B. Cochran, marrying Edward James, millionaire financier and great champion of surrealist art, and dancing in the ballet company, Les Ballets, that he formed for her. In 1932 Tilly landed one of two principal parts in Max Reinhardt's smash-hit London play, *The Miracle*, and she and James moved to a house on Grosvenor Square. The other star of *The Miracle* was Lady Diana Cooper, wife of Duff Cooper who, though an amateur, was a highly regarded actress and she was considered one of the great beauties of her age. There's no doubt that Porchey the theatre fanatic must have seen this production; it was an unmissable event and, besides, Lady Diana was a friend of his. In May 1939, now both divorced, Porchey and Miss Tilly Losch dined together in London. Porchey found her just as bewitching as ever.

Tilly might well have put on a good show at the dinner but in fact she was at a very low ebb. After her divorce in 1935, she had tried to make a jump to Hollywood. She featured in several films but the breakthrough never came. For a while Louis B. Meyer insisted he just needed to find the right role for her, but after two years, tired of waiting, Tilly had returned to the East Coast to dance with the New York City Ballet. A dancer's career is brief, though, and she was coming to the end of hers. Stuck for ideas about what to do next, feeling a failure and afraid of getting older, she developed severe depression and, in early 1939, booked herself into a sanatorium in Switzerland where she stayed for several months. When she dined with Porchey that night, at the Savoy, she was in fact far more fragile than he could have known.

He seems to have fallen for her almost immediately. A week after their dinner date, he invited Almina to stay at Highclere, which he tended to do at moments of crisis in his life. He needed to ask her opinion about something important. Porchey told his mother that he was thinking of getting married again, and that there were two ladies whom he favoured. Almina had suspected that something of the sort was in the offing, and confined herself to bland encouragements. She tended to be a supporter of the romantic decision and, in any case, neither of Porchey's prospective wives had either money or connections to recommend them. She probably told him to think hard about it but to please himself.

Porchey very much wanted to marry. Britain's preparations for war were now in full swing. No one doubted that conflict was coming; it was only a matter of what would trigger it, and when. Porchey's habitual sense that he would like someone he loved and who loved him by his side was becoming acute as the crisis approached. He appreciated Jeanne Stuart's beauty and kindness, but Tilly Losch was of a different order and, besides, he was sure of Jeanne, whereas Tilly was a challenge. Her visit to Highclere made up his mind for him.

Miss Losch arrived from London on the Saturday morning with two of Porchey's old friends, American-born Sidney Beer, a racing chum, and Leslie Hore-Belisha, an outspoken National Liberal politician who was by then Secretary of State for War in Chamberlain's government, and consequently a very busy man. In 1937 he had picked up where Alfred Duff Cooper, his predecessor, left off, in haranguing Chamberlain to embark on modernisation of the armed forces and a recruitment drive. Now he was central to Britain's preparations for war, which, since Hitler and Stalin were on the brink of signing a non-aggression pact, seemed imminent.

The staff had been surreptitiously watching to catch the first glimpse of the renowned Miss Losch. Robert Taylor was again standing in for Smith, whose health problems were worsening. He was delighted, as acting butler, to have the opportunity to welcome their charming guest alongside his employer, to open the car door and escort her to her room.

Tilly did not disappoint. Robert told the story of his initial impressions of her, many times. The first thing he saw was a perfectly proportioned leg extended from the car. She stepped out and greeted Porchey with a smile and kiss on the cheek. She was immaculately dressed, slim and elegant, with wavy dark hair framing huge, slanting green eyes. Porchey urged her to run back downstairs as soon as she was comfortably settled, and then Robert led the way across the Saloon and up the Oak Staircase. He turned right on the Gallery and opened the door to Mercia bedroom.

'But is this really my room?' she exclaimed, her voice husky from her beloved cigarettes and still bearing a soft Austrian accent. 'It is so beautiful!'

Ever the performer, Tilly twirled around, admiring the view over the park, the elaborate frame of the mirror, and the paintings, before throwing herself backwards onto the eighteenth-century four-poster bed in sheer, exuberant delight. Her dress rode up and Robert couldn't help staring—just for a moment; she really did have the most stunning pair of legs he had ever seen.

The weekend was a great success. Over dinner on Saturday night, for which Porchey had asked his new French chef Monsieur Pascal to make extra-special efforts, Leslie Hore-Belisha kept whispering to Porchey that Tilly was so divinely pretty. Had he noticed she had the most beautiful and expressive hands? It was difficult *not* to notice Tilly's hands. Her most famous choreographic creation was a hand dance that wowed audiences wherever she performed it, and she used them to great effect in conversation. As Porchey sat opposite her, watching her laugh at Sidney Beer's jokes, making graceful gestures, glancing at him from time to time and smiling, he found himself captivated. 'She would make a prefect chatelaine for Highclere; she's so elegant, so accomplished,' continued Hore-Belisha. Porchey quite agreed.

Hardly two weeks later, he decided to take the plunge. Over dinner in London, he quietly suggested to Tilly that they get married. She seemed surprised by the speed that things were moving, and not at all convinced. 'We hardly know each other, Porchey,' she pointed out, not unreasonably. 'And I'm not sure it's quite the right moment to marry. There's a war coming, after all.' Tilly's mother was in America and Tilly felt alarmed at the prospect of staying in England without her if Britain were about to go to war with Germany, especially since she was both Austrian and half Jewish.

Porchey was ready with a solution to at least the first of Tilly's objections and suggested they go to Paris to get to know each other better. Tilly looked tempted by the prospect of a trip to one of her favourite old stamping grounds, but made it clear that they would be staying in separate hotels. 'Porchey, darling, you've slept with most of my girlfriends and I am not going to bed with you unless we really are married.' Porchey felt his enthusiasm slightly dampened.

Despite doubts on both sides about the wisdom and purpose of the trip, they arrived in Paris on 24 August as a golden summer there was ending. The Nazi–Soviet pact had been signed the day before and now German troops were massing on the border with Poland. The Gare du Nord teemed with soldiers: the French army was mobilising. Porchey and Tilly's timing was a disaster. The next day they heard on the news that a call for general mobilisation had gone out in Britain, and they had to rush to book their tickets back to England. Tilly was seasick all the way back across the Channel and, when they arrived in London, having once more insisted on separate hotels, she announced that she was going to take three days to think about things and would then give Porchey an answer. 'If it's in the affirmative,' she told him, 'I think we should get married straight away.'

Torn between his infatuation for Tilly and the sense that things were not progressing as he would have wished, Porchey felt deeply apprehensive. But he tried to tell himself to hold his nerve. She was so beautiful, so lovely, such fun. He adored her. Having left her at the Ritz, he tried to think calmly about practicalities. If they were indeed to marry in the next few days, they would need a special licence.

Porchey lodged the application the following day. He must

have felt a sensation of familiar dread, having been here before with Tanis. In addition to his doubts about the fundamental wisdom of the marriage, there were familiar worries about the press getting hold of the information. Porchey completed the paperwork in the names of Henry George Alfred Marius Victor Francis Herbert and Ottilie James, in an attempt to throw any journalists off the scent. He gave her address as the Ritz hotel and his as Claridge's.

On 31 August, as Hitler ordered hostilities to begin against Poland the following day and Porchey waited for Tilly's answer, he tried to calm his nerves by travelling down to Brighton for the racing. He got back to Claridge's that evening to find a message from his not-quite-yet-intended, evidently very upset, summoning him to the Ritz. A diligent journalist had uncovered their special licence, put two and two together and trumpeted the news on the front page of that evening's edition.

When Porchey arrived at Tilly's room, he found her pacing up and down, while Sidney Beer sat, evidently feeling awkward, in one of the armchairs. She explained that she had been discussing the marriage with Sidney, and she still felt that there were pros and cons. There was also the little matter of money. Tilly looked at Sidney for his support, as he did his best to pretend he wasn't there. Turning back to Porchey, she said, 'I simply want to feel secure, darling.'

When Tilly explained that her definition of secure amounted to £1,000 a year, Porchey also began to pace. Now he felt really jittery. Tilly seemed to have discussed the marriage endlessly with their mutual friends and, frankly, the idea was losing all its mystique.

'Oh, I just don't know, darling,' Tilly said. 'But if you can get on to your lawyer and sort out the money, I do think it might be better to marry than not, don't you?'

Porchey, half wondering whether he should be backing out, but not quite sure how to do so, eventually agreed to pay Tilly £600 after tax, though his lawyers insisted it would only be for the duration of the marriage. The deed would be drawn up and they could sign it tomorrow, after the wedding ceremony. Porchey had previously made an appointment at the Register Office, just in case, for the earliest possible time on 1st September. Perhaps he was not convinced that, with another whole day to think about it, she would turn up.

Sidney was relieved to leave them to it. Porchey suggested to Tilly that they had dinner to celebrate their decision, at the Savoy Grill. They walked in to find two of Porchey's old friends, Alfred Duff Cooper and Harcourt 'Crinks' Johnstone, dining at an adjacent table and, perhaps feeling that they had talked quite enough to one another for one evening, decided to join them.

Tilly knew Alfred Duff Cooper from when she had starred in *The Miracle* alongside his wife, Diana. There had been considerable tensions between the two women; both famous, beautiful and used to the limelight. Relations sank to a frosty low when Tilly, in prankster mode, sewed up the arms of Diana's costume before she went on stage. This made Diana's key moment, the miraculous graceful descent from the pillar on which she stood resplendent as the Madonna, rather less impressive than it was supposed to be.

Duff Cooper's temper was famously explosive but short-lived, and he was incapable of remaining on bad terms with a woman as beautiful and charming as Tilly. Besides, there were more important things to discuss than old spats. The talk turned to war and a very sober estimation of the danger facing England. Porchey tried to be optimistic; Crinks was more truthful and gave the Germans odds of four to one on—they were so much stronger in terms of men, training and equipment. Porchey observed Tilly's demeanour becoming ever more withdrawn. He could just see her absconding on a boat to America in the middle of the night.

Porchey tried to reassure Tilly that Highclere was in a very safe part of England; in fact, that was why a nursery school was going to be billeted there. There would be no bombs at Highclere. 'I hope so, I do hope so,' she said very quietly, her Austrian accent seeming more pronounced.

Later that night, Porchey rang Almina to tell her the news of his wedding. 'Well, darling boy, God bless you. I've got a tiny present for Tilly, which I will give her when I have the pleasure of seeing her. Now. I have to ask. Are you quite sure in your heart of hearts that this is what you want?'

Porchey was lost for an instant reply. That night, he slept badly.

On 1 September, Nazi Germany invaded Poland and Porchey arrived early at the Register Office at Caxton Hall, Westminster. Half an hour later, and with less than five minutes to go, Tilly still hadn't shown up. The reporters were waiting. Porchey must have suffered paroxysms of anxiety and doubt, wondering whether he was doing the right thing, wondering whether he was about to be jilted at the altar for the second time in his life. To his immense relief, Tilly arrived just in time, looking pale but lovely and leaning on the arm of Sidney Beer. The registrar appeared and looked enquiringly at Porchey. 'Are you by any chance Lord Carnarvon?' 'I am,' he declared. 'Splendid. You're the first this morning. Be ready in three minutes.' Tilly smiled weakly and they entered the office together.

After the ceremony, Lord and Lady Carnarvon returned to Claridge's to sign the financial papers. Porchey felt a mingled sense of euphoria and panic and ordered champagne to steady everyone's nerves. Tilly cheered up immensely.

George packed His Lordship's bag and sent round to the Ritz for Her Ladyship's, and then they caught a train from Paddington to Highclere, where they were met at the station.

It was a beautiful late summer's day and, as they motored up the drive, the warm breeze carried the scent of cut grass. At the castle, the entire staff lined up outside the front door to welcome the Earl and his new Countess. Everyone was beaming; the maids could hardly believe this sudden injection of glamour, the male staff were scarcely less pleased. A stream of friends dropped in after lunch to wish them well and Porchey, observing Tilly in a more relaxed mood and exerting her usual powerful spell, began to feel more robust.

It wasn't until Tilly had suggested that they take their coffee outside to sit on picnic rugs in the sunshine, that they learned about the invasion of Poland. Smith informed his employer that twenty-seven evacuee children and four of their teachers and nurses had just arrived from Curzon Crescent nursery school in Willesden, northwest London. Oh, and there were several gentlemen of the press who would be obliged by a photo. The evening editions would be full of the news of invasion and a more cheering story was judged appropriate.

Porchey was stunned both by the terrible news, which seemed to confirm that war was now only a matter of days away, and by the realisation that he and Tilly would be sharing their home, from day one of their marriage, with dozens of strangers. When he was first informed about the plan for billeting the school on Highclere, he had asked his secretary Miss Stubbings to draw up plans for where the children would sleep, play, eat and take their lessons. Preparations had been made, but he could never have envisaged that they would be needed on his wedding day.

Following photographs for the press with the new Countess of Carnarvon, Mrs Saunderson and Miss Stubbings led the children, teachers and assistants out through the front door and round to the back of the castle. They were to use the staff entrance through the courtyard and then make their way up the second staircase, the Red Stairs, to the top floor. Mrs Saunderson and Miss Stubbings helped Miss Winifred Butler and her staff to settle the children in the old nursery and adjoining bedrooms, before showing them the Library that would serve as their playroom and the servants' hall where they were to take their meals. One imagines a slightly shell-shocked Porchey and Tilly dining that evening: Porchey making jokes about the ridiculousness of the timing; Tilly incredulous that her fears were being realised already. War seemed to be on its way to Highclere.

Porchey had invited his sister, Lady Evelyn, and Brograve, his brother-in-law, to come to stay for a couple of nights, to meet Tilly. Eve was a clear-sighted pragmatist, like Almina, and though she had adored Catherine, she wanted her brother to be happy. But both she and Bro worried that Tilly talked a lot about her fears for the future rather than her happiness with Porchey, and mentioned America a great deal.

On the morning of Sunday 3 September, the house party was driven down to Highclere Church for Matins. The building was packed and the mood was subdued. There was a sense of waiting for something to happen. Just after the service got underway, a note was passed to Lord Carnarvon, who read it and then handed it immediately to Mr Kent, the parson. Mr Kent fell silent, then cleared his voice to announce the news. 'At 11.15 this morning, the Prime Minister of England made a radio broadcast to the nation. Ladies and gentlemen, I am sorry to tell you that Mr Chamberlain has informed us we are now at war with Germany.'

14

We Are at War

After months of anxiety-inducing build-up and then last-minute hopes that the catastrophe could yet be averted, war had arrived. Congregations up and down the country received the news from their vicar; sermons were jettisoned and prayers for a swift victory were offered up instead. Millions more people, sitting at home, tuned in to the radio to listen to Neville Chamberlain's sober pronouncement. He, more than anyone, had staked everything on a diplomatic solution based on concessions. He sounded weary as he delivered the news.

At lunch at Highclere that Sunday, the talk was all of what might happen next. Porchey's great hope was that the war should be over quickly. If it were to drag on for years, his son would almost certainly be involved. Henry was now fifteen. His father must have been ruminating on the agonies suffered by his own parents when he joined up as an enthusiastic seventeen-year-old during the Great War. For everyone of Porchey's generation, especially those who had fought in that terrible conflict, there was a sense of history repeating itself. On 3 September 1939, the notion of a war to end all wars was exposed as a tragic delusion.

Porchey's other immediate worry, apart from Henry's safety, was that Tilly would bolt. They had been married for just three days and now their marriage, already so fragile, was being overtaken by global disaster. It was precisely the scenario Tilly had dreaded, and the events of the next two months would demonstrate that—despite Porchey's best efforts—she never did regard Highclere as a place of safety.

In the days after war was declared, there was a flurry of activity as people rushed around trying to determine what they could do to help. The country had been planning only half-heartedly for this eventuality; now everyone needed to buckle down and face reality. In the words of novelist Mollie Panter-Downes, who was writing from London for the *New Yorker*, 'The English were a peace-loving nation up until two days ago but now it is pretty widely felt that the sooner we really get down to the job, the better.'

The staff at Highclere were kept busy helping out with the nursery school. Monsieur Pascal, the chef, and the kitchen maids now had to prepare additional food for twenty-seven children and eight adults. The housemaids had extra fires to light and clear in the nurseries, bedrooms and schoolroom. Just as Almina's household staff had rallied round to support the nurses when the castle was turned into a military hospital during the First World War, now Highclere set about its war work with determination.

Miss Butler, the school's principal, was assisted by Miss

Soper, another qualified teacher, Miss Cowley, a teaching assistant, Miss Clarke, a nurse, and four trainee assistant nurses. Miss Butler was keen to establish a routine for the children as quickly as possible, to try to get them settled in and prevent the worst effects of homesickness. A schedule of lessons, meal and play times was drawn up, and the staff watched their charges closely for signs of unhappiness.

The children were aged between two and five and had left their families at a moment's notice when the first stage of the evacuation of London was ordered. Their mothers had time only to pack a change of clothes and a beloved toy or two in a small bag before they delivered their children, gas masks in boxes slung across their shoulders, to the train station for evacuation. Mollie Panter-Downes described the London mothers, 'left behind, standing around listlessly, waiting at street corners for the telegrams to be posted up in the various schools, telling them where their children were.' Some mothers could not bear to be separated from their children and insisted on travelling to the countryside with them. That doesn't seem to have happened at Highclere, perhaps because the Curzon Crescent school had been billeted before the declaration of war, and so the families at least knew where their children were going. They were assured that if it were at all possible, they would be welcome to visit in due course.

One imagines that some of the evacuees must have been distraught at the separation but, as Miss Butler and her colleagues quickly observed, most of the older ones seemed to be thoroughly enjoying themselves. For these north London children, who only saw the countryside once a year on a church outing or a trip to visit family, the big house and its huge parklands were an exotic playground. There must have been tears in the middle of the night when a child woke in one of those unfamiliar turret rooms and looked around for its mother, but during the daytime there was also fresh air and fun in abundance.

Porchey and Tilly had little to do with the day-to-day running of the school, but they crossed paths with children and teachers from time to time, in the Saloon or out in the gardens. Porchey was always genial and was known to the children as 'King Carnarvon', on the grounds that, as one little boy pointed out, only a king got to live in a castle. There are crayoned drawings by the evacuees depicting him as a skinny stick man with a crown and a big smile. One little girl particularly wanted to meet the queen, who she was sure lived somewhere in the house, and could not be persuaded otherwise. For the young teachers and nurses, Lady Carnarvon was even better than the queen. They joined the housemaids in hanging around on the Gallery at night, hoping to catch a glimpse of the famous former Miss Losch.

Porchey's immediate thought was that he should volunteer for service with his old regiment. He presented himself for assessment and was promptly declared unfit. His back problems, sustained from years of falls, had worsened, and he now had severe arthritis. He had suspected that he would not pass the medical but was nonetheless terribly disappointed. He set about writing to friends and acquaintances at the War Office, offering his services as an unpaid attaché. For a while he had high hopes that he would be appointed adjutant to Alan Breitmeyer, commanding officer of the 7th Queen's Own Hussars at Shorncliffe, a major army base in Kent, but a serving officer, Lord Amherst, was given the role instead. Porchey added his name to the list of reserve officers and tried not to give way to frustration.

Catherine and Geoffrey had been at home in Ovington Square when they heard the news of the outbreak of war. They had just returned from a morning stroll in Hyde Park to enjoy the Indian summer heat. As Chamberlain's radio broadcast ended, the air-raid sirens started up their wail. It was a test, they knew, but it sounded different from the tests of the previous weeks now that the country was truly at war.

Geoffrey wrote to his former naval unit to volunteer and had more luck than Porchey. At forty-one years old he was at the very upper age limit for active service and was instructed to report to Dartmouth Training College in a month's time to relieve the physical training officer. Geoffrey was slightly taken aback. He was fit and well but hadn't served in the Navy since he was twenty-one and felt he was out of touch with modern methods and past his physical peak. Surely he was not the best person to train 750 young cadets? His commanding officer countered with the argument that he would be required to teach combat skills, not a basic fitness course, and with his experience of naval battle he was as well placed as anyone. Geoffrey set off for Dartmouth still unconvinced. There was no suggestion that wives were welcome, and Catherine remained in London.

If Porchey and Tilly's timing was unfortunate, Catherine and Geoffrey's was not much better. They celebrated their first wedding anniversary two weeks after the declaration of war, having just heard from Dartmouth about Geoffrey's posting. Catherine, like millions of women all over Europe, had to find resources of stoicism to sustain her as she said goodbye to her husband.

Geoffrey wrote often, chatty letters in which he told her that the people he had met 'couldn't be nicer, all excellent fellows'. He missed her terribly, longed to hear the sound of her darling voice, but there was no point in her coming to visit him as he wasn't even allowed out for dinner. He was hopeful that he would not be in Devon for much longer as he was looking for another post. It was an excellent job but he was more sure than ever that he was not the right man for it. He simply didn't have the technical expertise to be instructing anyone on naval warfare in 1939 and he didn't want to be a liability.

Before long, it seems, someone agreed with him. In November he was transferred to Harwich. The port had been requisitioned by the Navy as a key point of defence for the eastern coast and was to be established as the base for a fleet of minesweepers. Geoffrey assisted with setting up command headquarters and awaited further orders. He knew they could not be long in coming. There was no land offensive imminent but the war had already begun for the Navy, with the declaration of a blockade of Germany's seaports and a counter-declaration by the Germans. The Battle of the Atlantic was underway. It was a relief to feel he was finally being useful and could also spend the occasional weekend with Catherine, but for Mr and Mrs Grenfell, as for the country as a whole, the relief was tempered with an uneasy sense that this relative calm couldn't possibly last.

Catherine, like Porchey, was worried about the war's impact on her children. Steeling herself not to think about what might happen to Henry if the war could not be won quickly, she decided that the most urgent priority was Penelope's safety. Henry was at Eton, close to London but beyond the area considered most vulnerable to bombing raids. Penelope was at school in town, though, and Londoners lived under a canopy of giant silver barrage balloons that were a constant reminder of the potential threat from the air. Catherine's anxieties for her daughter were calmed when the principal at the school attended by both Penelope and her cousin Patricia informed her that there were plans afoot to evacuate to Dorset.

When Penelope went to visit her father in October, she told Porchey that the move was imminent. Pen thought it sounded rather fun (this, after all, was the child who had remained unruffled by the fire that destroyed three bedrooms while she was staying at Highclere). All her friends would be there and she could return to the castle for some weekends and the holidays. Porchey promised to send the girls' two favourite ponies, Velvet and Robin (and Archie the groom, to look after them) to the school's temporary home at Lord Shaftesbury's requisitioned house in Dorset. It seems to have done the trick as both Penelope and Patricia settled quickly. Like the little Londoners billeted at Highclere, they welcomed the adventure of the change of routine.

Life for the residents of Highclere was settling into a form of 'business as usual'. The first few months of the conflict, which have come to be known as the 'phoney war', were relatively uneventful. Until the Germans pushed into the Low Countries and France in May 1940, for most British people the war seemed peripheral, like a threat not seen clearly, lurking in the shadows.

Porchey continued to cast around for a role with the Army but he was distracted by a series of problems with his household staff. In early October Smith, the butler, tendered his resignation. The extra work that came along with the nursery school meant that his long-standing health problems had finally got the better of him. It wasn't an easy moment to recruit men to non-essential positions, but a neighbour's retired butler declared he was ready to help out. Mr Pell arrived, slightly doddery but charming, and was duly engaged on a salary of £150 a year.

Just as he thought things were under control, Porchey had a rather more delicate situation on his hands, albeit one with a simpler resolution. His valet, George, was a charming, handsome and self-confident type, as befitted his position. Porchey found him good company and, as a result, had overlooked his tendency to overstep the mark on several occasions. The gravest of George's previous misdemeanours had occurred when he had passed himself off as a first-class passenger during a voyage with Lord Carnarvon in the Mediterranean. George had had a fine old time, right up until the moment he had docked and had to confess that he had spent His Lordship's entire cash float on wine and gaming. Somewhat incredibly, he was not dismissed for this, on the grounds that he had at least owned up. But in the autumn of 1939, his luck was about to run out.

In the interval between Smith's departure and Pell's arrival, George was acting butler. This seemed to have slipped his mind, however, for on the Saturday he invited several friends to lunch with him in the steward's room. Unfortunately for George, his festivities coincided with a lunch party upstairs. When he hadn't appeared in the Saloon by 1.30p.m., Robert Taylor was despatched to look for him. He found George hosting a party in full swing and very much the worse for wear. 'You go up, Bob—I'm enjoying myself down here,' said George, full of bonhomie.

'Luncheon is served, my lord,' Robert announced as he returned to the Saloon. Lord Carnarvon looked rather shocked as he realised that Robert, the first footman, had stepped in. Later, during the meal, Lord Carnarvon quietly enquired after George's whereabouts. 'He's downstairs, my lord, but I'm afraid he is not available,' replied Robert.

Miss Stubbings, Lord Carnarvon's secretary, was sent to investigate. Her reports of the uproarious situation in the steward's room were enough to seal George's fate. He was asked to leave immediately, and Robert was promoted to start straight away as Lord Carnarvon's valet.

Porchey's most pressing concern in the autumn of 1939, though, was to watch anxiously over Tilly for signs that she was happy in her new life. Partly in a bid to amuse her, he invited several groups of people to stay. The Duke and Duchess of Windsor had been expeditiously collected from France on 12 September by Lord Mountbatten and were staying in Sussex. Porchey immediately offered them Highclere's hospitality but the Duke regretfully declined the invitation. He wrote to say that he expected any day to be appointed to a military mission and sent back to France, which Porchey, the Francophile and fluent French-speaker, must have envied. The Duke of Windsor hoped that the outbreak of war would furnish him with a way to serve his country, which might in turn bring about a rapprochement with his family. This was not to be. At a time of heightened pressure and, given the persistent suspicion that he and his wife had been too close to Nazi Ambassador Joachim von Ribbentrop, the Windsors were more of a diplomatic problem than ever.

Randolph Churchill and his girlfriend of just a few weeks, Pamela Digby, did come, however, and announced their engagement to the assembled house party at Highclere on 26 September. Pamela was a nineteen-year-old debutante, the daughter of Lord Digby. She was flame-haired, pretty and confident, and had so captured Randolph's heart that he had asked her to marry him on their first date. There was not actually anything terribly unusual in that. Randolph was an inveterate proposer; one night he asked three women to marry him. But this time it was different, though probably more because of his fear that he would be killed in the war before he had acquired an heir than any of Pamela's admittedly considerable charms. Pamela might not have known the extent of Randolph's reputation for drinking and womanising, but she was surely not blind to the fact that he had a huge ego, derived from his sense of being the son of a great man. That was precisely his appeal to Pamela, who went on to have a long and illustrious career as the consort to powerful men.

Porchey was delighted at the happy news and promptly invited the young couple to return the following weekend so that Pamela could meet her fiancé's uncle and Porchey's dearest friend, the Duke of Marlborough. Porchey was fond of Randolph and was happy to help, but one can't help suspecting that he was probably also thrilled that his house guests were providing such good entertainment for Tilly. His new wife was an urban creature who required constant diversions. She had told him before their marriage that she was worried the country would be dull. Now here was amusing company, some of the grandest connections in the land and a love story to boot.

The Duke and Duchess of Marlborough were charmed by Pamela. Winston and Clementine Churchill were also thrilled, but principally were relieved at the news that their wayward son was finally settling down. The wedding had been planned quickly and the couple married on 4 October at St John's Smith Square, in the shadow of the Houses of Parliament. Lord and Lady Carnarvon were invited and the occasion presented Tilly with her first big opportunity to perform in her new role.

The setting was exquisite indeed: after the ceremony the guests made the short journey up Whitehall to Admiralty

House. The tradition that stipulated the bride's family should host the reception was set aside on this occasion, in recognition of the exceptional loveliness of the groom's parents' home. Alfred Duff Cooper had lived in Admiralty House during his time as First Lord of the Admiralty; he described it as the most beautiful residence in London, complete with paintings of sea battles and gilded mermaids swimming on the ceilings. On the day war was declared, Chamberlain had ended Churchill's ten long years in the political wilderness by appointing him First Lord of the Admiralty, the post that Duff Cooper had resigned in protest the previous September. It was an admission that Churchill's consistent petitioning for a more bellicose foreign policy and rearmament had been proved right.

Tilly could not fail to take pleasure in her first society wedding, and Porchey felt cheered as he watched her talking to his old friends, captivating them with her beauty and grace. Perhaps everything was going to be all right after all. He hoped so, but he had not been feeling that confident these last few weeks. Tilly had installed herself in East Anglia bedroom, a corner room with glorious views to the south and east of the park. It was one of the prettiest bedrooms in the house and the most comfortable, with a dressing room and bathroom attached, but Porchey wasn't fond of it. He couldn't shake the memory of the time one of his father's house guests had suffered palpitations brought on by some particularly unsettling events at one of the séances the 5th Earl conducted in the room. It also had the considerable disadvantage, from Porchey's point of view, of being the full length of the Gallery away from his own rooms.

At home, Tilly was often quiet and withdrawn. She had told her husband all about her health problems and her stay at the Swiss sanatorium. Porchey was beginning to develop the sort of hearty respect for his wife's nerves that Jane Austen's Mr Bennet professed. In truth, it was hardly surprising that Tilly should feel nervous. They were nerve-racking times and her recovery from depression had been very recent when she and Porchey rekindled their acquaintance and took their speedy and fraught decision to marry.

But though Porchey was sympathetic to Tilly's anxieties up to a point, he longed for some more signs from her that she was making a sincere effort to adapt to her new circumstances. There was a war on, it was true, but for Porchey, their evacuees were the perfect model of how to face up bravely to the challenges it posed. There was also the fact that Tilly did not always set aside her sophisticate ways and throw herself into the requirements of being Lady Carnarvon. The local newspaper, the *Newbury Weekly News*, reported delightedly on a charming entertainment given for Highclere wives of men in the armed services, which took place in the Armoury Room in Highclere village. Lord Porchester and his sister Lady Penelope were both involved and opened proceedings by singing the 'Lambeth Walk', in tribute to the London evacuees. Their cousin, Miss Patricia Leatham, followed with a recitation, and then they were joined by several of the children from the village in putting on a show of charades. The paper reported that the glamorous new Countess of Carnarvon enjoyed the whole thing but, to Porchey's mind, Tilly had seemed very strained in her reaction to the children's theatrical efforts. He knew she was a professional, but still, he didn't appreciate her reticence, especially when two of the enthusiastic amateurs were his own children.

On 26 September, Tilly received a letter from a former acquaintance, another escapee from London's theatrical world. Marie Rambert, the pioneering champion of ballet in Britain, had decided that since most of her male dancers and students were likely to be called up, she would move what remained of her company out of London for the duration of the war. She had settled at Grey House in Burghclere, the neighbouring village. 'I have suddenly discovered that we are near neighbours—how amusing and unexpected,' she wrote. 'Shall we meet and chat?' It took Tilly nearly five weeks to reply and, when she did, she was evasive, claiming ill-health and preoccupation with the evacuees. Perhaps Marie's letter had reminded her of her time with Les Ballets in 1933, when it was whispered that some of Madame Rambert's dancers rather outshone Miss Losch, the supposed star of the show whose powers were beginning to wane.

The bigger reason for Tilly's tardy reply was that she had been caught up in making a decision about her future. As she explained to Marie, she had such poor lungs and her doctors had advised her not to winter in England. She thought she might try Arizona, where the air was dry.

Porchey tried to put a brave face on things, but he was very hurt by Tilly's decision to go to the States. She assured him that she would be back in the spring, that she simply couldn't face a damp cold British winter, but they both knew that the air of Arizona was more an expedient excuse than anything else.

She sailed for New York in late November. Porchey accompanied her to Southampton and stood on the dockside to wave her off. They had been married for not quite three months. He returned to Highclere to find several of Tilly's unpaid bills, including a very sizeable one from Cartier. Judging from the stream of invoices that arrived from New York over the next few weeks, Tilly was in no hurry to leave the chill of that great city for the benefits of the Arizona desert.

It was a strange Christmas at Highclere that year. Porchey had been in downcast mood ever since Tilly's departure and in mid-December he fell ill with a severe throat infection. On the advice of his doctor he went up to town to have his tonsils removed, but the operation was bungled and he haemorrhaged so severely that, briefly, there were fears for his life. Almina nursed him back to health and by 27 December he was well enough to return to Highclere with Eve and Bro, where they all spent a very quiet New Year. Tilly had finally made it to Tucson, Arizona, and did not rush back to support her husband.

Despite the family's absence, the castle was full of activity. Another twenty-seven nursery schoolchildren and their accompanying staff had arrived at the beginning of December. Porchey left instructions that the usual entertainment for the village children should go ahead, and extra preparations must be made for the evacuees, who were spending their first Christmas away from home. On Christmas Day each child woke to find a stocking at the end of their bed stuffed with an orange, a ball, a chocolate doll, a penny, a small toy and some gums. The kitchen staff cooked a traditional lunch for the entire household and in the afternoon the nursery school assembled round the Christmas tree in the Library to receive a gift from Father Christmas, before singing 'Away in a Manger'.

For many of the evacuees, the best gift of all arrived on Boxing Day, in the form of their parents. That must have been a day of raw emotions: delight in seeing each other; agony as the hour arrived for the visitors to board the train at Highclere Station and return to London. By Christmas 1939, after three months of relative calm, there was a widespread feeling that the evacuation of London had been overhasty. There were no bombs and, meanwhile, families were suffering from having to live apart. Many parents reclaimed their evacuee children and took them back to the city. Again, Highclere's proximity to town and the consequent possibility of visits must have contributed to the fact that this didn't happen to the Curzon Crescent children. They and their parents were spared the awful fate of some Londoners, who brought their children home only to see them killed in the Blitz that battered the city between September 1940 and May 1941.

Porchey faced 1940 in a miserable mood. In November of the previous year, when Tilly left, he had written to Leslie Hore-Belisha enquiring about jobs in America. Some part of him seems to have accepted that his wife was unlikely to return to England, at least for a while. When that scheme too drew a blank, he decided that going south to recuperate from his operation might be a good idea. He would think again about looking for a military role when he was feeling stronger. And perhaps Tilly could even be persuaded to join him on the Continent. At the end of January he set off for Genoa, with plans to go on to the south of France, and was overjoyed when Tilly confirmed that she would meet him in Italy. She couldn't wait to see him, she promised. They could have a second honeymoon.

Tilly had spent the last two months enjoying herself. She was a tremendous hit as Lady Carnarvon, the subject of 'much lorgnette-peering', as one press cutting from her scrapbook puts it. She turned heads at the Ambassador Hotel in New York when she lunched there one day, appearing in a 'hand-knitted pink baby bonnet that she ran up herself, combined with a purple tweed suit and a pink blouse.' She was only outdone in outrageous ostentation by 'Mrs Charles

Laughton's blue felt hat covered with British military and naval insignia picked out in gold.'

Tilly was certainly making the most of her new profile, but she was not completely self-interested, nor had she forgotten Highclere and the evacuees. She toured several states, dancing at gala dinners to raise funds for the British war effort, urging American ladies to knit socks and vests for British soldiers and telling her audiences all about the thirty young evacuees at Highclere (which the American press reported as 'a hundred children at Newburg, England'). If this activity sounds frivolous, it should be remembered that at the time there was no support among the American public for the States to intervene in the war. The decisive event in favour of such an argument was of course the Japanese attack on Pearl Harbor in December 1941, but by that time the tide of public opinion had already begun to turn, in part due to propaganda efforts such as Lady Carnarvon's. Other friends of Porchey and Catherine also did their bit in this regard. Alfred Duff Cooper and his wife Diana undertook a four-month speaking tour, and Churchill later sent the Duke of Kent on a goodwill visit to President Roosevelt.

There's no doubt that Italy and the south of France were infinitely more appealing to Tilly than Highclere, which partially explains her decision to meet her husband there when she had avoided having to come back to England at the time of his acute illness. But in her defence, the first few months of 1940 were the phoniest of the phoney war, at least in mainland Europe, so by March there seemed less reason to be fearful of imminent invasion than there had been in December. It seems extraordinary now that people should have been dashing around on holidays when Europe was at war. The appearance of calm wouldn't last much longer.

Lord and Lady Carnarvon were reunited at Genoa and went on to Monte Carlo, where Tilly lost quite a lot of money in the casino. Porchey would have been happy to spend a quiet few weeks enjoying the sea air there. But Tilly was restless and began to suggest that it would soon be springtime in Paris, and they should not miss it. Eager to keep her happy, Porchey agreed.

Paris was a mixed success. Porchey thought that mostly it went quite well. They went to the races and had some amusing evenings with friends. But there were disquieting incidents as well. Tilly was furious when, leaning over the piano at which Noël Coward was playing, Porchey started to whistle along. She told him off for indulging himself in schoolboy tricks in the presence of the maestro. One morning Porchey forgot about her rule that he should not enter her bedroom without knocking first. He was walking in when Tilly spotted him in her dressing-table mirror and hurled a well-aimed heavy silver hairbrush at him. He ducked just in time as it cracked into the mahogany door and he hastily retreated, apologising.

The greatest proof of overall harmony, though, was that Tilly agreed to return to England with him. In late March the Carnarvons arrived back in London and headed for the Ritz as usual. Tilly's efforts to secure an ADC post for Porchey in Paris had come to nothing and had only succeeded in finally rousing his temper. He felt it was time to return to Britain and resume his quest for something useful to do, and he must have pressed his case forcefully enough to overturn any doubts on her part.

To his delight, when he got back to town, he learned that Baron Amherst had just been transferred, and the job of adjutant to Colonel Breitmeyer was now his if he wanted it. Porchey was heading back to the Queen's Own 7th

Hussars and he couldn't have been happier about it. Not even the little matter of having to live in rural Kent seems to have troubled him, though it must have troubled Tilly a great deal. Buoyed up by this change of fortunes, he was evidently in convincing mood, because he persuaded Tilly to accompany him and took a house for them close to the army base. It was also made plain to both Robert Taylor, his valet, and Jack Gibbins, first chauffeur, that they would be required to enlist. So with the Vauxhall car painted in camouflage, His Lordship's brass bedsteads (the frame for his bed) and other summary comforts (including Monsieur Pascal, the chef) transported, Lord and Lady Carnarvon set up house in Shorncliffe.

For the second time in his life, Porchey was taking a new bride to join his regiment. The trip to India with Catherine seventeen years previously must have seemed a lifetime away. Then there had been nothing more pressing on anyone's minds than winning at polo. Now the 7th Hussars were awaiting an uncertain future. They were stationed in a highly strategic part of the country, close to France and vulnerable to any bombing raids or, whisper the unmentionable, any invading army. Their role was still undefined: for as long as there was no land battle, nobody had to resolve the question of what purpose a cavalry unit might serve in a modern war. So they waited, and Porchey settled into his new role. He provided administrative support to Colonel Breitmeyer; though he was kept busy with regimental business, there was no possibility of being overstretched. A deep shelter had been built below the officers' mess for use during raids, but in the absence of any action, its chief attraction was that it had an extremely well-stocked bar.

Taylor and Gibbins spent much of their time in a battle of wits with the Regimental Sergeant Major. They were

Porchey began his relationship with the glamorous Tanis Montagu (neé Guinness) in 1934. She was beautiful, worldly and a fixture in Hollywood circles. They had a passionate but tempestuous romance.

Pa Found Tut; His Son Can't Locate Bride

Baltimore, Oct. 5. — British high-jinks by the blue-blooded Earl of Carnarvon, whose father uncovered the tomb of Tut-ankh-amen, and his bride-to-be

The Hon. Mrs. Tanis Guinness Montagu, who was going to marry the Earl of Carnarvon in Baltimore yesterday but didn't, somehow. Nobody knows why.

gave Wallis Simpson's home town a case of acute jitters today. He was to have married the Hon. Mrs. Tanis Guinness Montagu at the British Consulate today. He didn't.

At to what happened—whether Earl thought better of his protestations of love—no one knew exactly. Least of all the British consulate, where the attaches calling for ice-bags and sedat!

The broad-shouldered Earl

The Earl of Carnarvon
the bride-to-be stood him up at the altar, or whether the blue-blooded

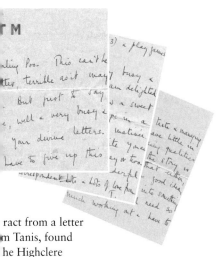

ract from a letter
m Tanis, found
he Highclere
hives.

Tanis's rejection led to public humiliation for Porchey.

LORD CARNARVON
HOME: Motoring from Southampton last night with his mother.

DAD FOUND TUT BUT SON CAN'T FIND OWN BRIDE

MARRIAGE OFF: EARL IS GLUM

Daily Express Staff Reporter
SOUTHAMPTON, Thursday.

THE Earl of Carnarvon stared glumly at the grey sea from the tender that met the Europa here today. He said to me:—

"The marriage with Mrs Montagu is definitely off. It is not a postponement. Everything is washed up. That is all. What else can I say?"

I showed the earl a cutting which told how Mrs Montagu, realising that marriage is for a lifetime, decided to let it go by. He read it, id to me—

"I cannot believe that Mrs Montagu really means that. Anyway,

the marriage is off. I am saying no more. I am very sorry."

The earl fixed his eyes more gloomily on the sea.

Last month the earl, 38, divorced in April, dashed across the Atlantic. He and the beautiful Mrs Tanis Montagu, 28, caught the night train from New York to Baltimore, Gretna Green of U.S.A., to be wed. There was a hitch. The earl caught the Europa home. Mrs Montagu is now crossing the Atlantic in the Normandie.

Although Lady Almina and Porchey's relationship had been strained at times, Almina dropped everything to meet Porchey when he returned from his abortive trip to America.

... d Porchester and his
... er Lady Penelope on
... ir ponies.

Porchey and his son,
taken in 1938 when
Henry was 14 years old.

Porchey described Robert Taylor as 'the perfect butler'. Robert worked at Highclere for fifty years.

Highclere staff sewing in Catherine's Rose Garden.

The Rolls-Royce Phantom III Porch bought in 1937. The current Lord and Lady Carnarv bought back the car and repainted it in the Carnarvo colours in 2012.

Lord Carnarvon was devoted to horses and was an excellent jockey until injury forced him out of the saddle.

King Edward VIII and Mrs Wallis Simpson in 1936. Porchey also attempted to persuade Edward not to abdicate, but in the end he chose Wallis over his throne.

Porchey was captivated by the Viennese ballet dancer Tilly Losch.

Tillie Losch in U. S. A.
*oses in Fashions at Ball to Aid Britain

Countess of Carnarvon (Tillie Losch, the dancer) is one of the members he Committee who will pose in American models at the Star Spangled Ball organised by the William Allen White Committee for Aid to Britain. will wear this dashing hat. The necklace and hat decoration advertise the hat as a U.S.A. product.

Tilly's good looks and aristocratic title ensured many column inches. Above right with Adele Astaire.

ïlly dressed as the part of angel in 'Everyman' at the mbassadors Theatre 1935.

The Earl and Countess of Carnarvon (Tilly) with Lord Stanley of Alderley en route to the wedding of Randolph Churchill and Pamela Digby, October 4th 1939.

Jeanne Stuart was a successful actress and movie star, married very briefly to Sir Bernard Docker after which she dated the actor James Stewart. She spent much of the war at Highclere after Tilly departed to the USA.

undergoing basic training and were not eligible for any leave, but they had worked out how to make up an official rubber stamp in Lord Carnarvon's name, which they used to stamp their passes for a night here and there. They would return to Highclere to re-provision the wine stores and the chef's supplies, as well as visit sweethearts and family. Robert and Joan were still courting, and in fact the war had made them think more seriously about their future together. Porchey turned a blind eye to these occasional jaunts. The Sergeant Major would be left red-faced and spluttering, yelling after them, 'I'll get you buggers in the end, I promise you!' as the men slipped the leash once again.

The war wasn't quite such a series of jolly japes for everyone, though. The Army was still in preparation mode but the Navy was already engaged, in the waters around Scandinavia. At the end of November 1939, Stalin's Red Army had launched an invasion of neutral Finland, expecting a swift victory. Despite their superior fire- and manpower, the Soviets were hampered by the fact that Stalin had purged the Army of most of its experienced senior ranks. The Finnish Army, by contrast, was efficient and determined. The Finns held out for two months before they succumbed to the might of the Soviet machine. They concluded a peace treaty in March, but by that time, the effectiveness of the Red Army was in serious doubt.

Hitler took note of Soviet Russia's vulnerability and the complete failure of Allied Supreme Command to come up with a coherent response to the invasion. Both things fed his confidence. By the spring of 1940 he had set his sights on Norway. The Allies too had planned to occupy the country, for the same reasons: its strategic importance in relation to the blockade that would prevent supplies from reaching

Germany by sea, and its coalfields. There was a significant build-up of both German and British ships. The British Admiralty believed their superior power would prevent any invasion, but tensions were rising, nonetheless. So while Porchey and Tilly set up house in Kent and drank cocktails in the officers' mess, Geoffrey was sent to Scotland to await imminent battle orders. For him and for Catherine, it was getting harder to ignore the threat lurking in the shadows.

15

Blood, Toil, Tears and Sweat

Geoffrey was posted to Glasgow in February 1940. That winter was one of the harshest anyone could remember, and in Scotland the mood among rank and file naval personnel was one of hunkering down to the fight. The rest of the country might have been labouring under the delusion that nothing much was happening, but for Geoffrey and his colleagues, the rapidly concluding peace between Finland and Soviet Russia augured badly. They had received orders to prepare for action.

British and indeed Allied military strategy in the first few months of the war was based largely on the conviction that an effective economic blockade would quickly starve Germany into submission and that meanwhile the first priority was not to rush to attack (despite Churchill's urging of a swift naval foray into the Baltic Sea to secure coal and iron deposits on which Germany depended), but to continue to rearm. Battles should be picked carefully, once the moment was right. Unfortunately, this eminently reasonable-sounding approach didn't take into account the Axis powers' willingness and ability to make numerous aggressive moves concurrently. That would come to cost the Axis dear in the long run, but it afforded them huge victories in the short term—victories that very nearly proved decisive. Norway was the first of the setbacks to overtake the Allies in 1940; the first of a series of miscalculations, losses and near-catastrophic lucky escapes that resulted in the fall of both British and French governments, the occupation of France and a rude awakening for the British people from their phoney war slumber.

Two weeks after his arrival in Glasgow, Geoffrey sent for Catherine to join him for a visit. She had only been there for four days when he received his orders. He was to take command of HMT *Juniper*, one of a newly commissioned class of trawler equipped with anti-aircraft and anti-submarine guns. He and his crew would be on patrol service. Catherine stayed for another week, as Geoffrey quietly set about getting to know his vessel and his men. Geoffrey had a gift for rallying people's spirits and a calm presence of mind, and one imagines that he must have lavished reassurance on his wife. But the escalation in tensions would nonetheless have been difficult to bear, especially since they both knew that, once Catherine left him, there was no knowing when they would see each other again.

Catherine went to stay with her sister at Cumlodean House in Scotland on her return journey to the south. She was trying hard to be calm but struggling, and she needed comfort. Philippa did her best, assuring her older sister that all would be well, but she was unhappy herself, and also without her husband since Lord Galloway had been down in town for the last two weeks. Philippa never expected much news from him when he was staying at his club. 'It's probably better not to know,' she explained sadly to Catherine. Philippa's marriage was not a happy one and her difficulties made worse by the fact that her little boy was not at all well. He suffered from epilepsy and his parents were at the end of their tether trying to find effective treatment. The Wendell sisters found some comfort in talking of family and their past. There was so little to enjoy in the present and so much to dread about the future.

Just six weeks after Catherine's departure from her husband in Glasgow, Germany launched its amphibious invasion of Norway, on 9 April 1940, and achieved nearly all its objectives by the end of the first day. King Haakon II had refused to authorise a handover of power to the Nazis and had broadcast a defiant message to the nation; he and his government had then fled Oslo and retreated north, just ahead of the Germans, to Tromsø. The Norwegian resistance was brave but ultimately hopeless. Hitler now had commanding access to the North Sea and the perfect staging post to launch air strikes against Britain. The Allies were caught completely on the back foot.

The first naval battle of the war took place on 9 April off the west coast of Norway. The Luftwaffe sank the destroyer HMS *Gurkha* and damaged two cruisers and a battleship. There was initial disbelief among British naval command before they rallied sufficiently to retaliate the following day, at Narvik, where they destroyed nine German vessels. But Allied Supreme Command was completely taken aback by the German superiority in the air and, above all, by the success of the ground operation. An expeditionary force of British and French men was sent to fight alongside the Norwegians; but in reality the land battle had already been lost. On 26 April the War Cabinet ordered a withdrawal from most of the territory, leaving only a rump force in the north of the country.

The Norwegian campaign was perceived as a disaster for Britain. It exposed radio networks that didn't work, lack of intelligence information and a complete absence of command structure between the armed forces. It was to prove Chamberlain's downfall. With confidence in his leadership failing, he offered his resignation to the King and advised him to appoint Churchill rather than Lord Halifax as Prime Minister. It was almost certainly Chamberlain's clear-sighted judgement and generous endorsement of a man who had been his nemesis for years, combined with Halifax's self-effacing refusal to push his own cause, that swung the decision in Churchill's favour. He was not the first choice of either the Conservative Party or the War Cabinet, and for months after his appointment he delivered some of his most famous speeches to a very cool reception in the House of Commons.

Churchill was sworn in on 10 May as the Norwegians battled on. Hitler ordered massive bombing raids on Rotterdam and the invasion of the Low Countries. The Allies were stunned. So were the Belgians and Dutch, who had hoped like the Finns and Norwegians before them to preserve their neutrality. They were occupied within a matter of days. As the German armies swept towards France, the Reich's military leadership was scarcely less incredulous. They had never imagined their audacity would be so successful. Panic ensued at Allied Command as lines fell and the British Expeditionary Force and a large segment of the French Army was cut off in northern Belgium, fighting for its life without even any transport with which to retreat. Churchill stood up in the House of Commons on 13 May and told the House, 'I have nothing to offer but blood, toil, tears and sweat.'

For the next two weeks the Allied armies were beaten back towards the English Channel and, despite heroic fighting along the way, it now seemed certain that they would be entirely overrun. The logistics and administrative corps were being shipped back across the Channel in desperate haste. The Germans were closing relentlessly in on the port of Dunkirk. The Allies put out the call for any and every seaworthy vessel to converge on the French port and bring the Allied armies back to safety. Between 26 May and 4 June, 930 civilian boats, barges, fishing trawlers and ferries answered the call. The flotilla of little ships was accompanied by 200 Navy vessels and defended by the Royal Air Force against the Luftwaffe, whose capabilities proved to be far less than they had promised the Führer. The seas were calm, which meant boats could be safely overloaded, and hundreds of them sailed back and forth between France and Britain until 338,226 British, French and Belgian soldiers had been rescued.

Operation Dynamo was a heroic aversion of collapse, but it was a hollow victory. Stores, ammunition and transport had to be abandoned on the beaches, destroyed where possible to prevent them from falling into enemy hands. The French army lost 290,000 men. The Allies were still in the war, but only just.

Hitler was triumphant. The French were fatally weakened; now he confidently expected that a chastened British government would see sense. But even as the Germans swept on into France, heading for Paris, Churchill made the nation's defiance plain. 'We shall not flag or fail. We shall go on to the end . . . We shall fight on the beaches, we shall fight on the landing grounds, we shall fight in the fields and in the streets, we shall fight in the hills. We shall never surrender!'

The rhetoric might have been unsurpassable, but the reality was grim. On 10 June, Mussolini threw in his lot with Nazi Germany and declared war on the Allies. As mainland Europe fell to the Nazis and Britain adjusted to the fact that it had escaped a similar fate by the skin of its teeth, the battle off the coast of Norway continued. Geoffrey had been assigned his mission. HMT *Juniper* was to be part of Operation Alphabet, another evacuation of Allied troops. The final British attempt to aid the Norwegians was over and the two forces, as well as the Norwegian royal family and government, needed to be transported back to Britain.

On 18 May Geoffrey sent an upbeat cable to Catherine telling her that he was 'busy but doing nothing dangerous . . . I am flourishing and do hope you are well and cheerful, my precious.' He told her that he had just heard they were to be deployed and so he would not be able to write for perhaps a fortnight. 'You mustn't worry, darling. The old mother country seems to be in a bit of a mess at present and obviously everyone must pull their weight. But I hope I shall get a week's leave in about a month or so.' He also wrote to his housekeeper, Miss Thorn, at Ovington Square, asking her to 'look after Mrs G. and to keep her busy!'

On 24 May, HMT *Juniper* docked in Tromsø. Geoffrey took the opportunity to write again to Catherine, looking forward to meeting her in London, fretting about rumours that there had been air raids over southeast England, sending her all his love. He also enclosed a letter that Henry had sent him, which had touched him very much. Catherine's son had written with several pages of news about the family's Easter holiday and to say that 'Mama was marvellously well, busy with Navy League work, but missing you terribly.' He included a rather charming sketch of 'Uncle' Geoffrey on the bridge of HMT *Juniper*, which resembles in Henry's depiction nothing so much as a rowing boat made for one.

Commander Grenfell was in actual fact in charge of a mostly inexperienced thirty-nine-man crew and a ship that was deeply uncomfortable in bad weather. While his officers and wireless operator were more seasoned sailors, most of his new recruits had had to learn as they went along. The North Sea has always been challenging, even for old hands, so Commander Grenfell's humour, confidence and decisive judgement were key to encouraging the crew in rough seas. Their work was made more difficult by the fact that *Juniper* rode the waves, rather than driving a path through them, as did larger vessels. The simplest of tasks became almost impossible in a heavy swell.

Geoffrey and his men awaited orders to evacuate from Tromsø. The British were expecting to transport the Norwegian government into exile and to escort the ships of the Norwegian Navy, then the fourth largest in the world, to safety. King Haakon was only very reluctantly persuaded to flee, by the British ambassador Sir Cecil Dormer. Under protest, he agreed, but he was adamant that, though he might leave Norway, the Crown jewels should never depart Norwegian soil. He enlisted Sir Cecil to help him bury the treasure in a cave that the two of them came across just outside Tromsø, for safekeeping. On 7 June he boarded HMS *Devonshire*, along with his family, his cabinet ministers and the country's entire reserve funds of gold. Haakon wasn't in the slightest bit sentimental about that. He didn't want the Nazis to get hold of it, and he knew his nation would need it later, when their territory was finally restored to them.

With King, government in exile, Allied troops and gold

all safely loaded, the convoy set off, pulling out of the fjords as quickly as possible. The Germans were patrolling, on the lookout for their rich prize.

Juniper had been assigned to escort the 5,600-ton tanker, *Oil Pioneer*. At dawn the next day, Commander Grenfell and his party were 300 miles west of Narvik when, to his dismay, he realised that they had been sighted by at least three heavy German warships. He sent urgent wireless signals reporting the development before radioing to the *Oil Pioneer* to sail independently. As a diversion, *Juniper* hoisted her battle flags and bravely sailed in to challenge the German ships. Commander Grenfell ordered *Juniper*'s twelve-pounder guns to fire on the *Admiral Hipper*, putting the enemy's fore turret out of action and inflicting some damage on the deck. The warship replied with a heavy salvo that tore through the bridge and superstructure of HMT *Juniper*. The British trawler was hopelessly stricken. Just four survivors were picked up later that day, one of whom was seriously injured. They were taken to a prisoner-of-war camp in Oslo. HMS *Devonshire* was luckier. The King, his ministers and his country's wealth made it to London after a top-speed race across the North Sea.

Catherine was oblivious to what had happened. The media's focus was on the 'miracle of deliverance', as Churchill described Dunkirk and, in any case, *Juniper* was a small vessel, the sort whose loss would not make front-page news. Catherine was no more anxious than usual. Geoffrey had told her that he would not be able to contact her until his return to Scotland, so she told herself she simply had to wait.

On 18 June, her waiting took on a terrible new dimension. Catherine received an official cable informing her that Geoffrey was 'missing in action, possibly a prisoner of war.' She had expected to tear open a letter from her husband, to read his typically positive account of events and to know for sure when she would next see him, on leave, in London. Instead, the brief words chilled her soul. She clung to the slim hope that Geoffrey was among the few survivors, but now every postal delivery, every knock at the door was a torture to her.

The phoney war was well and truly over. Churchill's most pressing concern was to re-equip the armed forces in the wake of the losses in northern France. Industrial production focused on munitions and, particularly, just five types of fighter planes. At Elliots of Newbury, a firm local to Highclere, a largely female workforce made components for Spitfires, De Havilland Mosquitoes and Tiger Moths. Nationwide the results were extraordinarily good. Output soared, rising from 256 planes in April 1940 to 467 in September. Remarkably, the RAF had more fighter planes at the end of the Battle of Britain than it did at the beginning. But this focus on aircraft manufacture meant that there were shortages of other arms. The British military turned to American firms to fulfil additional orders.

As the Battle for France unfolded just a few miles across the Channel from where they were stationed at Shorncliffe, a sombre mood fell upon the 7th Hussars. Robert Taylor and Jack Gibbins gave up on their flits to Highclere, and Porchey and Colonel Breitmeyer were poised to respond to the battle orders they expected any day. Tilly was petrified by the news of the German forces closing in relentlessly on the Channel ports, and Porchey had to devote a lot of time to reassuring her that as soon as he knew what was expected of the regiment, they could make plans for her to move.

The decision came soon enough, in the person of the Prime Minister himself. One of Churchill's first acts in office was to get out from behind his desk and go to inspect the troops. He was, after all, a career soldier and a veteran of the Boer War long before he was a politician, and he did not wish to rely on his generals for information.

Lord Carnarvon recalled the PM's comment as the 7th Hussars lined up for inspection, in his memoirs. It was entirely in keeping with the tone of all Porchey's exchanges with Winston. Churchill growled at the assembled men, pointedly directing his remarks at the commanding officer and his adjutant. 'Of all the ridiculous locations to be training a cavalry unit, I cannot imagine. You are right next to the aerodrome and if bombs fell among your horses they would stampede like the Gadarene swine and gallop over the cliffs into the sea. I shall have you moved immediately.' Within three days they were en route to Sherwood Forest in Nottingham, where they were to be billeted under canvas. Robert Taylor packed up. He and Gibbins and the bedsteads accompanied Lord Carnarvon in the Vauxhall, while Monsieur Pascal returned to Highclere.

It was all too much for Tilly. She refused point-blank to accompany Porchey and went instead to stay with her great friend Adele Astaire, now Lady Charles Cavendish, at Lismore Castle in Ireland. Porchey was relieved. He hoped that being far out of harm's way would calm Tilly's nerves. In fact, the distance gave her a clearer perspective from which to contemplate the fact that Britain's prospects looked a hundred times worse than they had when she had fled the country the previous November.

In early July, Tilly returned to London and the Carnarvons' usual suite at the Ritz. She asked her husband to meet her there so they could talk. The steel-framed hotel was promoting itself as a safer place to spend one's time as the city braced for the ferocious air battle that was daily expected to begin in the skies over southern England. The bar had become an air-raid shelter and at night it buzzed with rumour and conspiracy, defiance and conjecture. King Zog of Albania, who had fled Mussolini's invading forces in April 1939, had taken up residence at the hotel and was supposed to pay his bills in gold bullion. The atmosphere was febrile; it was hardly likely to calm Tilly down.

Porchey thought she looked radiant when he walked into her bedroom. She seemed delighted to see him, and for a moment he allowed himself to hope. But over dinner she produced a cable for him to read and he felt a familiar sensation, brought on by this repetition of a scene they had lived once before. The cable contained the offer of a part in a play on Broadway. Tilly had clearly spent the time at Lismore on the telephone to America. Porchey pleaded with her not to disappear from him for another six months. With everything hanging in the balance and the war certain to drag on indefinitely, she might not be able to return for years.

'You must let me go, darling. Look at what's happened in France. What if the Germans land here? You would be fine, but what about me, with my Jewish blood?'

Porchey tried to humour her but he only made her angry. 'Look, Porchey, I believe the Germans will win this war. You can't beat them, that's very clear now.'

Stung by her words, he flared up immediately. 'Nonsense. Things may not be too good at the moment, but you can be sure we'll defeat them, somehow.'

Tilly was unmoved. The Germans would be landing soon, it was only a matter of time; and she was convinced that, when they did, she would be targeted.

Completely depressed, Porchey went to see his sister and his mother to canvas their views on what he should be saying to Tilly. Porchey felt that his chance of married happiness was slipping away. Almina, as usual, was to the point.

She expressed the family view: Tilly had made it more than plain that she would not stay and now she had to go.

It was infinitely harder to arrange a passage for her than it had been nine months previously. Porchey went to the Passport Office to try to procure a visa and found hordes of people attempting the same thing. Tilly was obviously not the most pressing case, but Lord Carnarvon managed to persuade the official. Ever resourceful, he slipped some banknotes into her passport and secured the necessary stamp. Tilly was a picture of radiant happiness when he returned, mission accomplished, to the Ritz hotel. Porchey, by contrast, was struggling to contain his sadness at the suspicion that his marriage was failing. This leave-taking had an air of finality.

The Countess of Carnarvon set sail on the liner *Duke of Atholl*, arriving in Canada after nine days at sea. The crossing was not without risk, but the Battle of the Atlantic had not yet quite entered its critical phase. From late July onwards, the ferocious fight to protect the convoys, which were bringing the imported goods on which Britain was dependent, stepped up a gear. The battle at sea, which lasted the duration of the conflict, underpinned the whole war effort, and the nation's survival. Blockade and counter-blockade: both sides knew the war would be won or lost at sea and so it eventually proved. But Britain's victory came at a huge price: 3,500 merchant ships and 175 warships were sunk, compared to just 783 German U-boats lost. Tilly was fortunate to travel when she did.

Despite the fact that the crossing passed off without incident, they were an anxious few days. People were fleeing in circumstances that forced them to wonder whether they would see their loved ones again. Like most of the other passengers, Tilly was in charge of a party of small children sent to Canada for their safety by worried parents. Having handed her charges over to the authorities on arrival, she travelled down to New York and reinstalled herself in the life she had left six months before. She continued with her rounds of fundraising, in between theatre performances, and maintained to Porchey that if all went as well as he claimed to believe it would, she would be back at Highclere in the spring once her contract finished.

Porchey was increasingly resigned to whatever might happen. In the meantime, he had barely returned to Sherwood Forest when he received two pieces of news. The 7th Hussars were to be disbanded. The matter had been settled: there was no role for the cavalry. With a heavy heart, he set about the business of winding up the regiment's administration and writing once more to everyone he could think of in search of something useful to do. Then, he heard from Catherine. She wanted to settle the question of their daughter's future. It seemed that she felt it was time to take up her American relatives on their offer of sanctuary. Porchey had just secured a passage for his wife to travel to the States. Now Catherine wanted him to help her make arrangements for Penelope to make the same crossing.

Catherine's cousin Arthur Wendell, who lived in Rahway, New Jersey, had written to them both back in May, offering to do whatever he could to help. He and the rest of the family would find houses for them all in the States and schools for the children, though he was at pains to say, 'Please don't think any of us have lost faith in the ultimate outcome of this struggle.' Catherine and Porchey had discussed it and decided to ask Arthur to look into a school for Pen. Arthur wrote to Porchey some weeks later about an 'outstanding American school near Marian's [Gar's] cousins—hunting country. It has splendid equipment, capable teachers, two of

Penelope's friends already there.' The school was Foxcroft, in Virginia. Catherine had sent Pen the prospectus.

Neither of them wanted to send Penelope so far away, but now that the threat to Britain was closer, they felt they must. Catherine was suffering the agonising wait for news of Geoffrey, with every day sapping her reserves of hope. She dreaded the prospect of being without her daughter, and without Doll—she had asked her if she would accompany Pen. But her personal sense of the encroaching dangers had been sharpened to an almost unbearable point. She would have to find a way to bear the separation. With the Battle of Britain raging in the skies above southern England, her mind was made up. Porchey agreed. They must act now, before it became too dangerous to travel.

On 24 July, as the Battle of the Atlantic entered its first critical phase, Pen, Doll and her beloved dog Baba left from Southampton. Catherine had said goodbye to her daughter at home in Ovington Square. She couldn't bear to leave for fear that the cable would arrive with news of her husband while she was away. It was Porchey who once again made the sad trek to wave from the dockside.

Pen promised to write the moment she arrived. She was worried about leaving her mother but her grandmother, Gar, had told her, 'I'll look after your mummy for you, don't you worry, my darling.' Her Uncle Jac and Aunt Eileen were close by in London, too, and her mother had told her repeatedly that she would be quite all right. But it must have been an awful wrench. Pen was just fifteen years old. She had watched her mother sink into a state of depression and become reliant on alcohol during the divorce from Penelope's father. She must have worried how she would bear up under this even greater pressure of not knowing whether Geoffrey were alive or dead. So far, Catherine seemed to be staying strong without any recourse to drink, but even so, it was a worry. Pen would also miss her cousin, Patricia, hugely. The girls had always been close and had become allies in the strange new circumstances of their wartime lives.

Patricia was to stay on at their evacuated school, where she missed her cousin terribly. The ponies went back to Highclere, as did Patricia for her holidays. She had troubles of her own. Her parents were living in London since her father was an MP and spent long evenings in the House of Commons. The workload and strain of being in such a position of responsibility during wartime was starting to tell on Bro. He was becoming utterly exhausted. Patricia knew her mother, Eve, was worried about him.

Pen and Doll arrived safe and sound in New York, where they stayed for a few days before travelling to Arthur Wendell's house. The city must have seemed almost overwhelmingly carefree compared to London, which was gripped by anxiety about the outcome of the aerial battle being fought over its head. New York was pure heady glamour next to the austerity of wartime London, with its blackout and air-raid shelters and gas masks, not to mention its rationing. Pen didn't go short when she was with either of her parents (after all, there was caviar for dinner at the Ritz throughout the war) but school food was very plain indeed. Now she and Doll enjoyed trips to the cinema and the shops, and lunched with Tilly. Pen was pleased to see her, and to receive some money that her papa had sent her, care of her stepmother. One hundred dollars was a fortune to a fifteen-year-old schoolgirl. She (or perhaps Catherine, on her behalf) might have been a bit put out if she had discovered that Porchey had sent Tilly $2,000, with instructions to share it with Pen when she arrived. Strictly speaking, of course, Tilly did.

Even had she known, Catherine had far bigger things to think about. Her son spent much of the summer at Highclere training with the Local Defence Volunteers, or the Home Guard as they were rechristened before long. Two and a half months earlier, when the threat of a land invasion had looked alarmingly imminent, Anthony Eden, Secretary of State for War, made a wireless broadcast calling on all men between the ages of seventeen and sixty-five who were not in military service but wished to defend their country, to enrol in the LDV at their local police station. A wave of patriotic enthusiasm carried 250,000 volunteers to sign up in the first seven days; by the beginning of August, 1.5 million men were enrolled. Catherine was proud of Henry, of course, but the knowledge that, at seventeen, he was now just nudging into the age bracket that made him eligible to serve in the military was terrifying to her. The Home Guard was one thing, but she didn't know if she could bear it if he were to join the regular Army. She was relieved when the academic year started again and Henry went back to being a schoolboy at Eton.

In his absence there was tremendous excitement for the Guard and everyone around Highclere when a German Heinkel plane crashed near the estate. It had been damaged by anti-aircraft fire near Bristol and was trying to get home. The crew of five bailed out as the plane went down and the Home Guard were called out to search for any survivors. Two Germans were picked up almost immediately, and then a member of the search party who had gone to relieve himself in some rhododendrons in the Park inadvertently found two more. The last German airman was caught a few days later when, preferring capture to hunger, he decided to hand himself in. A passing lady motorist found him on a roadside close to Highclere Castle and drove him to

Newbury Police Station, where she asked them to give him a good meal.

The war in the air was entering a terrible chapter. On 7 September the Luftwaffe launched a massive night-time raid on London. They bombed the city for fifty-seven consecutive nights. The Blitz, in which sixteen British cities suffered major attacks, went on for eight months, between September 1940 and May 1941, and claimed about 40,000 lives in total.

Londoners had been preparing for such an attack—but it was still devastating when it came. After two weeks, Catherine's nerves were at breaking point. Gar decided they should move out of the city to somewhere safer, for the sake of her daughter's health. It took some effort to persuade Catherine that any news from the Navy about Geoffrey would find them, that there were central information systems they could access. Catherine was also anxious not to give up her voluntary work for the Navy League, serving lunches in their canteens. Gar made enquiries and discovered that she would be able to continue down in Torquay, on the Devon coast. At the end of September, Catherine, Gar and Mrs van Celst, Catherine's housekeeper at Wilton Crescent, moved to the Imperial hotel, situated atop the cliffs overlooking the bay.

By the end of October 1940, the Luftwaffe had lost the Battle of Britain, defeated by the heroic efforts of the RAF fighter pilots. Operation Sea Lion, the German plan for an invasion of England, was mothballed. The British public rallied; for the first time in long months of despair and disaster, there was a definite sense that the war could be won. The Americans started to think so, too, despite Ambassador to London Joseph Kennedy's pessimistic bulletins to Roosevelt. Now the word was that Britain could survive, and deserved every support in her efforts.

The Blitz continued but at the end of 1940, the nation could look back on a year in which so much had been sacrificed and conclude that perhaps it had not been in vain. Catherine wrote to her daughter, went up to London to visit her son and to see friends. Porchey phoned her several times and thought she seemed in reasonable form, all things considered. Catherine tried to summon up the strength to begin a new year without Geoffrey, still lost in the limbo of not knowing what had happened to him. Her waiting was almost over. On 8 February 1941, Catherine Grenfell received a letter from the War Office. Her eyes clouded as she struggled to read the words. 'All hope of his having been rescued must be abandoned. Your husband, Lieutenant Commander Geoffrey Seymour Grenfell, must now be presumed to have lost his life.'

16

Coming Through Darkness

Once Catherine had read the letter from the War Office, she handed it to her mother and went immediately to bed. The wait was over and now there was no hope left, nothing to be done. For the next three days she drank the tea that Gar brought her and responded calmly when asked how she was feeling, but she refused to speak to the friends who had started to telephone to offer their condolences. Gar was half frantic with worry.

When Catherine did get up, the first thing she did was cable Penelope, and then her cousins in America, via Arthur. 'Dear *Trois Anges*, Have just received official announcement that darling Geoffrey was killed in gallant fight against great odds . . . Please tell family.' Arthur duly passed on the news. To his cousin Edith he wrote, 'I met Geoffrey two years ago. He was a splendid man in every particular, devoted to Catherine.'

One of the first to write to her was Porchey, who knew how wretched she would be but trusted in her 'faith and nobility of spirit'. He was going to see their boy at Eton, and ended the letter with 'all love, God bless you'. Catherine had already written to Henry. The letter is touching for the way her pride in Geoffrey's bravery is already the dominant theme she clings to. 'It is a very fine story,' she tells Henry. He wrote by return, trying to cheer her up, urging her not to be too 'miserable, I am sure Uncle Geoffrey would not want you to be.'

Countless friends, including Almina and the Duke and Duchess of Kent, wrote to express their sympathy for her loss and their admiration for Lieutenant Commander Grenfell. 'I hope one day the story of [*Juniper's*] action will be told.' 'I feel so sorry for you losing him, because he was such a good chap.' Dr Johnnie, who had been part of Highclere's life for forty years, penned a note in a spidery hand offering his prayers and best wishes. Sibell Lygon wrote from Madresfield inviting Catherine to stay and saying she was 'so sad that those months of anxiety should end like this.'

Geoffrey's father was not very well and Catherine was worried about when to break the news. Geoffrey was Riverdale Grenfell's only son. In the end she managed to compose a brief but heartfelt note. Her father-in-law wrote to Catherine that he was 'suddenly overwhelmed by pride . . . pride that he belonged to me and you. [He] belongs to that brave band of Grenfells who have given all they could to their country and to all those who loved them.' She had brought great happiness into Geoffrey's life and must always remember that she still had him and Olive [Geoffrey's step-mother]. 'Darling, we do both love you so.'

Catherine's first few attempts to reply had to be abandoned when the page became blotted with tears. Eventually she managed, 'He taught me to think the right way and to face the world anew. I will try to keep that spirit of gaiety and courage in my heart for ever.'

The Grenfell family knew what it was to read the worst news in the world. They understood the anguish that Catherine felt at not being able to bury the man she mourned because he had died in the seas off Norway, just as his cousins had died in the sea of mud in northern France. Julian Grenfell and his brother—that 'brave band of Grenfells' referred to by Riverdale—had perished in the last war.

In her reply to Geoffrey's father, Catherine enclosed some lines from a poem written about Julian, who was killed at Ypres in 1915.

> Because of you we will be brave and gay
> Remembering you we will be brave and strong . . .
> And you will speed us onward with a cheer.
> And wave beyond the stars that all is well.

Catherine and Gar stayed on at the Imperial hotel. Catherine loved the sea-sprayed air and listening to the sound of the waves on the cliffs below. As long as she was by the sea, she felt connected to the waters off Norway where her husband lay. Now, more than ever, she wanted to keep up her involvement with the things that had mattered to Geoffrey. Every day she left the hotel and walked down into Torquay to work in the Navy League.

Her family were worried that she would collapse under the strain, or that she would turn once again to alcohol to numb her pain. But Catherine seems to have been determined to live out her assurance to Geoffrey's father that she would honour her husband's memory by keeping in her heart the courage he had taught her. She and Gar would sometimes settle themselves in the hotel bar and watch the sun set into the sea. Prompted by her mother, Catherine would recount the details of her day down at the League over a gin and tonic. There might have been a second but there were never more than two. Gar could write to Pen, who felt the burden of being so far away very keenly, and tell her that her mother was impressing everyone with her fortitude.

On 2 April 1941, Catherine received notice of her war widow's pension and read again the words 'the late Lieutenant Commander Grenfell'. She felt her resolve not to give in to despair faltering and decided that it was time to return to the refuge provided by her beloved Catholic nuns. Gar went to Wilton Crescent in London. The Blitz was still raging but, with Catherine in safe hands, she wanted to be near her son, Jac, and her grandchildren.

The rituals of worship, the peace and quiet for reflection, the nurturing atmosphere of the retreat all healed Catherine's mind, and her soul. She was grateful for the loving support she received and started to think seriously about converting to Catholicism. The stumbling block, and it was a big one, was the Church's refusal to recognise divorce. As far as the Catholic Church was concerned, Catherine was still married to Porchey and her subsequent marriage to Geoffrey was invalid. The nuns treated her with nothing but kindness and sympathy as they talked to her about her loss, but the institution's inability to recognise the fundamental importance of Geoffrey in her life made her hang back from taking the steps to convert.

Catherine spent two weeks at the convent in Highgate, north London, before returning home at the end of April.

She went straight to Ovington Square, where Geoffrey's housekeeper of many years was at the door to receive her. Charged by Geoffrey with caring for his wife, in Catherine's absence Miss Thorn had looked after the house, which was immaculate despite the devastation across London. Fewer bombs fell in the western districts than in the east, which was nearer the major target of the docks, but no part of the city was spared. Bombs had been dropped on landmarks such as Buckingham Palace, Downing Street, many of London's great churches and in front of the Bank of England. Catherine hailed a cab from the station and picked her way through dust and debris, horrified by the blackened craters where houses had been, the bomb sites that still smoked.

It must have been an emotional homecoming. Outside was destruction; inside too, since she was alone. But at least she was back in the house where she had been so happy for one sweet year, surrounded by her beloved's possessions, his clothes hanging in the wardrobes still carrying his scent, his books on the shelves where he had left them.

Catherine knew she could not stay in the house, that it would have to be sold. She spent a few days dealing with Geoffrey's trustees and arranging for things to be packed up and moved to Wilton Crescent. How fortunate that she had retained that home of her own. Then, not yet able to face her former life in town, she decided to take a lovely quiet house called Byeways, just outside Ascot, so that she could be close to Henry at Eton. Catherine felt she needed the calm of the countryside, to pick the berries in the hedgerows and collect wood for her fire. She volunteered at a canteen in Windsor and spent as much time as possible with Henry. She did small things to make herself content and put off all major decisions for later, as she relearned how to live alone.

Catherine took comfort from good news, wherever she found it. Penelope's letters (and her school reports) cheered her. They were full of accounts of how hard she was working at Foxcroft and how much she enjoyed America, despite her longing to come home. Henry was happy and well, though Catherine had asked him not to talk to her about his plans to join up when he left school later that year. She would have to bear it when the moment came, but she didn't want to think about it until then.

There was good news too, on the course of the war. The last major bomb attack on London occurred on the night of 10 May, the day before Catherine's departure for Windsor. The Blitz was over and the country had survived with its manufacturing capacity, Air Force and spirit intact, despite the terrible loss of life and destruction of homes and livelihoods.

The immediate problem was money, or lack of it. Britain was fighting the war virtually single-handed and it was costing a fortune. Churchill made an appeal to Roosevelt for financial and material support in December 1940, to which the President responded by exchanging fifty destroyers for ninety-nine-year leases on British bases in the Caribbean. This decision triggered a debate in the United States over whether the nation should actively support the Allies or maintain its neutrality. A majority of public opinion favoured support in the form of loans, but without active intervention in the conflict. On 11 March, Roosevelt signed the Lend-Lease legislation into law, and the transfer of billions of dollars' worth of supplies began.

It was a critical moment for Britain, with the attacks on convoys in the Atlantic sapping its ability to keep fighting. Churchill wrote in his diaries that the threat of the German blockade was perhaps his greatest fear. Rationing had been in place since January 1940, but the self-sufficiency pro-grammes in food and other agriculture instigated at the outbreak of hostilities were only now starting to yield results. Britain needed more of everything: food, steel, armoured vehicles, ships, munitions. Churchill was overjoyed at the conclusion of Lend-Lease. He knew that the Americans had effectively entered the war on the side of the Allies.

When Porchey returned to Highclere, in the wake of the 7th Hussars being disbanded in the summer of 1940, he found virtually the whole estate had been requisitioned for the war effort. Porchey was disconsolate. Tilly had left him, Pen was about to set off for America and once more he was searching around for a way in which he could contribute. For the next four months, in between fruitlessly importuning Tilly to come back, he had to be satisfied with helping wherever he could at home. There was a lot to do.

As well as the nursery school in the castle, which now numbered fifty-five children and sixteen staff, there were hives of activity in every corner of the estate. Agriculture was a major focus, as it was up and down the country. The Dig for Victory campaign had urged the nation to turn vegetable gardener in their back yards, with impressive results. There were 1.7 million allotments yielding fresh produce by the end of the war. The bigger estates were subject to compulsory land-use orders. When the government directed that any potentially viable arable land must be ploughed up, Highclere's gardeners and tenant farmers took to the paddocks, the cricket pitch and the golf course. Most of the land was very poor and the wheat harvest scarcely justified the efforts involved so, under the watchful eye of the Potato and Carrot Division of the Ministry of Food, the Highclere staff concentrated their efforts on extending the castle's kitchen gardens. Before long they were supplying vegetables to schools, hospitals and shops all over the local area.

The stud had been in government hands since the beginning of 1940. The buildings housed a constant stream of different battalions as they carried out training exercises. RAF Bomber Command requisitioned another part of the estate, on the far side of Siddown Hill, as a practice area.

Bomber Command had been formed in 1936 when it was regarded as a virtually impregnable force and essentially a deterrent. But in comparison to Fighter Command it had received insufficient investment, either in planes or in training. In May 1940, when the Germans violated agreements not to attack civilian targets by flattening Rotterdam, it became clear that a major air battle was approaching. The unit needed more and better planes, more pilots and more practice.

The bombing alley at Highclere ran south to north in a valley leading up to the chalk downlands. Two brick towers were constructed as lookout posts and became favourite hideouts for local boys, who used to go out to collect detritus after the practice runs. Planes swept up and over Siddown Hill, aiming their bombs at the dummy target, an Avro Anson positioned halfway along, before practising their only defensive manoeuvre: a tight corkscrew dive that the German Messerschmitts could not follow. The de Havilland Mosquito was one of the fastest aircraft in the world but early on in the war it was also prone to wing failures. One afternoon a Canadian Air Force Mosquito came very fast down through the valley and went to pull up but failed to clear the top of the hill. The wings sheared off and the cockpit slammed into the trees not twenty yards from the Home Guard's hut. Both the pilot and navigator were killed.

Life expectancy in Bomber Command, both in combat

and also in training, was so short that Churchill censored the information. A staggering 44 per cent of Bomber Crew members were killed, and the odds of surviving a whole tour of thirty missions were just one in six. It wasn't until American funding and supplies arrived, from the summer of 1941 onwards, that the unit received the investment it needed. The Lancaster and Halifax bombers, introduced in 1942, were the workhorses of the latter half of the war. With their higher speeds and bigger bomb loads they made Bomber Command's task somewhat less suicidally risky. But by then the unit had already secured its reputation for outstanding valour. Despite the appalling odds, its pilots kept flying. Of the 182 Victoria Cross medals—the British military's highest decoration—awarded during World War Two, RAF Bomber Command earned nineteen, one of the highest tallies of any single unit.

In the November of 1940, Porchey's job-hunting efforts paid off. He was approached to head up the local division of the military's Claims Commission. Britain had become a vast training camp with troops scrambling through hedges, tanks trundling across farmers' fields and dummy bombs unleashed on private land. There were constant disputes about rights and damage. Lord Carnarvon was in many ways the perfect man for the job. He had demonstrated himself to be an able administrator during the process of disbanding the Hussars, and had first-hand experience of the sorts of negotiations that he would be required to adjudicate. He was disappointed, though; he had hoped for something more exciting. In a letter to Arthur Wendell he wrote, 'I am not looking forward to it very much', before asking him to 'kiss Penelope for me' and assuring him that he was grateful for everything Arthur was doing for his daughter.

Porchey had been recommended for the post by his old

friend General Alexander, who had been his superior in both Gibraltar and Constantinople, back in the days before he married Catherine. Alexander had supervised the retreat from Dunkirk and had just been appointed General Officer Commanding-in-Chief of the Southern Command, with overall responsibility for defending southwest England. General Alexander took the time to meet Porchey and to offer encouragement, describing the work of the commission as 'vital to retain the goodwill of the people, especially the farmers who are growing the food we desperately need.'

Porchey knew he was right but couldn't quite dispel his yearning for something a little more romantic than form filling and dispute resolution. He made one last-ditch attempt when he wrote to his friend Brendan Bracken at Downing Street. Bracken was a confidant of Churchill's and a member of the Privy Council, and in 1941 would be appointed Minister of Information. Porchey admitted it was 'an audacious request but [he] wondered whether there was a role for [him] as a personal ADC to the Prime Minister.' It was not to be, and at the end of the year Porchey knuckled down to his duties at the Claims Commission.

Christmas 1940 was subdued. Porchey was missing Tilly. Everyone was missing Pen. Henry and his cousin Patricia were at Highclere and handed around treats at the traditional children's party. That year the numbers had swollen to 140. In the afternoon they read stories to the evacuees in the Library.

Almina arrived in the morning to spend the day with her family. She was much loved by all her grandchildren. Patricia still remembers the delicious lunches and the crème de menthe she was given on visits to see her at Alfred House, before the war. By 1940 Almina had closed her beloved London nursing home. When war was declared she had hoped to turn it into a military hospital, but the rules governing such things were far stricter than they had been twenty years before and it simply wasn't possible. She was not about to give up on nursing, though, and established two more small homes: the first in Hove; the second in Barnet at a house called The Glebe where she lived herself.

Almina, in common with many people, enjoyed an easier relationship with her grandchildren than she did with her son. She had a gift, much appreciated by all of them, for saying exactly what was on everyone's mind. Before returning to The Glebe that evening she told Porchey, not unkindly but quite firmly, to buck up. He was lucky to have a useful job that didn't expose him to danger. 'And darling, I suspect you're right that Tilly isn't coming back. But just think how much worse it could be. Poor Catherine is still waiting to know whether Geoffrey is alive or dead.'

As always, Porchey found it intensely irritating to be bossed and patronised by his mother, especially when he knew she was right. He did indeed buck up. By the summer of 1941 he had been promoted to Major in recognition of his effectiveness in carrying out an unpopular job with charm and persistence. And of course, when Catherine's world fell apart in February that year, he was on hand with sincere sympathy and offers of practical help. He had loved her; he respected her and was fond of her still.

In the midst of all the endings, one love story was entering a new, happy phase. Robert, who the previous year had been serving as Lord Carnarvon's personal servant and flitting off from basic training down in Shorncliffe, had asked his long-standing sweetheart, Joan, to marry him. The couple wanted to get married as soon as possible but Robert was too busy with the next, rather more serious, stage of his military career.

After his not altogether glorious association with the cavalry regiment ended with the disbanding of the 7th Hussars, Robert joined the Royal Armoured Corps, one of the British Army's tank divisions. He excelled on the wireless course, so much so that he was singled out to be an instructor. He had hoped to be sent into the field, but accepted that training was essential work. And there were compensations for remaining at home, such as the possibility of leave and the fact that he would be posted to Bovington in Dorset, relatively close to Joan, in Highclere. (It seems reasonable to assume that Joan saw no disadvantages whatsoever to her beloved being an instructor rather than a combat soldier.) Perhaps the couple could finally plan their wedding.

As soon as he arrived at Bovington, Robert applied for a pass for two weekends hence, to marry Joan. He was told the pass would depend on his progress and performance over the next two weeks. Wartime weddings were arranged in a jiffy to take advantage of even the smallest amount of leisure time. This was the best opportunity Robert and Joan were likely to get for a while. Mr Kent, the parson at Highclere Church, agreed that in the circumstances a single week's worth of banns would suffice and the wedding was fixed for Saturday 12 April.

Only on the evening of the Friday was Robert granted his pass. There was no way of contacting Joan, so he simply set off, hitching a series of lifts to reach Winchester. He arrived late that night and asked a policeman at the station to help him find a lodging for a couple of hours' sleep. At 6.00 a.m. he caught a milk train from Winchester to Highclere. Walking through the park to the castle, where Lord Carnarvon had promised him he was welcome to wash and change his clothes, Robert stared around at unfamiliar faces and noise, army tents in the fields, rickety fences criss-crossing the land, military trucks parked on broken verges. The castle soared in front of him and he was pleased to see that, from a little distance at least, it looked exactly the same as ever: pale gold stone and ranks of windows, Gothic turrets and the tower atop the square body of the main house. When he walked through the courtyard to the staff entrance, though, he saw that no one had time to sweep it any more.

Pushing open the back door and setting off down the corridor, he looked in on the kitchens, where a cook he didn't recognise was directing a new maid to hurry up with boiled eggs and toast for fifty-five evacuees. Robert Taylor nodded his greetings and headed to Mrs Saunderson's sitting room to ask her to show him to a room in which he could dress. Judging from the warmth of his reception, the entire household was pleased by the news, and happy to help.

Before he made his way up the back stairs to a room in the men's quarters, Robert wondered whether he might take a quick look at the Saloon, to see how the place was keeping.

'Of course, be my guest,' said Mrs Saunderson. 'It's all changed, you know. We have any number of people running about all over the place: schoolteachers from London and army types and everything.' She gave him a smile that suggested she was rather pleased at the bustle.

Robert took the few stairs from the housekeeper's sitting room, round a corner and up to the small passage that links the study and Lady Carnarvon's sitting room to the Red Staircase and then the Saloon. A small child dashed past him into the Library. The great leaded windows over the Oak Staircase were boarded up. 'What happened there?' he asked Mrs Saunderson, who had followed him. 'Machine-gun damage. Two planes were practising and they got a bit close, blew out some of the lead, broken glass everywhere.' Mrs Saunderson shook her head. 'We were lucky. Only one of the children was slightly scratched.'

On his way to the back stairs, Robert saw Lord Carnarvon emerging from his study. 'Ah, Robert, glad to have bumped into you. Congratulations!'

'Thank you, my lord. It's very good of you to let me come here to change.'

'Nonsense, least we can do. The castle's full but there's always room for an old hand. Now, you'll need to get on your way.'

Joan must have woken that morning and wondered whether or not this would be her wedding day. Robert had told her that he would find out only at the last minute whether he had been granted a pass, too late to send a note or go to the Post Office to place a call. She dressed in the silver and white brocade gown given to her by a friend's mother, which she herself had altered to fit. Then she set off on her father's arm, followed by her family and the villagers, to walk the short distance to the church. Halfway there one of the village boys, who had run ahead, returned at full pelt. 'He's come! He's waiting for you.' Joan fairly skipped down the aisle to meet her bridegroom.

Lance Corporal Robert Taylor and Miss Johanna Streeter were married in Highclere Church on Easter Saturday, 12 April 1941. Mr Keen played the organ and the first hymn was 'Lead us heavenly father, lead us'. Afterwards there was a reception for about fifty guests at the Pheasant, their friend Ruby Benson's father's pub. The bride and groom had just that one day and one night together before Robert had to return to camp, but for them as for thousands of wartime couples, it was time made sweeter for having been so long anticipated, and it would be long treasured in the memory. When they parted on Sunday Robert promised to write often and to come to see her as soon as possible. Now that they were married, he could apply for married couple's accommodation at camp. Joan was too happy even to suffer. They would be together soon.

During the Easter Holiday Henry returned to Highclere to train with the Home Guard. Like his father before him, he was an enthusiastic and patriotic lad and, though he tried to be sensitive to his mother's anxieties, especially in the wake of her loss of Geoffrey, he had all the self-assurance typical of youth. He couldn't wait to join up. In the meantime, he wanted to do his bit with the Home Guard. Charles Maber, the head gamekeeper, and Frank Soper, the head forester, were the two company officers, men he had known all his life.

The duties of the Home Guard were various but could be boiled down to two essential functions: protecting vital infrastructure such as post offices, factories and fire stations, especially where they were vulnerable to bombing, and keeping an eye out for anything suspicious. Even as the threat of invasion faded, there was a real fear of fifth columnists. The Guard checked people's ID cards and removed signposts so that any German spies wouldn't be able to identify their surroundings. They scanned the night skies for enemy activity of all kinds.

The Highclere Home Guard had built an observation hut on top of Siddown Hill to the south of the castle, which commanded an excellent view across the downlands towards the port of Southampton. It was carefully concealed within the beech trees, and on the nights when Bomber Command wasn't practising, it was a peaceful spot. A rota was worked out to ensure at least two guards manned it each night and Henry enthusiastically took his turn.

One night in the early summer, by which time Henry was back at school, an accident occurred. The kerosene heater was knocked over, the wooden hut caught fire and the two guardsmen were unable to put it out. Enemy planes to the south saw the fire and swooped down to attack the hut. The Guard had to run for cover. The following morning there were two very sheepish individuals as reports were made to superior officers.

No real harm had been done, but the incident could have been designed to feed the criticisms—some good-natured, some less so—made by the Home Guard's detractors. The vast majority of recruits were men too old to serve in the military. In 1941, this meant anyone over the age of forty-one, and there were plenty of highly capable men of middle age serving. By 1942, when the age limit for conscription had been raised to fifty-one for men, the average age of Guards shot up. The soubriquet Dad's Army was applied and a reputation for bumbling attached itself. In fact, accidents such as the one at Highclere notwithstanding, the disorganisation that certainly was typical of the Guard in its early days derived more from the fact that the service had been raised at speed and at a moment when there was a serious shortage of arms and equipment, than the age or capabilities of its recruits. With more and more proper training and better equipment being made available throughout the war, the Guard proved its worth many times over.

Retaining younger men at Highclere was a particular concern for Miss Stubbings in 1941. She had taken over as Lord Carnarvon's agent from Marcus Wickham Boynton at the end of 1940, when he was called up. Now she spent a lot of her time applying on behalf of the estate to hang on to a few younger men to help with the heavier work in the gardens and on the farm. Many of the workers keeping Highclere going were over sixty years old. Haines, the plumber, was sixty-three; Frank Sheerman, the carpenter, was seventy-one. Miss Stubbings drew attention to the fact that there was a school as well as various army units billeted on the estate and put in a special plea for Jack Day, the electrician, on whom the nursery personnel were particularly reliant for all their small jobs. She seems to have been at least partially successful, as Jack remained at Highclere throughout the war.

Miss Stubbings' expanded role was typical of the way that women were required to take on tasks traditionally handled by men. Over the next four years nearly 10 million women entered the workforce, many in direct support of the war effort. Women worked in munitions factories, delivered Spitfires for the Air Transport Auxiliary and were recruited by Special Operations as spies. Though it dealt out a great deal of heartbreak, the war also provided women with opportunities to participate in public life and serve their country on an unprecedented scale.

On 22 June 1941, Hitler reneged on the non-aggression pact that Nazi Germany had signed with Soviet Russia in 1939. Four million troops from the Axis powers, the largest military force ever assembled, began the march to Moscow.

For Britain, Hitler's decision to wage war on Soviet Russia meant the creation of a major ally. For the first time since the fall of France in June 1940, Britain was not fighting alone. Churchill was famously anti-Communist, but he quipped that 'if Hitler invaded Hell, I would at least make a favourable reference to the Devil in the House of Commons.' Churchill was still actively pursuing good relations with the United States in the hopes that they too could be persuaded to come in formally with the Allies. But even without the Americans, in the summer of 1941 there was a sliver of breathing space, more than there had been for a year.

In America Penelope and Doll spent most of the summer with Wendell relations. They also dropped by to see Tilly when they were in New York. Tilly seems to have been genuinely fond of her stepdaughter; Pen in turn enjoyed Tilly's aura of exuberant glamour and appreciated the fact that she was still using her position as Lady Carnarvon to raise funds and support for the British war effort. Porchey found some small comfort in this, too, though even the $10,000 his wife raised at a gala in Cleveland wasn't enough to stop him from preferring her presence at Highclere.

Pen had hoped to return to England to visit her family, but the situation in the Atlantic remained far too dangerous to allow it. Convoys were being attacked every day by 'wolf packs' of German submarines, and her parents absolutely forbade her to come. It was torture for Pen who, though she enjoyed school and being in the States, missed Patricia, her father and her brother, and worried terribly about her mother. Arthur Wendell wrote to Catherine to reassure her that they were all 'treating Pen as if she were our very own. She has won the affections of everybody.'

If Penelope was desperate to come back to England, Tilly remained evasive on the subject of her own return. Several times she had apparently been on the brink of booking a passage but it never quite happened, and for the last year she had been ready with excuses every time she spoke to her husband. It was not that Porchey actually wanted her to put her life in danger by crossing now, at the height of the crisis in the Atlantic, but he would have been pleased to see any sign at all that she was really sorry about the situation or serious about coming as soon as she could.

In early September, Mrs Saunderson received from her employer a list of names of house guests who were expected the following Saturday morning; it was to be the largest house party in several months. Porchey had rekindled his friendship with actress Jeanne Stuart, the one who hadn't quite made the final cut as the new Lady Carnarvon two years previously. He had persuaded her to come for a couple of days away from the grimness of London, to enjoy the fresh air, peace and good food at Highclere. Rather sad, he rang Tilly to tell her his plan. 'The thing is, if you're going to abandon me, you can't expect me not to look for other company.' She replied that she quite understood. His brother-in-law was also staying. Bro was terribly in need of some relaxation himself as his work as an MP continued to take its toll.

The party was a success. Porchey felt lighter and more himself than he had since Tilly's departure. He invited several of his closest friends, all of whom commented on his more cheerful aspect and said how much they enjoyed Jeanne's company. It was the start of a long-standing relationship between Porchey and Jeanne, one that lasted far longer than his marriage to Tilly.

In the closing months of 1941, Britain's attention was concentrated on the war in North Africa that had been waging since Italy's opportunistic invasion of Egypt in May 1940. Following initial British successes against the Italians, Hitler had despatched Rommel into battle; his Afrika Korps troops had proved far more effective than the Italians, and the British had been fighting tough battles for months. In November General Auchinleck launched Operation Crusader to try to secure a decisive victory and relieve the Siege of Tobruk, a port city vital to the Allied war effort. On 7 December the good news for which Churchill had been desperate arrived on his desk. The siege had been broken and Rommel's troops had fallen back.

The good mood lasted a matter of hours. Later that day Downing Street received a communication from the White

House. The Japanese had launched a surprise attack on Pearl Harbor, the US naval base in Hawaii. Four US Navy battleships had been sunk and another four seriously damaged. One hundred and eighty-two aircraft had been destroyed; 2,402 American servicemen killed and more than a thousand injured. The following day US Congress voted 470 to one in favour of declaring war on the Axis powers. The United States was now fully engaged.

While he acknowledged the horrific scale of the attack, and the loss and fury felt by the American people, Churchill could not help but reflect that with the United States' entry into the conflict, the Allies' chances had just been given a war-winning boost.

17

Shoulder to Shoulder

Overnight, Pearl Harbor galvanised virtually unanimous American public and political support for the Allied war effort. There was profound shock, and a sense of outrage that Japan had attacked without a formal declaration of war. On Monday 8 December the United States of America declared war on Imperial Japan. Recruitment offices all over the country stayed open throughout the night as tens of thousands queued to join up. On 11 December Germany declared war on the United States.

The speed at which the US armed forces recruited and mobilised troops, and with which the United States shifted its economy on to a war footing, was astonishing. In 1939 the US Army numbered 100,000 men. By 1945, 14.5 million Americans were in uniform.

The attack on Pearl Harbor was part of a wider strategy

to advance Japan's interests in southeast Asia. It had been making inroads into European-controlled areas in Thailand and the Philippines throughout 1941. But the Allies were totally unprepared for Japan's attack on Malaya on 8 December. It took the advancing Japanese Army two months to push the Allies up the Malayan peninsula to Singapore, site of the supposedly impregnable Royal Naval base, which it captured in just over a week along with 80,000 British, Indian and Australian men, who were enslaved in Japanese internment camps for the rest of the war. Churchill described the fall of Singapore as the 'worst disaster' and 'largest capitulation' in British history. It triggered total war in the Pacific.

Tilly had spent the last two and a half years hoping that the States would afford her a place of safety. Now the Japanese had brought the fight to America. The Wendell family had been urging Catherine to join them for eighteen months; she had always refused, feeling her place was in her adopted home country, with her immediate family. But she and Porchey were immensely grateful to have American relations who could offer a refuge to their daughter. Except that, at the beginning of 1942, it seemed there were fewer and fewer refuges left anywhere in the world.

Churchill urged the country to hold steady, and there were determined efforts in every sphere to keep morale up. At Christmas, three weeks after Pearl Harbor, Porchey's friend Sidney Beer and his wife came to stay at Highclere. Beer was an obsessive music fan, a generous patron of the arts and an excellent amateur conductor, as well as being a wealthy impresario and racehorse owner. One evening, listening to gramophone records over port and Stilton, Sidney told Porchey he was going to do his bit by funding an orchestra. Good as his word, that year he formed the National Symphony Orchestra. With his own contacts and those of his friend Malcolm Sargent, the most famous English conductor of his era, Sidney's orchestra comprised some of the best musicians then working in London. Many of the wind players performed in between their duties in the RAF Central Band or the various Guards' bands.

Highclere continued to be a hive of activity. Porchey plugged away at the Claims Commission, making endless rounds of inspections of his area, taking a sandwich lunch and a Thermos of tea to have in the back of his car. He had been assigned a driver, Trooper Bloss, who was a Yorkshireman of extreme adaptability and mildness of temper. He was adept at swapping rabbits shot on the estate for a parcel of contraband lamb chops under the counter at a local butcher's. He was also sanguine in the face of Lord Carnarvon's irritation when he repeatedly got lost as they were trying to find the site of some complaint that needed investigating. On one occasion, when they had circled helplessly on unmarked roads outside Devizes for what felt like hours before Porchey recognised something and managed to navigate them in, Bloss remarked to a furious Lord Carnarvon that if His Lordship had known the way all along, he could perhaps have said so.

Porchey was extremely fond of Bloss, who proved his worth repeatedly. It was his suggestion that they mount a small red and blue pennant (the colours of Highclere Castle's flag) on the Vauxhall, with the happy result that army convoys thought the car belonged to a general and moved their vehicles to one side when Porchey swept past. Bloss would load for Henry when he went out to shoot for rabbits or other game at Highclere. His bluff Yorkshire humour tempered young Lord Porchester's natural enthusiasm for the coming fight with some down-to-earth common sense. Bloss's attitude was that duties must be done, but you might as well try to stay alive. Porchey's advice was similar: he reminded his son that 'a live subaltern was better than a dead Victoria Cross'.

In June a division of Canadian troops arrived to train at Highclere. They caused Miss Stubbings no end of headaches as they drove across crops and left piles of empty petrol cans and trees cut down to no purpose across the park. The number of men billeted at the stud was now stretching the capacities of the local utilities; the estate's water reservoir was perilously low.

If the Canadians were not terribly popular with Miss Stubbings, she was probably the only woman for miles around to feel indifferent to their charms. For many of the young nurses and teachers attached to the nursery school (to say nothing of local girls and the Highclere maids), the Canadians were very welcome indeed. Taking their charges for walks through the village or to church on a Sunday afforded plenty of opportunity for interaction with handsome young men in uniform. Before long, their possibilities for assignations received a significant boost thanks to a change of routine up at the castle.

The bombing campaign against Britain was ongoing, despite the failure of all-out Blitz. Hitler needed to secure Britain's surrender, and the sooner the better. So blackout continued to be a way of life for all Highclere's residents. The castle was never deliberately targeted by the Germans, but they seemed to think the old lime kilns at Burghclere, just four miles from the Castle, were an arms dump, so plenty of bombs fell on the estate.

One night, after the Home Guard had cranked up the siren for yet another air raid and the nursery school staff had frantically shepherded their charges all the way down from the castle's turrets to its cellars, the decision was made to move the children's sleeping quarters. Their cots were set up in rows in the Library. Most of the teachers and nurses remained in their bedrooms on the top floor of the castle, but a den with a sofa was established in the northeast corner turret of the Library's gallery, and every night a single member of staff took a turn to keep watch over the children. The turret's windows were easily wide enough to admit a soldier determined to meet his girlfriend, the main thing was to slip quietly across the gravel and avoid the night watchman Stratford, and his dog. The new sleeping arrangement was judged a complete success, much better for everyone.

In between the occasional love affair, the nursery school staff were run off their feet and often cold, tired and hungry. In the wake of the move, the children's playroom had to be shifted to the Dining Room. (From now on the family took their meals in what had been Catherine's sitting room.) Restrictions on coal meant that it was hard to keep their bedrooms warm at night, and hot water either for themselves or the children was often in short supply. Baths were shared, with the cleanest going first and the grubbiest small child going last.

Feeding the children continued to be a challenge, both in terms of logistics at mealtimes down in the servants' dining hall, and in getting hold of enough supplies. Monsieur Pascal had been succeeded by Monsieur Pavillard, who brought in his son and had two additional ladies to help as kitchen maids. The school's presence meant that Highclere's kitchen staff had been receiving extra rations ever since January 1940, but by the summer of 1942, the entire household must have looked back on those early days of rationing with longing. At first it was just bacon, butter and sugar that were restricted. Gradually more and more items were added to the nation's coupon books. By the mid-point of the war, virtually every-thing was rationed: milk, cheese, eggs, tea, jam, biscuits, breakfast cereal, sweets, canned fruit and all meat including offal and sausages. The only things that were—in theory—freely available were fresh fruit and vegetables, fish, game and bread, though in practice most people's ability to get hold of fish and game was very limited: by 1945 supplies had dropped to just 30 per cent of their pre-war levels. Highclere residents were lucky on that score: the estate's market garden kept them in carrots, potatoes and spinach, and its woods and downlands kept them in rabbits and game, from partridges to venison. The efforts of Highclere's game-keepers and the wily Trooper Bloss were very much appre-ciated. So too were the members of the Women's Land Army, who worked in the market gardens and up at the stud, looking after the few remaining horses and staffing the farm.

On 23 August the Axis powers launched an offensive to gain control of Stalingrad in the southwestern Soviet Union. It would prove to be probably the single most decisive battle of the war; even at the time, everybody knew it was a stra-tegic showdown. Churchill and Roosevelt had no confidence that the Russians would be able to hold the Germans off, but Stalin staked his country's survival on the battle.

Two days later there was shocking news for Catherine and Porchey. Catherine was sitting down to listen to the wireless at her cottage in Windsor. Gar had come to visit and the two were just about to have tea when the headlines were announced. The Duke of Kent was dead, killed in a tragic accident in Scotland when the Sunderland flying boat he had been travelling in, on his way to inspect RAF bases in Iceland, had crashed into a hillside in thick fog.

Catherine was distraught. She had seen the Duke and Duchess of Kent only two weeks previously, when she had gone back to London to stay for a few days at her house on Wilton Crescent. Princess Marina had given birth to

Michael, her third child, on 4 July, and Catherine had been anxious to congratulate her old friends in person. Now Prince George was dead, leaving Princess Marina with a six-week-old baby and two other children.

The Duke of Kent's funeral took place at St George's Chapel, Windsor Castle, on 29 August. His widow was inconsolable; most of the congregation was in tears. Both Porchey and Catherine attended, and though Catherine was devastated, she said afterwards that she had found it impossible to cry at the time. It was all too dignified and it was so impressive the way the Royal Family stood united in grief. Later, though, she wept uncontrollably, firstly for the loss of her friend of twenty years' standing, who had been her champion and seen her through the dark times of her divorce and Geoffrey's death. She also cried for the loss of Geoffrey, whom she had not been able to bury; one of the many millions of war dead who lay where they fell.

By the time of the Duke of Kent's death, Catherine had been in Windsor for a little over a year, volunteering in canteens near Slough and spending time with her son. She'd made the decision to delay her return to London until after Henry had finished first school and then his military training. The plan was that he would join the Blues and Royals, the Royal Horse Guards, in the summer of the following year. Most of his courses would take place in barracks close to Windsor.

Catherine tried hard to be cheerful, but between the death of one of her dearest friends and the sense that she was in limbo, waiting for Henry to join up and be deployed, the autumn of 1942 was a long struggle against melancholy. Porchey did his best to distract her by taking her on visits to the cinema. Her correspondence with Pen was always a tonic for her spirits. Penelope was still thriving at Foxcroft but more and more insistent that she must come home. She would be eighteen in March of the coming year, and she wanted to celebrate her birthday with her parents and her brother, before Henry left for the war. She hadn't seen any of them for more than two years. Porchey and Catherine were still wary about the dangers of allowing her to come, but they were desperate to see her, and Pen's argument that she couldn't possibly miss Henry's send-off carried a lot of weight. Three years of war had taught them all that the opportunities to embrace the people one loved must be seized.

Pen had been taking a secretarial course as preparation for finding useful work when she returned to Britain. Porchey wrote to her that he was immensely proud of her determination to contribute to the war effort. In his day there would never have been any suggestion that girls of their class should seek employment, but the war had changed everything. All women between twenty and thirty without children were required to carry out war work. Penelope was still too young to meet the age requirement, but she had no thought of waiting two years for her name to come up on a recruiter's list. She, like her brother, was full of patriotic energy. Two years in the States without her parents had also made her independent. Apart from her desire to do her duty for her country, she must also have relished the prospect of a job in London, her own money and the freedom the two things would bring. She couldn't wait to get back.

Catherine wasn't alone in feeling low that autumn; Porchey was also badly hit by the death of the Duke of Kent. The two men had been comrades in arms in their youth, in the days of trips to the theatre and evenings at the Embassy Club, but they had relied on each other in more weighty matters, too, whether at Porchey's wedding to Catherine or his attempt to plead on George's behalf with Edward VIII during the abdication crisis.

Porchey decided he wanted company, and in September and October a steady trickle of visitors came to Highclere. There were no big house parties, but Jeanne was frequently there, and several old friends—who were in need of time away from London and the stress of war work—took Porchey up on his offer of peace, quiet, some early shooting and a good meal cooked by Monsieur Pavillard.

Harcourt 'Crinks' Johnstone was one of the most prominent Liberal politicians in the National Government. He had unexpectedly returned to government in 1940 (despite the fact that he was not a Member of Parliament at the time), thanks to his friendship with Churchill, who considered him an extremely able man and appointed him Secretary to the Department for Overseas Trade. Two months later the irregularity was cleared up when Johnstone was elected MP for Middlesbrough West. He was renowned for his love of good living and spent much of September 1942 enjoying the hospitality of Highclere. The following month Alfred Duff Cooper also came down briefly for a couple of days away from his desk. The three men had known each other for twenty years and the company of old friends was just what Porchey needed to lift his mood.

In November there was a massive boost to Allied morale and prospects when General Bernard Montgomery and his men secured a decisive victory over Rommel at the Second Battle of El Alamein. This was the turning point in the Western Desert Campaign, which Montgomery had long ago correctly predicted would be a war of attrition similar to the battles of the First World War. Monty had proved to be just the injection of energy and confidence the 8th Army needed. He was also an extremely astute and able commander, much to the surprise of Churchill, who had only reluctantly appointed him.

El Alamein was the Allies' first decisive victory over the

Axis powers on the ground and the last battle fought solely by the forces of the British Commonwealth without American input. Churchill briefly forgot his dislike of Montgomery and allowed himself to be jubilant. Back at Highclere and throughout Britain the church bells were rung in celebration. It didn't take long for the Prime Minister's acerbic wit to reassert itself, though. After his capture, General von Thoma was taken back to Allied HQ where, to the subsequent disapproval of the British public, he dined with General Montgomery. Churchill remarked, 'I sympathise with General von Thoma: defeated, humiliated, in captivity and . . . dinner with Montgomery.'

Despite the breakthrough, the desert war sputtered on into the following year. Rommel, ill and exhausted, fell back to Fuka and was finally allowed to leave Africa on 9 March. Only when his successor General Hans Jürgen von Arnim was captured along with 230,000 troops on 13 May 1943 could General Montgomery declare that the job was done and turn his attention to his next campaign, the one in which young Henry would serve: the invasion of Sicily and the battle for Italy. Elsewhere in North Africa a joint Anglo-American force had launched Operation Torch on 8 November. The object was to take control of Vichy-French North Africa (Morocco, Tunisia and Algeria), thereby consolidating the Allies' grip on the region and drawing more troops away from the Eastern Front.

That Christmas, the moment that Catherine had been dreading for years finally arrived. Henry had left Eton and put his name down for the Army.

Catherine worried that she would be unable to bear the strain. She had lost her beloved husband in the opening months of the war, one of her dearest friends when the Duke of Kent perished and had been separated from her daughter for two years. She tried to keep busy with her voluntary work and to take comfort in her faith and the support of her many friends but she was very fragile. There were millions of women like Catherine all over the world, wondering how they would find the strength to brace themselves for the possibility of more tragedy.

Porchey tried to be stoical, as was his way, but he too had hoped against hope that his son would not have to fight. Now, as the number of people pulled under by the tow of catastrophe grew ever larger, it was plain that Henry was going to have to do his bit. Despite American involvement, the war looked set to drag on for years.

In January of 1943 Henry turned nineteen. He would start officers' training in the summer but, for now, he decided to spend some time with his father at Highclere. Porchey had invited friends for a few days' shooting and Henry was looking forward to going out with them, but there were other attractions, aside from sport.

Monica Sheriffe, one of Porchey's great racing friends, was coming to stay and had announced that she intended to bring her new best friend. Elvira de la Fuente Chaudoir was Peruvian, extremely chic, and an inveterate gambler, who was particularly fond of the casinos of London and the south of France. She was born the daughter of a Peruvian diplomat and had been brought up in Paris. Highly intelligent but easily bored, she made a brief marriage to a Belgian exchange trader but decided in 1938 that running away with one of her many rich lovers to gamble in Cannes was much more fun than life in dreary Brussels. When the Germans invaded, she and her friend escaped to England, where Elvira was turned down for a position with De Gaulle's Free French government in exile on the catch-all grounds of being 'unsuitable'. MI6 didn't think she was unsuitable at all, and in 1940 she was recruited over a game of bridge at Hamilton's in Mayfair.

Elvira was perfect spy material. Thanks to her Peruvian passport it was relatively easy for her to move through Occupied Europe. Her father's diplomatic status helped there, too. She spoke fluent French, English and Spanish and was attractive to both sexes. Above all, she had the overwhelming advantage of appearing more stupid than she was. Elvira looked like a well-connected party girl, which indeed she was, but she was also brave, resourceful and smart. MI6's deputy director, Charles Dansey, sent her off into France with the express purpose of attracting the Germans' attention and making her into a double agent. By the time Henry met her at Highclere, she had been laying false information trails for the Germans for nearly two years. He was fascinated by her, and thoroughly enjoyed her indiscreet conversation and losing to her rather heavily at bridge.

At the Casablanca Conference in January 1943, Churchill, Roosevelt and De Gaulle met to decide the Allies' strategy for the next phase of the war in Europe. With the Battle for Stalingrad reaching a climax, Stalin was unable to attend. The leaders agreed that they should move their focus to southern Europe. The other priority was dealing with the U-boat threat in the Atlantic. In December 1942, Bletchley Park cryptologists had broken the latest generation of the German naval Enigma code. Extra resources in the form of aircraft and escort boats were committed. The Allies also took the fight into the German ports. The combined results of all these strategies were fast and impressive: the seven million tonnes of Allied shipping that were sunk in 1942 were three million in 1943, one million in 1944 and less than half a million tonnes in 1945.

On 2 February Stalin was vindicated when the remnants

of the German Army that had been holed up in the city of Stalingrad in a state of siege since the end of November 1942 finally surrendered. The Battle of Stalingrad was extraordinarily brutal. Somewhere between 1.7 and two million combatants died, as did countless civilians; but it was also, in the end, effective. It brought to a definitive stop Hitler's campaign to defeat the Soviets. The war in Russia had been the Führer's number one priority; now the Axis powers had lost in both North Africa and on the Eastern Front.

In Newbury, Highclere's nearest town, no one felt that the Nazi powers had been shaken or that war was receding. Quite the opposite. On the afternoon of 10 February, the town was bombed with the loss of fifteen lives; three of the casualties were children. The bombs fell very close to the school by St John's Church; the whole area was devastated. Up at the castle they heard the faint sound of explosions. By now everyone was familiar with the sound of a hit, and from the maids in the kitchens to the teachers up in the schoolroom, there was a sickening sense that it had been a big one.

Mrs Stacey lived with her family in one of the estate cottages, The Pens. On that day she had been visiting her sister in Reading and was just setting off from Newbury station to bicycle home when she heard the explosion. As she approached St John's Church she saw the smoke and broken glass blown out of the windows and asked a policeman what had happened. 'Jerry paid us a visit,' came the answer. And then the information that made her heart practically stop beating. 'The council school was bombed.' Two of her boys attended the school.

Trying to control her rising nausea and her useless legs, which seemed to have turned to jelly, she cycled furiously. The place was mayhem; the fire service was battling to put out the conflagration. Other desperate parents were milling around looking for their children. It was half an hour or so past the end of the school day and most of the school's pupils had already set off for home when the bombs fell. But there would have been stragglers. Mrs Stacey clutched the arm of a teacher whose face she recognised. Where were her boys? They left before the attack, the teacher assured her, before wandering off in a daze. Powered by her need to believe, Mrs Stacey pedalled homewards, past Wash Common down the Andover Road, into the woods and at last through the park and along the muddy track leading to her little cottage. There they were, both of them shaky and tearful, but unharmed. Sobbing with relief, Mrs Stacey hugged her children to her. It was at least five minutes before she could pull herself together enough to make tea for them all.

Three of her sons' schoolmates were not so lucky. Two of their teachers who were still working when the bombs dropped were also killed. Forty-one people were injured, twenty-five of them seriously. It seemed likely that the German bomber simply wanted to unload his unused bombs so he could get home faster.

Just over three weeks after the bombing, Henry Lord Porchester set off to Newbury to learn a very useful trade. A local garage, Wheeler's, had been turned into a military training centre for vehicle mechanics. It was Porchey's idea for Henry to attend. While he was waiting for the officers' training courses to start in the summer, he needed something useful with which to occupy himself. And a skill such as vehicle maintenance would be a good complement to his other training courses. Henry was keen to do whatever might come in handy in the field and readily agreed. He passed out three months later as Vehicle Fitter Class II.

A week after Henry started at Wheeler's, the Carnarvon family had the best reason to celebrate in more than two long years. Penelope was home. She had been so determined to make it back in time for her eighteenth birthday, but in the end it simply wasn't possible. Cousin Arthur had been lucky to secure any passage for her and Doll; everyone thought that it would be summer before they returned. Arthur was full of scepticism about the wisdom of crossing the Atlantic at all: even though the situation was stabilising, it was still fraught with risk of attack by U-boats. But Pen had been pushing to go home for months and Porchey and Catherine finally gave in to her pleas and agreed. The only tickets Arthur could obtain were to Lisbon in Portugal. From there Pen and Doll flew with BOAC back to an airfield just outside Bristol. This last leg of the journey was also fraught with stress. In theory both Allied and Axis powers respected Portugal's neutrality, but in reality several civilian planes had been brought down by the Luftwaffe over the Bay of Biscay in the first few months of 1943. Pen and Doll were extremely relieved to land at Bristol and board a train to London.

They must have chattered all the way up to town, delighted to be back on British soil, to see the landscape they loved, to be among their fellow countrymen again. But it would surely also have been shocking to see the evidence of bombing as they passed through Reading and the strain on people's faces. At Paddington, Penelope scanned the crowd for her mother's face. She had promised to meet them and Pen could hardly bear to wait another second. Catherine was tearful as she caught sight of her daughter and ran the last few steps to embrace her. Two and a half long years had elapsed and so much had changed. She had lost her beloved husband and then worried almost out of her mind that her daughter too would be killed on her journey back, but now here she was—taller, more confident, so much more grown up, and laughing as the two of them clung to one another.

The following day Porchey took his beloved daughter to dinner at the Ritz and they toasted her eighteenth birthday in champagne. That weekend they travelled together to Highclere and Penelope wept as they drove past London Lodge, which had been damaged by a stray bomb, and caught the first glimpse of her childhood home.

Safely back in England, Penelope started to look around for employment. Before long she found an administrative post at the Foreign Office, which she had thought sounded a rather glamorous place to work, though in reality the job was mundane with very long hours. It didn't pay much, either, but Penelope was happy. She had moved into Wilton Crescent, and Catherine was making preparations to join her later in the year when Henry finished his training.

Henry was in exuberant mood. His much-loved sister had returned, considerably more grown up but just the same unflappable and sweet-natured soul she always had been. He knew that she had wanted above everything to see him before he left for the war, and he was deeply touched. Once his mechanics course finished in early summer, he was itching to get on with training.

In the first week of August, Henry and several of his closest friends from school arrived at the Acton Recruiting Office to enrol in the Blues and Royals. Part of the household cavalry, the Blues are regarded as the senior regiment in the British Army, thanks to their status as the monarch's private bodyguard.

During the war, abbreviated training courses were run so as to maintain a steady supply of newly qualified officers. Henry and his friends were about to embark on a punishing schedule of highly compressed information and skills training. Their first port of call was Combermere Barracks, Windsor, where the regiment were instructed in the use of armoured vehicles and combat. From there they would be sent to Caterham, to Pirbright and finally to the Royal Military College at Sandhurst, all close to Windsor. Henry had an exceedingly tough few months ahead of him, and Catherine wanted to be on hand for any brief time he could find to slip away for tea, toast and chat. Penelope frequently came down form London on Friday afternoons after work. Despite her anxiety about Henry, Catherine was happier than she had ever been since Geoffrey's death. With her two children teasing one another over toast and their mother's homemade jam, she felt a surge of hope for the future.

Scarcely three months later, Henry Porchester was awarded the Belt of Honour, presented to the most promising cadet of his class. As Catherine watched him command the passing-out parade, she was so incredibly proud that she almost forgot that it could only be a matter of weeks at the most before her son was sent abroad. For now, Henry and his class were posted back to Combermere Barracks.

A graduating officer cadet is typically designated a Second Lieutenant, but in the Royal Horse Guards, in his first most junior rank he is referred to as a 'cornet'. Henry Porchester had achieved the goal, passionately wished for, of his last three years. He had distinguished himself in training and was facing the beginning of his military career with steadiness as well as enthusiasm. Less than two weeks later, he got the call he had been waiting for. The new officers of the Blues were shipping out to the Middle East to join their regiment and await the expected order to deploy to Sicily and thence to mainland Italy.

Henry was granted short leave to say goodbye to his family and went first to see Catherine and Pen, who begged a day off from the Foreign Office in light of exceptional circumstances and travelled from London to Windsor. She planned to stay overnight with her mother, whom she knew would be in need of encouragement.

Both his mother and his sister wanted Henry to have something of theirs to take with him into battle. Catherine gave her son one of her old watches, a hip flask and a map case; Pen gave him a chain. When the time came for him to leave, everyone did their utmost to be brave but, afterwards, when her boy had disappeared from view, Catherine cried. She felt that all her happiness was in the lap of the gods.

From Windsor, Henry made his way to Highclere to say goodbye to his father. Porchey's present was his advice on how to handle active service, dispensed as the two men rode side by side around the estate. One imagines that though Henry must have been grateful to his father, he struggled to pay full attention. Everywhere he looked he saw his family's heritage, his inheritance. What would happen if, unimaginable thought, he didn't come home?

When they got back to the castle the light had faded to dusk and father and son took a drink in the Library. Porchey handed him three letters of introduction to friends of his in Cairo, and then it was almost time for Henry to go. He went to say goodbye to the estate and household staff, shaking hands with each person, receiving the curtseys of the women and the hand-clasps and back-slaps of the men—only the old men, now, whom he had known all his life. The last thing he did was fetch his semi-automatic Winchester .22 rifle from the gun room. His father embraced him for a second and then Henry set off, back to barracks to pick up his kit and be on the road to Glasgow and the troopship SS *Leopoldville*, bound for Alexandria.

Porchey stood at the main entrance to the castle and watched his son and heir walk away. Then he turned to go inside and Pell closed and locked the door behind him.

18

To Play One's Part

The SS *Leopoldville* arrived at Alexandria with no incident, just a few submarine alerts that didn't amount to anything. On Christmas Eve 1944, her luck would run out when transporting American soldiers to the Battle of the Bulge. Attacked by U-boats, she would sink with the loss of approximately 763 men. Fortunately, the only trouble Henry encountered on this voyage was a nearly disastrous boxing match, in which he lasted one and a half rounds against a sergeant in the Royal Irish Fusiliers, whom he later discovered was the army welterweight champion. Henry had been an excellent boxer at Eton but was relieved when the fight was stopped. He had much more success playing bridge against his school friend John Ewart, whom he continued to relieve of money throughout the forthcoming campaign.

Henry was full of anticipation as he disembarked in Egypt.

It was his first visit to a land with which his family had special ties. He had grown up hearing his father's stories about the Curse of Tutankhamun and his grandfather's devotion to the country's heritage. Now he was here to see the place for himself. The circumstances were hardly conducive to tourism, it was true; but nonetheless his first sight of the Pyramids thrilled him as it does every visitor. He must have felt a frisson of pride at the thought that the discoveries made by the 5th Earl and Howard Carter had revolutionised Egyptology.

Lord Porchester and his group of friends were stationed on the outskirts of Cairo at Abissaia. The young men were very much focused on their deployment to Italy, where the Allied Expeditionary Force had been slogging their way up the peninsula for nearly three months. The fighting was brutal, made worse by atrocious weather, the difficulty of the mountainous terrain and the fact that the Germans had dug in to defend their positions with increasingly sophisticated booby traps. At its close, in April 1945, the Italian campaign had claimed more lives on both sides than any other on the Western front.

The young officers of the Blues had no idea when they would be deployed, but they took a step closer when they were ordered to join the main body of the regiment at Jebel Mazar on the border between Syria and Lebanon. From there they would push on to Jerusalem in British-controlled Palestine before returning to Egypt. By the winter of 1943, the region was quiet, but it had been the location of very fierce fighting two years before when the Allied armies battled those of Vichy France. The Syria-Lebanon campaign had seen huge casualties among the Australian, Free French, British and Indian troops, but on 12 July 1941 Beirut fell. Two days later an armistice was signed with Vichy, and a Free French government installed.

The Blues and Royals were able to practise manoeuvres in peace while they waited for their orders. They were busy but not in any danger—yet. Henry wrote to his mother from the mountains of Lebanon, apologising for not having had time to write before. He was now posted to 'C' Squadron, he told her, and with a note of pride mentioned that he had been the first among his group of friends and fellow officers to be given charge of a troop. He signed off with 'tons of love to Gar' and asked Catherine to please 'continue to write your lovely newsy letters' before sending her 'tons and tons of love'.

Catherine must have suffered agonies as she waited to hear from her son. She tried to distract herself from worrying by taking pride in his accomplishments (as well as his command of Troop No. 4 he had been acting as wireless operator to his squadron leader), but towards Christmas she went once more to stay at one of her favourite retreats, to pray for Henry's safety and a speedy end to the war, and to closet herself away safely from her demons.

Gar did her best to support her daughter but she was anxious herself, though she put a brave face on it. On 7 December she was staying with Catherine at Windsor and wrote to thank Henry for the lovely photo. 'God will guard you, my darling, and bring you safely back to us.'

Perhaps it is harder to be the one left behind waiting for news than it is to be the one out facing whatever the world may bring. Compared to his family at home, Henry was on fine form that Christmas. He was granted some leave and set off for a day of shooting at Lake Ekiad. He stayed the Friday night at Shepheard's hotel in Cairo where his grand-father always stopped en route to and from his archaeological digs in the Valley of the Kings. Throughout the war the graceful old hotel was Cairo's main meeting place for diplomats, high-ranking soldiers and spies, but Henry didn't stay for long enough to see anything terribly exciting. Very early the morning after his arrival he set off in convoy with the other guns: His Excellency the British Ambassador Lord Killearn, Sir Alexander Keown-Boyd, who was director of the Ministry of the Interior, Lord Cadogan, his second-in-command, Prince Galitzine of Russia and various others. In a letter to his father, who he knew would appreciate the details, Henry wrote, 'We arrived, were dished out with 200 cartridges apiece and then we started off to our butts with a couple of mallard decoys each.' He shot one of the best bags of duck and snipe and then they returned to Cairo for an excellent dinner. Porchey was much cheered by Henry's letters. He, like Catherine, depended on the exchange of news to keep his worries at bay.

The gathering at Highclere for Christmas was somewhat sparse, with Henry serving abroad and Pen stuck in London. The Foreign Office granted her just one day off so she spent the 25th lunching at Claridge's with some Wendell family connections. One of them, Gerrit van der Woude, made himself particularly charming. He, like Pen, was the child of an American who had moved to Britain. Gerrit was serving in the Grenadier Guards and cut quite a dash in his uniform. When they parted, he asked whether he might take her to the theatre the following week. Pen didn't hesitate to say yes.

Eve and Bro arrived at Highclere with Almina, who was on powerful form, wanting to talk of nothing but how her beloved grandson was getting on out in Egypt. Bro's health was worsening. He had developed a serious heart condition brought on by overwork and lack of sleep. The strain was making Eve rather tetchy; she too had been working very hard, helping with liaison between British prisoners of war abroad and their families at home. Patricia was too busy with stories of her new job to pay her mother that much attention. Patricia had joined the Wrens, the Women's Royal Naval Service, and was working as a junior administrator at Bletchley Park, the soon-to-be legendary centre of the Allies' work to break the German Enigma code. She came down in her smart new uniform. On Christmas Eve, Dr Johnnie and Jeanne arrived. Jeanne was mightily relieved that her ENSA tour had been postponed until early February. The Entertainments National Service Association, formed in 1939, sent many outstanding actors and singers all over the world to perform to troops in the field. Gracie Fields, Vera Lynn, Joyce Grenfell, Laurence Olivier and Ralph Richardson all did their bit to boost morale. Jeanne was keen to go but much preferred to spend Christmas at Highclere getting some rest first. She was supposed to be heading for Cairo and everyone was excited at the thought that she might be able to see Henry.

Despite their collective anxiety for him, the Carnarvons (and indeed the country as a whole) were starting to dare to hope that the war would be won. The Axis powers were everywhere on the retreat. Japan had sustained huge losses in its naval battles with the US Navy and the new command in India under Lord Mountbatten was gaining the upper hand in the battle for Burma. Italy was defeated. The Germans were still strong, it was true, but they were falling back from Italy and Russia. The mood at the start of 1944 was so much more hopeful than it had been a year previously.

Porchey was very unwell with flu in the first week of January and spent several days in bed writing letters. To Henry he wrote that Jack Gibbins, his former chauffeur, had been poached by the royal household and would now be 'driving their majesties whenever they go out in the Daimler.'

He kept his son up to date with news of how the horses were shaping up for the flat season ahead and how well his horse, Stonehenge, was looking.

Henry was rather more concerned by the news he received from his mother that she had been knocked over by a lorry coming out of a shop in Highgate, near the retreat, on Christmas Eve. Catherine assured her son that she was quite well now and had only been a little shaken. She hadn't been paying attention, had been turning over so many things in her mind. Pen's letter a fortnight later reassured him that their mother was absolutely fine; she had suffered just minor bruises. The reason for the pre-occupation was also revealed. Catherine had formally converted to Catholicism on 25 January, just after Henry's birthday. Having made her decision she now seemed peaceful and content, Pen reported. Penelope's letter was full of her own news. Gerrit van der Woude had indeed taken her to the theatre and to several dinners and was now definitely her favourite beau. There was a rather nice American lieutenant she had liked for a while, but Patricia had pronounced him not very handsome, even if he was amusing. He had evidently been eclipsed.

There were a great many young ladies in the area around Highclere who were far more enthusiastic about the presence of American personnel. As Henry had been leaving for Alexandria at the end of October the previous year, the United States Ninth Air Force had been sending an advance party to prepare the newly constructed Greenham Common airfield for its troops. The base was just a few miles from Highclere and, before long, romances were being struck up between the Americans and local girls. The exotic incomers arrived trailing associations with Hollywood, a free and easy new-world charm, and lots of money in their pockets to

Lt. Commander Geoffrey Grenfell, Catherine's second husband.

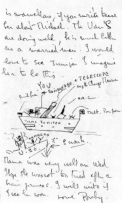

A letter from Henry, Catherine's son, to her husband Geoffrey who was serving in the Royal Navy.

The Home Guard at Highclere in 1944.

Children's dormitories were created in the bedrooms on the top floor of the Castle.

Highclere welcomed several dozen evacuees from London during the Second World War.

glamorous Tilly, Countess of Carnarvon, with the evacuee children September 1939.

Lord Carnarvon   and   Lord Porchester

this is their house.

Nurses working at Highclere with their young charges.
The Castle must have seemed like a fairytale to the young visitors,
although touchingly this handmade card from one of the evacuees
shows they thought of the Castle as a home like any other.

The 6th Earl of Carnarvon in uniform in 1943 and Henry,
Lord Porchester, in uniform in the same year.

Porchey, The Earl of Carnarvon, had re-joined the 7th Hussars.
Shorncliffe, Kent, spring 1940.

WEDDING OF LADY PENELOPE HERBERT

AT HIGHCLERE PARISH CHURCH

Great interest was taken in the wedding of Lady Penelope Herbert to Lieutenant van der Woude, Grenadier Guards, which was celebrated in the Church of St. Michael the Archangel, Highclere, on Saturday afternoon.

The church, which was decorated with a profusion of flowers and blossom—white lilac and pink tulips, spring blossoms and azaleas from the gardens at Highclere Castle—was crowded for the occasion.

THE BRIDE AND BRIDEGROOM.

It was quite a simple country wedding. The Castle party was made up principally of near relatives, the bride's father, the Earl of Carnarvon, her mother Mrs. Geoffrey Grenfell, who arrived at the church with Almina Countess of Carnarvon, the mother of Lord Carnarvon; others of the party included Lord Porchester,

Patricia Beauchamp and Lieut. Jack Wendell. The only relative of the bridegroom was his mother, Mrs. R. G. A. van der Woude. There were a few Highclere residents present, including Lord and Lady Teviot, the heads and those on the estate, and the villagers of Highclere. While the congregation was assembling the organist Mr. G. H. Keen, L.R.A.M. played Purcell's two Trumpet tunes and air, Mozart's Serenade and other music.

Lady Anne Penelope Marian Herbert is the only daughter of the Earl of Carnarvon, of Highclere Castle, Newbury, and Mrs. Geoffrey Grenfell, of 5, Berkeley House, Hay Hill, London, W.1., and Mr. Reinier Gerret Anton van der Woude is the only son of Mr. and Mrs. R. G. A. van der Woude, of Heronden, Estrey, Kent and New York.

The service was fully choral. The bride entered the church on the arm of her father to the strains of the hymn "Lead us, Heavenly Father, lead us." The officiant was the Rector of High... N. B. Kent. The psalm ... lift up mine eyes unto the ... then the hymn "O Perfect Love" being sung kneeling. As the ... being signed the organ ... "Jesu joy of man ... Mendelssohn's Wedding ... pealing out as the ... couple left the church.

The bride was dressed ... pearl satin cut on long ... with veil and orange ... only ornament was a st ... Her bouquet was of pale ... pale pink roses and lilie ... Mrs. Geoffrey Grenfell ... gown of marocain in a ... of cyclamen, with silve ... a smart dark blue beret ... Beauchamp was in brow ... Countess of Carnarvon ... shade of old gold sand ... was Lord Porchester. The Earl of Carnarvon, the bridegroom, best man and Lieut. J. Wendell, who acted as

Lady Penelope Herbert married Captain Gerrit van der Woude of the Grenadier Guards in April 1945.

Highclere Parish Church.

Mrs Geoffrey Grenfell (Catherine), Porchey, their son Henry and Almina, Countess of Carnarvon at Penelope's wedding April 21st 1945.

Porchey lived life
to the full in the
1950s and 1960s.

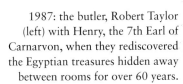

1987: the butler, Robert Taylor
(left) with Henry, the 7th Earl of
Carnarvon, when they rediscovered
the Egyptian treasures hidden away
between rooms for over 60 years.

When Porchey wrote his memoirs in the 1970s he described Catherine as his 'beloved wife', he had loved her deeply for many years. Catherine's portrait hangs once more back in her sitting room at Highclere Castle.

spend on their dates. Britons had been living with rationing for three and a half years by then and had got used to going without. These young men had seemingly endless chocolate, cigarettes and—totem of glamour—nylon stockings to give away. All over the country there were highly appreciative British girls having more fun than they'd ever had before. The description of the GIs as 'overpaid, oversexed and over here' captures the sense of frustration among British prospective suitors.

The US Air Force set up wing headquarters in requisitioned Bowdown House, on the edge of the airfield. The elegant house, designed by Edward Lutyens, had belonged to the family of Sir Cecil Dormer, former British ambassador to Norway, who had fled the country with King Haakon back in 1940; it had in fact become the refuge for the Norwegian royal family after they had escaped to Britain. Mrs Dormer was given twenty-four hours to find alternative accommodation for everyone. Ever enterprising, she moved the entire household to Foliejon Park, near Windsor.

She had to enlist the help of the Norwegian attachés to help dismantle everything she possibly could, to get it out of harm's way before it was overrun by the US Air Force. The Dormers had spent evenings playing bridge at Highclere; they were cousins of the Carnarvon family and many of the precious paintings now being hastily stored were of shared ancestors. When she returned a month later for a few things she had forgotten, there were trestle tables covered in maps and cigarettes, model planes suspended from ceilings and tanks parked across what were once lawns.

American airmen were soon the latest in a long list of military personnel to exasperate Miss Stubbings, Lord Carnarvon's agent, as they practised all over the estate. But on one dreadful day an accident occurred infinitely more serious than any carelessness with gateposts up at the stud. Two planes were practising airborne gunfights, swooping above the Highclere village school. Mrs Stacey, the tenant whose boys had narrowly escaped the bomb in Newbury, had three daughters at the school. Later, her oldest, Sylvia, told her that her friend Hazel had been playing cat's cradle outside the schoolroom during their break when Sylvia heard a plane whoosh overhead and saw Hazel fall to the ground, as if she were having a fit. The school's two teachers rushed out when they heard the children's screams but there was nothing anyone could do. A bullet had passed through her arm and entered her heart. Sylvia was numb with shock. Just ten minutes earlier Hazel had lent her her bike. Now she was dead. At the little girl's funeral, the Stacey children sang her favourite hymn, 'There is a green hill far away' with the rest of the congregation. Their mother found them in bed that night, all sobbing inconsolably. Sylvia remembered that her redoubtable mother got them straight up and put them to baking a cake with their precious rations because Hazel had always loved cake so much and they thought she would have appreciated it.

Having recovered from flu, Porchey contacted his solicitors about the recalcitrant Tilly. She had cabled at Christmas saying that she hoped to obtain a passage back to England shortly, and sending all love both to him and her stepchildren. It was not enough to mollify Porchey, who had spent a great deal of the previous six months putting it to his wife that with the threat of U-boat attacks in the Atlantic now receding, it might be a good moment for her to at least visit. She had promised so many times that she was going to buy a ticket that very week, and by late 1943 he had quite given up all hope.

He heard rumours that she was having an affair with a

Hollywood producer, a Mr Foy, who ran the B-movies unit at Warner Brothers. This was too much for Porchey. He had been so humiliated when Tanis jilted him for Howard Dietz six years earlier and he was damned if he was going to let it happen again without a fight. He decided to engage the services of a private eye. He wanted to know the worst, and then to instigate divorce proceedings.

At the end of January 1944, William J. Burns International Detective Agency were hired to tail Lady Carnarvon for two weeks. The agents spent hours sitting behind a newspaper in the lobby of Tilly's hotel and followed her to Radio City Music Hall, on a shopping trip to Saks, and to lunch with a girlfriend. There was no sign of any male acquaintance whatsoever until the afternoon when an agent was thrilled to observe Lady Carnarvon enter the lobby with a tall handsome Latino type and head for the elevator. The detective resumed his watch and was slightly disappointed when the handsome Latino reappeared an hour later looking distinctly unruffled and headed off. The subject then went to a restaurant, alone, and read a magazine over dinner before returning to her hotel. The gentleman was nowhere in evidence. This potential breakthrough turned out to have a rather workaday explanation. The agency informed Lord Carnarvon that the suspected target was in fact Lady Carnarvon's press agent, engaged to help her promote her forthcoming exhibition of paintings. William J. Burns' international detectives argued strongly in favour of another period of surveillance (they seem to have been rather struck by the loveliness of Tilly), but Porchey decided he'd learned enough to satisfy his peace of mind. Mr Foy was, as it turned out, in Los Angeles. Meanwhile Porchey was being billed to follow his wife as she racked up yet more bills, many of which were still getting sent to him. It wasn't the most rewarding way to spend either time or money. For now, he decided, there really wasn't much to be done.

At the beginning of March, Henry wrote to his mother to tell her that he and his troop were now on official standby for deployment. Their training continued: lots of shooting practice with mortars, machine guns and small arms, and occasional surprise fifteen-mile route marches, which everyone hated. Henry was playing football to stay fit and to relieve the boredom. He was evidently still playing a lot of bridge as well because, having thanked Catherine and Doll for the books they had sent him, he asked his mother to please also send him some cards and pencils. 'They are an important factor for my income.'

At the end of the month, the orders finally arrived. On 3 April the regiment travelled by train to Port Said and, having spent the night in a transit camp, sailed early the following morning on P&O liner SS *Strathnaver*, one of a convoy of twelve transport ships. Henry never forgot sailing through the Straits of Messina, the snow on Mount Etna's peak clearly visible. On 16 April they arrived at Naples harbour, the port looming suddenly out of a deep mist. Everyone fell silent. It was impossible to tell how much of the devastation had been caused by Allied bombing, how much by the retreating German Army, but the result was the same. Naples was reduced to living on her wits and on booty begged or stolen from the occupying Allied forces.

The Blues and Royals barely had time to catch their breath or realise that they had finally made it to Italy before they marched out of the city and, having taken delivery of a fleet of armoured vehicles, headed to a camp at Salerno where they were to spend the rest of the month.

Henry's experiences are a reminder that, for much of the time, war consists of waiting around for things to happen, for orders or supplies to arrive. He and his friends had just swapped one training ground for another. For the next two weeks they played more football, shot more targets, swam in the sea. It was starting to get warm and Henry's troop had to go on patrol in their winter-in-the-desert army issue sheepskin coats. They were waiting for summer-in-Italy uniforms to arrive.

As Henry and the Blues and Royals were landing at Naples, preparations were well under way for the long-anticipated invasion of France. It would be the key Allied attack of the war, an enormously complex joint operation between American, British and Commonwealth, Free French, Polish, Dutch, Free Belgian, Free Greek and Norwegian air, land and naval forces. It had been well over a year in the planning, but by April 1944 the plans were all coming together.

The US 368th Fighter Group arrived at Greenham Common in March and started to fly their first combat missions over France, attacking key infrastructure such as bridges and highways, anything that might slow down German troop movements. The 438th Troop Carrier Group replaced them a few weeks later and prepared to fly their resupply and reinforcement missions, and to evacuate casualties. Assault gliders were arriving flat packed from the States and being assembled at the rate of twenty a day before being delivered by the Auxiliary Services to other airfields. Bomber Command stepped up the number of raids on German cities, including daylight raids on Berlin that made many British people, who remembered the Blitz only too well, rather uncomfortable. Every day the skies above Highclere were busy with hundreds of aircraft flying in the direction of France and Germany.

Surprise was judged to be a crucial element of the planned invasion. A key part of the build-up to the invasion was therefore a campaign of misinformation and false trails code-named Operation Fortitude. Dummy landing quays, fake camps complete with fake camp fires, mock-ups of tanks—all along the southern coast there were decoys, intended to keep the Germans guessing about the location of the landings that they knew were coming.

Elvira de la Fuente was back at Highclere in April but she didn't stay long. She was too busy. As Agent Bronx she was feeding a carefully plotted stream of false information to her German handlers, who were avid for every scrap she had to give them. She was laying a decoy for a landing at Bordeaux and thereby keeping the feared German 17th Panzer Division well away from the Normandy beaches. Elvira's efforts and those of countless other agents were far more successful than even MI6 had dared to dream. Operation Fortitude therefore paid off. Though the casualties of the June invasion would indeed prove to be very heavy, they could have been far worse. The Germans maintained elite forces at Pas de Calais, for example, miles away from the Normandy beaches, until well after the D-Day landings had finished. Their false intelligence told them that there were more Allied forces to come and the Germans stubbornly sat there waiting for them, rather than joining the fight.

On 15 May the Allied commanders met in London to discuss the launch of Operation Overlord, as the Battle for Normandy had been code-named. General Eisenhower was in overall command of the operation and on 6 June 1944 he signalled that it was beginning. There had been a last-minute doubt because of the weather, which was unusually bad: the landings would be scuppered by heavy seas. But if the Expeditionary Force missed this window of opportunity, it would be a month before the next full moon allowed for another go. The build-up of hundreds of thousands of men couldn't possibly be concealed for that long. Eisenhower gave the order to press ahead.

All over the south of England, people came out of their homes to watch as tens of thousands of aircraft headed for France. Catherine had recently moved back to London to rejoin Pen and Gar at her house in Wilton Cresent. The three women ran to a window to stare, to hope that this was indeed the beginning of the end. The nursery teachers, the evacuees, Mr Pell and the entire household staff, Mrs Stacey and her children, the Home Guard up on Siddown Hill: at Highclere everyone poured out of the castle and watched as the sky turned black with the mass of tiny triangular dark outlines, streaming towards France. One person in particular was transfixed by the sight. Joan Taylor knew that this meant the invasion had started and that somewhere on the rough seas between England and France, her husband Robert was sitting in his tank, waiting for a landing craft to dock and the order to advance.

In fact, Robert embarked from Southampton three days after the initial assault. By that time more than 200,000 men had been offloaded from landing craft onto the beaches of Normandy or dropped inland from aircraft. Around 60,000 vehicles and more than 120,000 tonnes of supplies had also been shipped. In many places the hard-fought-for element of surprise made all the difference: German officers were off duty, the troops scrambled to meet the invading forces. On other beaches, notably the one code-named Omaha, Allied losses were devastating. The US forces landing at Omaha lost fourteen out of sixteen tanks and all the men inside them.

Robert was with the 7th Tank Regiment. They were destined for Gold beach, with eighteen Churchill tanks, 25-pounder guns strapped to them, as well as barrels of oil and extra ammunition for gunners already in France. As the landing craft pulled out of the lee side of the Isle of Wight, the seas grew rougher and the men eyed one another nervously. Soon the waves were battering the shallow-hulled ship. First one tank broke loose and then another. The guns were smashing against one another, several barrels of oil burst open and a slick oozed into the sea. Robert held his breath as the captain assembled everyone on deck. He was on the brink of giving the order to abandon ship. Then, as they neared the French coastline, the winds dropped.

The landing craft had to reverse to have any chance of offloading the tanks. The cruiser HMS *Ajax* and the destroyer HMS *Argonaut* were shelling the German gun emplacements high up above the beach, trying to give the tank regiment some cover as the men waded onto the sands. They had to work in the oily slick of the waves to free the tanks as quickly as possible, a cacophony of shells exploding all around them. Almost before he knew it, Robert was rumbling forward to do battle. The regiment was detailed to move towards a crossroads at Ouistreham. As they left the beach and started up a hill, their liaison officer was standing with his head out of the turret when his ear was cleanly sliced off. They lurched to a halt and Robert ordered Corporal Duck to bandage the man's head. They left him by the side of the road in the hopes that a medical team would pick him up. Robert assumed command of his tank.

When they reached the top of the hill, he gave the order to slow so he could scan the low woods 100 yards in front. The crackle and boom of battle sounded infernal. He could see the enemy, straight ahead. Robert ordered his gunner to open fire. They had only fired three or four shells when the tank to their left received a direct hit and the turret was carried into the body of the vehicle, destroying everyone and everything. It was as if the men had never been.

Robert hardly understood, it had all happened so fast. Then the tank to his right was hit. Suddenly there was a roar as a shell passed through his tank from underneath him. It decapitated his operator but passed straight through the armour and out of the other side without exploding. Corporal Duck called up to Robert, 'Are you all right?' Robert was concussed, half unconscious. He put his hand up to his face—it was covered with bloody gore and brains. 'My god, my face has gone,' he whispered.

'Get out, get out!' yelled his corporal. The gunner was still alive and climbed out through the hatch as Robert scrambled down behind. The gunner was only eighteen years old. He started to scream and wouldn't stop. Robert realised in that instant that he could still see, and hear, and that it was not his brains all over his face. Pain began to spread through his shoulder and hands where they were full of splinters of metal. He grasped the boy's shoulder firmly and told him, quietly, to hush. The three men tore off strips of their shirts to make rudimentary dressings to staunch the flow of blood and started to crawl back to the first-aid station. They passed more eviscerated tanks on their way, averted their eyes from the bloody fleshy mess that used to be their comrades.

When Robert got to the medical station he was cleaned up, given drugs for the pain and told that he would be flown back to England and taken to a military hospital in Derby. He nodded his head but he couldn't take anything in. 'How many died?' he asked. 'Did any get through?' 'We don't know yet,' the nurse told him. 'We don't know much.' The next thing that Robert remembered was arriving at Derby. When he asked again how his unit had fared, this nurse looked away when she answered him. 'Pretty well, I think.' The 7th Tank Regiment had in fact lost more than half its men within two hours of landing on Gold beach.

Robert was in hospital for nearly a month. By the time he was discharged at the end of the first week of July, approximately one million men had been landed on the beaches of Normandy and were pushing further into France, driving the Germans back relentlessly but at heavy cost.

Joan Taylor came to visit her husband in Derby. He looked bloodied and bruised but he was alive and she wept to have him safe. The thing that scared her most, as she kissed his scratched face and stroked his hair, was the glassy look in his eyes. Robert knew that he and his corporal and gunner had only survived because the shell that struck their tank had exploded outside rather than inside with them. For the rest of his life he remembered the way the tanks around him had disintegrated, their cargo of men evaporated along with them. Nothing left to identify, nothing left to bury. He smiled at his wife when she asked him, 'Tell me what happened, darling', but he never did, not properly.

Robert spent a few days with Joan at Highclere, where Lord Carnarvon congratulated him on a brave job well done. Robert wasn't sure about that but there was no time for reflection. He was declared fit enough to return to his unit; the battle to liberate France was ongoing and he was needed. So he took his leave of his wife and headed back to France, just in time for the Battle of Falaise.

In Italy news of the extraordinary Allied achievements in northern France cheered Henry Porchester and his men. Their own battle was slow, tricky work that was wearing everyone down. Henry was set to have a dangerous summer.

19

The Beginning of the End

Between the beginning of May and the end of September 1944, Henry Porchester and the Blues and Royals inched their way along the broken roads and through the booby-trapped medieval hill towns of some of the most beautiful countryside in Europe. As the cold wet winter gave way to a warm spring, there were days of startling loveliness; days that might have been a pleasure, in another time, if it weren't for the fact that they had to creep into houses looking for the remnants of the German Army and hoping they wouldn't step on a mine or get shot in the back.

Henry and his troop were part of a reconnaissance unit, pushing cautiously onwards ahead of the rest of the 8th Army up the eastern flank of the country. They were searching for signs of where the enemy might still be in hiding or where they might have left a little trick to catch the Allied forces out. The Germans had become experts in laying traps, some of them extraordinarily ingenious, and Henry was part of the intelligence-gathering team that had to send information back down the line. Whole towns had been turned into obstacle runs and killing fields. Buildings were demolished to slow access and machine-gun nests set up to mow down the Allied soldiers as they picked their way through the rubble. Abandoned vehicles were fitted with trip wires that set off charges the moment a door was opened. Explosives were strung through trees so that whole avenues would explode around the advancing troops. Anything movable might be wired: Jerry cans, oil drums, abandoned rucksacks, a tempting crate of wine. Anticipating and evading the Germans' latest strategy was dangerous, exhausting work. One thing that helped enormously was that some of the soldiers Henry and his troop were fighting alongside were veterans with a stock of hard-won experience. Some of the Blues and Royals had been out in the field for four years and in Italy for a year. They were deeply familiar with the Germans' tactics. Even so, it was a battle of wits and nerves and it took its toll.

On 16 May a detachment was ambushed and Ian van Ammel, a friend of Henry's, was taken prisoner. Henry wrote to his father that it 'seems so odd since I was playing bridge with Ian three weeks ago.' Two weeks later, on 1 June, Gavin Astor's jeep was found just outside Gamberale. It was a total wreck, burnt to pieces and perfect booby-trap fodder. Henry Porchester was sent out to reconnoitre the area. He reported that there were no signs of blood on or around the wreckage. He could only hope that Gavin was now a prisoner of war.

On the opposite side of the country, the US 5th Army had finally taken Monte Cassino after four long, bitter months and four waves of attacks that cost 55,000 Allied soldiers' lives as against 20,000 German. General Clark diverted from pursuing the fleeing German Army, and on 4 June marched into a virtually abandoned Rome. The empty gesture, in direct defiance of the orders of his commanding officer, astounded his subordinate officers. The result was that the Germans were allowed to fall back and dig in again across the country from just north of Pisa to south of Rimini. The Italian campaign was set to rumble on for many more exhausting, bloody months.

Catherine wrote to her son in June, thrilled that the Allies were nearing Rome. 'I hope and pray St Peter's will be spared—and my dear Father the Pope.' Rome was indeed spared, though since it had been declared an open city by the two opposed armies, it had never been targeted. There was in fact a startling consensus that the great historic towns of Italy should be protected. Aside from Rome itself, Florence, Siena and Orvieto were also relatively unscathed. Not that Italy escaped devastation: Naples was not the only great historic city to suffer carnage, and of course the human cost of the campaign was vast, but there were considerable efforts made to preserve the exceptional fabric of Italy. Catherine would surely have been delighted, if perhaps rather confused in her loyalties, to learn that two German officers had in the autumn of 1943 convinced Church authorities and their own commanding officers to use German army vehicles to remove the contents of Monte Cassino's library and picture gallery to Rome for safekeeping. Local people were paid in extra food rations and cigarettes to assist in the removal of the entire community of monks and more than 80,000 books and manuscripts and 100,000 prints, as well as countless paintings by Old Masters. The abbey had been founded in 529 AD and its library was described by historians as 'a treasure literally without price'. This prescient forethought saved more than a hundred lives and an irreplaceable resource for humanity.

Catherine was about to start new work and had just bought a flat when she wrote to her son. Penelope's return to the UK and to living with her had revitalised her desire to be in London, but though she loved the house at Wilton Crescent it was really too large for her, Pen and Doll. The new flat was on Hay Hill, just off Berkeley Square, Catherine told Henry. She was about to start work with the Women's Legion in a soup kitchen down at the docks in the East End, where some of the poorest people in London were still struggling to recover their lives in the aftermath of the Blitz. One gets the sense that Catherine was finally starting to come through the dreadful sadness brought on by her loss of Geoffrey, and even to manage her anxiety over Henry. Her faith undoubtedly helped her, and she reported to her son that she had been seeing lots of friends and felt really well. She had even been learning to cook, under Doll's supervision. The previous night Doll had bought a week's meat rations and hovered at her mistress's side as Catherine attempted a mixed grill of liver and kidneys. The results were pronounced extremely delicious.

Porchey came to have tea with her and inspect the new flat. He was preoccupied with his divorce. Catherine gathered that he'd served notice on Tilly and that he and Jeanne had had a farewell party as they were not supposed to meet in public while the case was being put together. 'She's madly in love with me,' Porchey confided to Catherine. 'And do you know, I think she's absolutely wonderful.' Catherine was sanguine and also a little sceptical. After all, she did know Porchey really quite well and she suspected that he might grow restless again once the divorce was settled. She was not the same woman she had been when they were married. Her experience as Geoffrey's wife, and above all as his widow, had given her great confidence and skills of self-reliance. She only smiled at his comments and wished him well.

The main topic of conversation at Porchey and Catherine's meeting, though, was not his divorce but their daughter's marriage. At the beginning of June, Gerrit van der Woude had telephoned Lord Carnarvon at Highclere: he would very much like to give him a drink at the Ritz the following week. Porchey was not at all surprised. Pen had been fizzy with joy for the last few months, talking of Gerrit in terms that suggested he was indispensable to her happiness. Gerrit had now won over both Penelope's parents—it was impossible to argue with the evident happiness of their daughter. Besides, she was a sensible girl with sound instincts and not inclined to flights of romantic fancy; they trusted her judgement.

Porchey gave his blessing over drinks at the Ritz. His only concern was that they should not rush into marriage until the war was well and truly over. In any case, Penelope couldn't countenance getting married until her beloved brother was home, so the young couple agreed to a slightly longer engagement than they really wanted. For now it would be kept a private matter. The public announcement would wait until they could set a date for the wedding. Two days later Almina came to lunch with Catherine to discuss the wonderful news and both Pen and Catherine wrote to Henry to tell him. 'Your father found Gerrit absolutely charming,' wrote Catherine. 'We are all really so happy and Pen is almost beside herself. The only thing now is that we so desperately look forward to you coming home.'

Penelope went to Highclere two weeks after she became

engaged, for ten days' holiday. It was the first time off from the Foreign Office she'd had since her day at Christmas and she was exhausted. Her father had told her that Robert Taylor was recuperating at the castle and she went to see him and meet his wife, Joan. She found them both tense, unable to let go of each other's hands as they talked. Pen was moved by Joan's fortitude despite the prospect of her husband's imminent return to the battlefield. Beneath the carefully upbeat general conversation was a thick anxiety. There were no illusions left for Robert. He knew what the battle that was waiting for him looked like. He had been so lucky once; could his luck possibly hold long enough for him to see the end of the war?

Pen found Harcourt 'Crinks' Johnstone down there too, also resting up, but there was plenty of activity. Her father was busier than ever with Claims Commission business, and to his delight he had just been promoted to Colonel. He hosted a meeting on post-war agricultural policy. People were starting to believe that the war would actually end, and to prepare accordingly.

One visitor to Highclere during Pen's stay who certainly had no doubts about the war having entered its final stages was General Patton. Since playing his part in Operation Fortitude to perfection, he had been given command of the US 3rd Army as they readied to make their push south and southeast from the Normandy beaches. He was now preparing to leave for northern France to meet his troops, who had been moved across throughout July. He and Porchey must have met when General Patton was out raising morale among the US troops who were waiting to be sent to France. In between his work on Operation Fortitude, Patton visited a great many US bases. Porchey travelled all over southern England for his work and was often at military functions.

One imagines that they would have recognised something of the kindred spirit in each other. They were both bluff and direct, with an irreverent sense of humour. Porchey had suggested that he come to lunch at Highclere if he found himself in the area.

General Patton arrived on a beautiful summer's day accompanied by his ADC and laden with goodies—golf balls, crisps and tinned food, mostly—for Lord Carnarvon to pass on. The power of American largesse was still proving effective, even as the conflict started to draw to a close. The golf course was still a wheatfield but at least Porchey could practise some driving shots.

There were just eight for lunch and it was a small and convivial group. Patton was on excellent form, his spirits restored by the prospect of getting back into the field. 'When we get to Normandy,' he confided to Porchey, 'I have one plan and one plan only. I don't care what Monty says, I'm determined to get to Berlin before those goddamned Russians.'

In between battle strategy, Patton was overflowing with wisecracks until he was stopped in his tracks by his ADC's reaction to Mr Pell the butler. Asked whether he would prefer red or white wine, he responded, 'I'd like a glass of milk, please.' A silence descended on the table before Pell smoothly despatched a footman to see to it. Patton directed a powerfully dirty look in his unfortunate ADC's direction, whereupon the lad went beetroot red, but the General managed to contain his normally forthright language.

Patton left the UK for France at the end of July. Robert Taylor left Highclere to rejoin his regiment just a few days before. The Battle of Normandy was in full flow; Lieutenant General Montgomery was moving steadily inland. Monty had been transferred from the command of the 8th Army in Italy just before Christmas the previous year and had been put to planning the British ground forces' participation in the D-Day landings. Now, bolstered by the triumph of D-Day, he and his Army had fought their way stubbornly through Caen and were holding the Germans there as the US 3rd Army pushed its way east. The Germans were being driven back on two fronts, forced into an ever smaller area. True to form, Hitler refused to countenance a retreat when there was still time to avoid disastrous loss of life. The Allies seized the opportunity to encircle the Germans and trap them in what became known as the 'Falaise pocket', a scrap of land around the small town of Falaise that was transformed into an inferno of fighting.

It was a devastating battle. It raged for just nine days from 12 August but those days were a matter of pure survival. Robert was in command of a flame-throwing tank and was called forward to incinerate roadblocks as the Army advanced. The noise was a roaring that he couldn't stop hearing for hours afterwards; the smoke that was belched back into the tank stained the men's skin black so that it looked like charred leather. He saw remains of horses blown into trees, of carts and guns in twisted piles, rows of trenches where dead soldiers still seemed to stand and everywhere was the stench of death and exploding shells.

The tanks were not suited to this type of warfare. Many of the battalions had trained in England on wide, undulating spaces such as the estate at Highclere. The landscape of Normandy was a patchwork of high hedges, orchards and sunken roads. As a tank went steeply up over the crest of a hill it provided an excellent target.

The pocket was finally closed, after days of brutal hand-to-hand fighting, on 21 August. Approximately 100,000 German troops were left in the area, of which perhaps half managed to escape while the rest either perished or were taken prisoner. Thousands of civilians also died, along with countless horses and cattle. The villages and towns Robert and his regiment passed through were nothing but piles of rubble with blackened tanks lying askew and, everywhere, the bodies of the dead. General Eisenhower was conducted on foot through the area to review the damage two days after the battle ended. 'Falaise was unquestionably one of the greatest "killing fields" of the war . . . I encountered scenes that could be described only by Dante. It was literally possible to walk for hundreds of yards at a time, stepping on nothing but dead and decaying flesh.'

Falaise was the decisive battle of the Normandy campaign. The Allied armies' progress was now relentless: Robert was part of the force pushing eastwards through Belgium towards the border with Germany. Patton's determination to get to Berlin first fuelled his Army's remarkable two-week dash across Lorraine. But, as one force went east, another smaller one went south towards Paris. The news that the Allied Army had scored a decisive victory sparked an uprising by the French Resistance and, three days later, the 2nd division of the Free French Army swept into western Paris in triumph as the 4th US infantry division cleared the eastern sections. Vast crowds of ecstatic Parisians greeted them, and the following day the Germans signed their surrender as General de Gaulle made his first speech as President of the Provisional Government of the French Republic.

Robert's unit pressed on in pursuit of the Germans as Operation Anvil began: the invasion of southern France. Many of the troops had been transferred from the Italian campaign, leaving Henry Porchester and his men tightly stretched. Unconditional surrender had been declared the Allied goal more than eighteen months before but, so far, the Germans were showing very little sign of being willing to surrender on any terms. Von Cholitz, the military governor of Paris, was unusual. Most German officers obediently followed Hitler's orders for counter-attacks and no surrender. As a result the Allies would have to fight for every inch of ground as they pushed the Germans through the battlefields of the First World War, back towards their own borders.

Morale was high, despite tough fighting, heavy casualties and food and fuel shortages. The speed of the initial Allied advance, combined with the fact that so many ports were out of action, led to huge logistical problems. There were two types of food packs that got delivered intermittently in cardboard crates and were labelled 'A' and 'B', containing different tinned rations. Robert and his men were grateful for either, but they always kept an eye out for the remains of an allotment where they might find some carrots or tomatoes.

The other great supplement to army rations was the hospitality of local people. As they made their way northeast through France and towards Belgium, Robert and his troop were met by euphoric and grateful crowds. People came out waving flags, singing their national anthems and offering coffee, champagne—and even, on one blessedly happy occasion, a plate of salty, crunchy chips.

The whole of Britain rejoiced at the Allies' wins on the Western Front and the liberation of Paris. On the Eastern Front the Red Army was also pressing towards Germany, liberating Poland as it went. Finally it seemed that victory was a matter of when, rather than if. But the Soviets' advances were also revealing horrifying evidence that confirmed persistent (and persistently overlooked) stories about a Nazi programme to annihilate Jews, Roma, homosexuals and other so-called 'undesirables'.

The first concentration camp to be liberated was Majdenek, near the city of Lublin in Poland. Soviet troops were struck dumb by what they found: barely a thousand skeletal survivors, gas chambers and burial pits. Approximately 79,000 people had been exterminated in its gas chambers and hundreds of thousands more were worked to death and died of disease and starvation.

Majdenek was the first of dozens of camps that would be liberated over the next nine months. Its discovery was widely reported in the press; Western and Soviet correspondents entered the camp along with the Red Army. H. W. Lawrence, a journalist with the *New York Times*, wrote, 'I have just seen the most terrible place on earth.' Somehow, these reports were not given the full import they merited. The horror and the staggering scale of the Nazis' Final Solution were impossible for the public to take in, even as more and more evidence built up. It would be many more months before, with Germany's defeat secured, the world could set about the virtually impossible task of confronting the aftermath of the Holocaust.

That summer London was struggling to cope with a new German weapon of terror, albeit one on an infinitely smaller scale than the machinery of death in Eastern Europe. On 13 June the first V1 flying bomb was launched towards London from a site on the Pas de Calais coastline, part of a last-ditch attack on Britain. It landed next to a railway bridge in Mile End in the east of London and killed eight civilians. Between then and October, when the last launch site was destroyed by the Allies, more than 9,500 of what the British quickly christened doodlebugs rained down on southeast England, and London in particular.

The doodlebugs were extremely effective. They were difficult to intercept and destroy in the air and, though their impact was relatively limited, their capacity to inspire terror was not. A great many air-force resources were diverted to trying to shoot them down safely and, meanwhile, the bombs kept falling. Before long Londoners' nerves were shot to pieces. The only warning of an imminent attack was the bomb's pulse engine giving out, which meant the thing was about to drop. Everyone, from theatre audiences to school-children to office workers, grew adept at keeping one ear out, first for the trademark buzzing and then for the awful silence. If a doodlebug cut out over your head you had less than a minute to dive into an air-raid shelter and hope for the best.

On 20 August, ten minutes after Pen had left for work from Catherine's new flat near Berkeley Square, she heard the dreaded buzzing overhead. She stood still in the street and looked up, scanning the sky. There it was, a chubby, cigar-shaped missile bearing nearly 2,000-pounds' worth of explosives. It was still moving. Then it stopped. The whistling it made as it fell was demonic. Pen felt its blast and knew it couldn't have been very far away. It seemed to have landed in the direction of her mother's flat. She started to run. When she got to Catherine's street she saw broken glass all over the road but the bomb had not hit. It must have fallen a few streets further on. She rushed upstairs and Doll let her in, trembling. Catherine had been blown right across her bedroom by the force of the blast but remarkably she hadn't been hurt at all, not even by the shattering glass from her window.

The three women knew they were lucky and tried to comfort one another, but though Catherine had recovered her calm by the end of the day, Pen was totally unnerved. She went to sleep on a mattress in the corridor for the next couple of nights, away from windows, tossing and turning and unable to relax. When she telephoned her father to tell him of the near escape he was sympathetic and reminded her that she could always come to Highclere. 'I know it's pretty bad up there. Poor Jeanne's driving me mad,' he added. 'She's so nervous from the damn doodlebugs that she's really quite snappy with me.'

Things got even worse when the Germans developed the next generation of flying bomb, the V2, which they began to use in September. This flew at such an astonishing speed that it was impossible to shoot down and it fell without any warning whatsoever. It had a longer range than the V1 so it could be launched from German territory, and V2s terrorised London right up until the end of the war. Some 13,000 were fired, day and night, and killed approximately 9,000 people.

In Italy the Allied armies had been twice depleted: first by the transfer of several divisions to the D-Day landings and then again when men were sent to participate in the invasion of the south of France. In August Henry was asked to liaise with one of the more colourful special military units that worked alongside the remaining forces. Popski's Private Army, officially known as No. 1 Demolition Squad, was a small force under the command of Major Vladimir Peniakoff. It had been formed in Cairo in October 1942 as an 8th Army special forces unit, tasked with attacking Rommel's fuel supplies in the build-up to El Alamein. Peniakoff, who gained the nickname Popski because British intelligence operators had trouble with his surname, was a Belgian-born Anglophile and had studied philosophy at the University of Cambridge before enlisting as a gunner in the French Army and serving in the First World War. He was commissioned into the British Army in 1940 and proved himself to be a remarkably skilled and courageous special agent, who left the North African campaign with a Military Cross for his three-month stint behind enemy lines gathering intelligence on Rommel's fuel dumps. From North Africa he and his men made their way to Italy as part of a special advance party. They specialised in intelligence gathering and clandestine operations and worked closely with partisans, but they could turn their hand to regular soldiering if required and held a section of the Allied front line when the D-Day landings diverted large numbers of troops. Officially they were eighty men, but they acquired a lot of strays along the way including Russian, German and Italian POWs. The international make-up of the unit meant that French was the common language. Henry spoke excellent French so he was tasked with liaising with Popski's men as the Blues and Royals continued their advance towards Rimini, attempting to break the last line of German defence. The Blues had themselves built up extensive experience of reconnaissance and the two units swapped a great deal of knowledge and information.

As the Allies prepared to launch their attack on Rimini in late August, the Germans sent a small force into the neutral territory of the tiny republic of San Marino, just southwest of the city. When the Allied attack met with the usual severe resistance, the Indian and British forces, including the Blues, opted to push west towards San Marino, looking for a weak point where they could burst through the line. On 17 September, after a day of fierce fighting, they took control of the hills on the territory's borders and started to press on towards the territory's tiny capital city. Henry's troop was the second to enter San Marino city on 20 September. By the afternoon the German surrender had been secured. Both armies suffered heavy losses in the course of the battle but at least it must have been a relief to be away from the defensive line, in neutral territory, and therefore in an environment free of the booby traps that had been testing their ingenuity and courage for the last six months.

San Marino was virtually the last action Henry saw. Three days later he wrote to his father to say he had heard 'some interesting news'. All correspondence was heavily censored, so typically Henry confined himself to asking his 'Darling Pups' for news of the family, staff or the racing. He couldn't divulge any details, but both Porchey and then Catherine, who received a similar letter, intuited that the news their son had heard was good. It was indeed. Half of Henry's regiment had not been home for four and a half years. It was confirmed that those men and officers would be leaving Italy before the end of October. The question for the other half of the regiment was whether they would be amalgamated with another unit or sent home alongside their comrades.

At the beginning of October, Catherine received the letter telling her that Henry was coming home. She had been longing for this moment for so long that when it came she could hardly believe it. She started to cry, tears of sheer relief that brought Doll running to her, asking frightened questions. But this time, the news for Catherine was the best it possibly could be. Her boy was coming home. On 10 October 1944, the Blues and Royals boarded the HMT *Monarch of Bermuda* at Naples; they left port three days later, on Friday the thirteenth. Despite the inauspicious date, the only trouble they encountered was overcrowding. There were 5,000 men and 560 officers loaded onto three troopships and six destroyers and the officers were packed nine to a cabin intended for two. Henry and his friend John Ewart were too happy to be going home to mind. By some miracle the food was excellent and the sun was shining. They had survived one of the most brutal campaigns of the war and had the satisfaction of leaving at a time when the Allies seemed certain to achieve their objectives, not just in Italy but everywhere. With a mixture of euphoria and relief they set about playing bridge with their customary gusto. John was still losing, Henry still winning. Two weeks later they docked at Liverpool and were told they were going straight to Aldershot but would be discharged the following day.

Back in Italy, Popski and his men were still battling on. In November they took part in the liberation of Ravenna, where Popski was awarded the Distinguished Service Order. Two days later he lost a hand to a German grenade. In Belgium, Robert Taylor's tank regiment was held up in the stalled Allied push towards the German border, waiting for fuel supplies, bracing themselves for the last stage of the war. They knew it would be bloody. The Germans were clearly not going to give up until they had exhausted every resource, every tiny chance to resist what now seemed inevitable. But for Henry Porchester the war was over. He was on his way back to Highclere.

20

Celebrations

On 19 January 1945, three months after his return from the war, Henry Lord Porchester turned twenty-one. His father took the opportunity to throw as lavish a party as was possible in wartime, to celebrate his son and heir's coming of age. It was held not at the castle but in the Armoury Room in Highclere village; this was a public celebration for the entire local community. There was a buffet prepared by Lord Carnarvon's chef, a conjuror performing tricks and a dance band that played late into the night. Wine and beer flowed in abundance.

Lord Carnarvon made a speech saying how lucky he was to live at Highclere and to have such wonderful friends around him to share his good fortune with. The festivities were shot through with awareness that Henry had been spared, and now the years of sacrifice were coming to an end for the whole nation. There was a heady atmosphere of gratitude, of gladness simply at being alive. Lord Carnarvon's declaration that 'the English way of life is a priceless heritage' was received with cries of 'hear, hear' and when he said he was sure his son, as his successor, would 'keep the lights burning brightly' there were cheers. Lord Carnarvon appealed for quiet as he had a very special announcement to make. 'I know you will all be as delighted as we are by the news that Lady Penelope is shortly to marry Captain Gerrit van der Woude of the Grenadier Guards.' The cheers reached a crescendo as Penelope gazed around at the mass of smiling faces, clearly moved by this outpouring of goodwill.

The staff and tenants gave Lord Porchester an illuminated address to mark the occasion. He rose to thank them and then asked if they would toast 'one who was as dear to them as to him'—his sister, Lady Penelope. As everyone rose and held their glasses high, the room brimmed with happiness.

Of course, the war was not yet over, either at Highclere or in the wider world. The stud had been decommissioned in November 1944 but the bombing run in the valley was still operational, and full of huge craters. Some of them contained live material; the bomb disposal squad was kept busy at Highclere well into 1946. Miss Stubbings and Lord Carnarvon started to lodge claims for damage and to address the dilapidated state of the park roads and the destruction of the stud buildings and paddocks. Porchey knew better than anyone that funds were limited, and accepted that most of the money to put things right would have to be found from the estate's budget. It was going to be a long time before everything was back to the way it had been.

Joan Taylor had been as thrilled as everyone else by Henry's safe return, but for as long as Robert was still in Belgium, she couldn't even begin to think of a post-war life. Her husband wrote to her at Christmas, telling her that he was sure he would be home soon. In fact, he and his unit were still waiting to make their final push, and still short of supplies. As winter set in it grew harder to stay cheerful. For millions of troops out in Belgium and France there was a job to finish and they just wanted to get on with it.

In mid-December the Germans caught the Allies off guard when they made their last great counter-attack of the war through the Ardennes region of Belgium, France and Luxembourg. As the Allies' front line was squeezed in on itself, the bulge on the maps produced by news agencies gave rise to the battle's most enduring name: the Battle of the Bulge.

The Germans' aim was to take advantage of their opponents' preoccupation with planning their final offensive, and of the heavy fog, which meant that the Allies' superior air power would be grounded. They almost succeeded. The German Army advanced sixty miles, splitting the Allied armies into two sections and surrounding two pockets of US troops at Elsenborne Ridge and Bastogne. Hitler sent a representative to Major-General Anthony McAuliffe, at the Bastogne garrison, with an ultimatum to surrender or face annihilation by German troops, which massively outnumbered the Americans. McAuliffe's one word response, 'Nuts!', made him famous throughout America and Britain. The cost of this defiance was high, though. It was only the heroic determination of the US 1st Army that held the Germans for long enough that reinforcements could be sent.

Eisenhower ordered Patton to turn his US 3rd Army around and march to the north. He was going in to counter-attack against the southern German flank. It was pure aggressive risk-taking, precisely the sort of thing that Eisenhower had sent Patton back into the field to achieve, and it worked. The pressure points were relieved and shortly afterwards the weather started to clear a little, just enough for the Allies to launch heavy aerial attacks. The trails of smoke from the planes lifted the hearts of the infantry, who had been fighting hand-to-hand through snow and sleet for nearly two weeks. It took until 24 January for the Allies to declare victory and it was a bitter victory indeed for the US Army: 124,000 American soldiers were killed, wounded or captured. Winston Churchill's verdict when he spoke to the House of Commons was clear: 'This is undoubtedly the greatest American battle of the war and will, I believe, be regarded as an ever-famous American victory.'

From 23 February the Allies began to cross the River Rhine, Germany's ultimate line of defence, and from there to fan out through the country and advance along a front that stretched from the Baltic Sea in the north to Austria in the south. Robert Taylor was part of the British push to the northeast. The 2nd Canadian division were following along immediately behind Robert's tank unit. They had fought to liberate Holland, where the civilian population was starving, and incurred heavy casualties. The troops that had trained at Highclere three years previously, crashing into the buildings at the stud and sneaking into the Library to meet their sweethearts, were now battle-hardened and weary.

Robert was grateful that finally, after months of dismal stand-off, they were on the move again; the war was in its endgame. But the sense of relief and determination to press the victory home was tempered by the misery he witnessed as they marched on to Hamburg. He saw a country in ruins. There were no walls left in the towns they passed through, just acres of twisted rubble populated by skeletal citizens too wasted to bury the dead. Why hadn't Hitler given the order to surrender? Robert had seen enough, lived through far too much. Now he just wanted to get home to his wife, to Highclere.

Back in London, Gerrit and Penelope had been making plans. They had discovered that Gerrit's regiment, the Grenadiers, would very soon be sent to Germany with the occupying forces that would be tasked with running the British sector in the wake of Germany's defeat. He had just three weeks of training left to complete before he would be eligible to be posted, and only two Sundays. The only place where the banns could be read that quickly was at Penelope's home parish of Highclere. So, most unusually, the Carnarvon family was planning a country wedding with the celebrations at the castle, rather than a grand spectacle at St Margaret's Westminster and in Mayfair. This suited Gerrit down to the ground. He was a reserved man and not at all keen that his wedding day should feature in the press, especially during wartime. The date was set for 21 April.

It would be the first time Catherine had returned to her former home since she left it on the day she walked out of her marriage, ten years previously. She and Porchey had long ago ceased to hurt each other. They had always been courteous and reasonable in their shared duties as parents, and in recent years they had even become friends. But still, Catherine felt nervous at the prospect of returning to the scene of her old life, to the house where she had been so happy, and so wretched. If Geoffrey had been with her it would have been different, but she couldn't help slightly dreading the prospect of arriving, of stepping into the Saloon and greeting her ex-husband in what had been their home.

She tried to set these thoughts aside. Catherine had been in a bubble of happiness ever since Henry's safe return from the war and she was determined not to let her nerves spoil the wonderful occasion. After all, she would have her son, Gar and Doll for support. Meanwhile, she concentrated on preparations and supporting her daughter. There was a lot to do in a short time, and many things were made more difficult by the fact that an exhausted Britain was now suffering from acute shortages of all sorts of things that when Catherine had planned her own wedding she had taken for granted.

Pen managed to find some beautiful pre-war white satin with which to have her dress made, but she and Catherine discovered that there was no tulle for a veil in the entire city. Every day for a week, Catherine finished her shift in the canteen at the docks a little early so that she could jump on a bus back to the West End and hunt through every haber-dashery store from Soho to Knightsbridge. In one place the assistant practically laughed in her face. White tulle? There hadn't been any since 1940! The following day, as Catherine was listening to the same thing from yet another shop assistant, the lady standing behind her tapped her on the arm. 'Excuse me, I couldn't help overhearing. I have some tulle at home that might do. Would you like to see it?' Astounded, grateful, Catherine accompanied the stranger to her flat. The lady had bought a long length of soft white tulle in 1939 and hadn't used it. She gave a sad smile when Catherine handed over the money. 'I hope it brings her a great deal of joy.'

Catherine had equal difficulty finding a dress for herself. The boutiques were practically bare and no couturier could make anything in such a short time. Eventually she bought a dress in Peter Jones in a very pretty cyclamen pink and managed to get it fitted despite the short notice. By this time, though, her nerves were a little strained. When Henry rang up and she described the dress to him, he said, 'Oh, Mama, you can't possibly wear that colour! It sounds awful.' Catherine had always been a supremely confident dresser and was used to receiving compliments; now she was crushed. The following day, having fretted all night, she set off again on the hunt for the perfect dress in which to make her reappearance at Highclere. Eventually she found a bluish grey one. When she pressed Doll for her opinion, Doll said quietly that she thought it not very sparky. Penelope agreed. When Henry came to lunch at the weekend to discuss what still needed to be done, his opinion was sought on the two options. He loved the cyclamen pink one. 'You look lovely, Mum! Now all you need is some orchids for a corsage.' Catherine had a charming hat made to match and organised her make-up, shoes and clutch bag. Doll had squirrelled away some fabric the year before, but in her rush to get her own dress made, she had bought the wrong size pattern; she had to cut it by hand, then spend every evening for the next week determinedly sewing.

On Friday 20 April, Catherine, Penelope, Henry, Doll and Doll's dog Pixie (bathed especially for the occasion) caught the 10.30 train from Paddington. Catherine and Penelope were both fluttery with nerves. They were met at Highclere station by the Rolls-Royce and driven past London Lodge, still crumbling from the impact of a bomb that only just missed, along the drive, past the Temple of Diana until Catherine caught her first sight of the castle's familiar tower rising above the tree-tops. Her heart was beating sixty to the minute as Mr Pell opened the car door with a huge smile. 'You must be Pell, thank you so much,' she said as he handed her out of the car. This was the moment she had been so nervous about: she knew that once it was all under way she would be too happy for Penelope to think of anything else. Catherine, the Countess of Carnarvon, as she had been the last time she stood here, Mrs Geoffrey Grenfell, widow, as she was now, took the few steps through the front door of Highclere Castle and into the Gothic Saloon.

Pell informed them that Lord Carnarvon would be with them in a moment and two seconds later Porchey appeared, all smiles. He greeted them all warmly and laughed as he excused himself for not having been there to meet them himself. He had been talking to Tilly's lawyers in New York. 'She's making a fuss about money, as usual.'

They all went to have lunch in the Dining Room, Porchey and Catherine sitting opposite each other as they had done in the old days and their children just delighted to have their parents in the same room and everyone back together again. Catherine was so buoyed up by the jolliness of the occasion that she found she was no longer nervous. After lunch Penelope went to wash her hair and try to relax a little, sitting outside as it dried in the strong spring sunshine. Henry went with both his parents for a walk to inspect the stud. Doll admired her mistress's evident calm and dignity. She must have been relieved; she had shared in every nervous conjecture for the past three weeks. Almina, Eve, Bro and Patricia arrived at tea-time and that night the whole party went to bed early in preparation for the big day.

Catherine woke on her daughter's wedding day and realised that—though she felt the absence of all the people she wished were here to share it with them: Geoffrey, her brother Reggie, her father Jac—she was happy; happier than she had been since Geoffrey's death. Seeing her son, the future Earl of Carnarvon, walking around Highclere arm-in-arm with his father gladdened her heart. She was so proud of both her children.

When Doll came to open the shutters, sunshine streamed into the bedroom and the bright spring greens of the park seemed like a promise of happiness for Gerrit and Penelope. Later, as they sat down to lunch, Penelope opened several gifts of exquisite jewellery from her family. Gerrit had given

Henry a beautiful ruby brooch to present to his fiancée. Henry then slipped away to Newbury to perform his best man's duties: lunch and several glasses of champagne for the groom.

Penelope and Catherine went up to dress. Doll helped Catherine, as she had done almost every day for the last twenty-five years. The cyclamen pink dress was pronounced indisputedly the right choice; the whole effect, with her hat perched to one side and her fur shrug, perfectly chic. Catherine set off for the church with Almina, Eve and Brograve as Doll knocked on the door to Penelope's bedroom.

The bride was already in her dress. It shimmered with just the faintest trace of pink, like an oyster's shell. The skirt was a simple A-line shape, the three-quarter sleeves and bateau neckline contributed to an effect of perfect elegance. Pen's thick hair was set in perfect waves, the diamond earrings her grandmother Almina had just given her sparkled at her ears.

Doll had come to help with the finishing touch, the veil. She had pleaded with the very exclusive French lady who made wreaths of orange blossoms in an atelier just off Berkeley Square, to make one for Lady Penelope at incredibly short notice: there was no one else in London who could possibly do it like her. Eventually the appeals to patriotic pride won out and the delicate wreath had been transported in a hatbox down from London. Doll fixed the lace-edged veil in place and set the wreath on Penelope's head. 'You've never looked so pretty,' she told her. 'No, don't cry, you'll get puffy eyes!'

Penelope had no bridesmaids to attend her: there hadn't been time to arrange any more dresses. It was Doll who carried the train of her veil as Penelope walked round the Gallery and descended the Oak Staircase. Lord Carnarvon and Pell were waiting in the Saloon and had broad grins on their faces as she stepped down the last stair. 'You look beautiful, my darling girl,' Porchey told her. 'I'm so proud of you.'

Pell could only nod appreciatively and clear his throat to wish her a wonderful day and a very happy married life. Then Penelope and her father walked out arm-in-arm to the polished Rolls-Royce waiting on the gravel by the front door. Jack Gibbins had taken a day off from his duties with the King and Queen to drive them the short distance down to the church. As he saw Lady Penelope, his face creased in a smile. 'You look lovely, my lady.' Penelope couldn't stop smiling herself. 'Thank you, Gibbins, you're so kind to do this.'

Catherine arrived at the church at the same moment as her sister Lady Galloway and a group of Wendell cousins and friends of Penelope's from London. She was delighted to see Philippa and, as the sisters embraced each other, Philippa whispered in her ear, 'You look marvellous, darling, so very strong.' With those words to fortify her, Catherine entered the church. She couldn't help remembering the Sunday services she had attended every week for more than twelve years as she saw the same faces of employees and tenants. There were many in the congregation who remembered her generosity and smiles and their obvious pleasure at seeing her buoyed her up. She had worried that she would be overcome by memories of her brother's funeral, but this was, after all, such a happy occasion that Catherine had no room in her heart for anything else.

She saw her soon-to-be son-in-law standing at the altar, with her son by his side. Gerrit had a serious expression but looked so handsome in his uniform. The church was a bower of flowers from the gardens at Highclere, with lilac, azaleas, rhododendrons and apple blossom everywhere she looked. Then, as the music for the bride's entrance started up and the congregation stood, Catherine could no longer stop her tears. Pen looked so wonderful, her smile of happiness clearly visible beneath the veil that Catherine had found for her.

Catherine thought of her own two wedding days, so different, and wished with all her heart that her beloved daughter would be happy, as she had been.

After the ceremony the congregation made for the castle. Chefs in white hats served a buffet of sandwiches and cakes with tea or champagne, from tables in the Saloon. Penelope and Gerrit stood with their arms twined about one another's waists as Bro Beauchamp proposed a toast for the bride and Gerrit replied in a neat little speech, and then suddenly it was all over. Pen slipped upstairs to change into a navy going-away dress and then the couple were climbing into a car to be driven to Gerrit's family house in Kent for a week's honeymoon. Everyone came outside to cheer them off and Henry attached a huge silver horseshoe to the car's bumper. Doll had slipped another smaller one into her darling Penelope's dressing case.

Late in the afternoon, as all the excitement faded, Catherine and Philippa walked down the drive, past the dairy yard to the family chapel and their brother's grave. Catherine placed one of the orchids she had worn pinned to her dress onto his tombstone, and they both paused to weep a little and to remember.

Gerrit and Penelope's honeymoon coincided with the final days of the war. Victory, and peace, were now only days away. Hitler committed suicide on 30 April; Hitler's successor, Karl Dönitz, ordered General Alfred Jodl to sign an unconditional Instrument of Surrender at Reims, at 02.41 on 7 May 1945. The decimation of German lives, communities, cities, industry, culture and reputation was complete. As the news spread across Europe, church bells were rung in every village and from every cathedral; people flocked to give thanks for deliverance and to pray for their loved ones who had not lived to see this day. In the United States, Americans woke to the news. It was President Harry Truman's birthday and he dedicated the victory to the memory of his predecessor, Franklin D. Roosevelt, who had died of a cerebral haemorrhage less than a month before, on 12 April.

At Highclere, Joan Taylor wept with relief. Until now she had not allowed herself to picture Robert appearing at her door, or to imagine what it would feel like to run into his arms, for fear of jinxing his return. In London, Catherine cried when she heard the news, too; tears of relief that – though she had lost her beloved husband—her son had been spared. She welcomed Henry for lunch that day. He had come up to London to take part in the celebrations that he was certain would erupt once the Prime Minister had spoken to the nation.

On V-E Day, the horrors of the recent past were put aside as people burst into spontaneous celebration. Churchill made his broadcast to the nation on the morning of 8 May, declaring that the ceasefire had come into effect the previous day. Hundreds of thousands of people poured onto the streets of London. Mollie Panter-Downes, still filing her columns for the *New Yorker*, described a day that 'when it finally came was like no other that anyone can remember', though the mood of the celebrations was perhaps like one 'vast, happy village fete'. Young servicemen and women in uniform danced with their arms around one another, American soldiers and London girls did the conga up Piccadilly. Anything that could be climbed, from lamp posts to the scaffolding and sandbags around the statue of Eros's pedestal, had at least two or three young people hanging from it, shouting their joy to the world. Whole families decked out in paper hats of red, white and blue milled between Trafalgar Square and Buckingham Palace, determined to see the King, and Mr Churchill. When King George VI and Queen Elizabeth appeared on the balcony of the palace with their daughters, the Princesses Elizabeth and Margaret, the ecstatic crowd yelled their approval. The royal family had won enormous respect and affection for their decision to stay in London throughout the war. They had been bombed at Buckingham Palace, they had visited the docks and the tenements of the East End during the Blitz, had stayed to share in the suffering and the fortitude of the British people. But the biggest cheer was saved for Churchill. Mollie Panter-Downes wrote that when the crowd saw him there was 'a deep, full-throated, almost reverent roar'.

Henry kissed his mother goodbye and went looking for his friends. A group of them made their way to the palace. Princess Elizabeth and her sister Princess Margaret begged for permission to leave the balcony and go with their cousins, Henry Porchester and others to mingle with the crowds. It was an exceptional day; smiling, the King gave his assent. Virtually incognito thanks to their uniforms, the girls melted into the mass of people and ran with their friends through the streets, laughing, crying, singing, doing the hokey-cokey. It was all a joyful madness. The Mall was packed with revellers and it took them ages to battle their way back down to join with the multitudes standing outside the palace and scream, 'We want the King! We want the Queen!', who duly obliged. Down below, their children hugged each other, sharing their elation alongside thousands of others.

Tomorrow there would be time to plan for the future; tonight, all anyone could think of was that the long years of stoicism and anxiety were over. Churchill's rallying cry at the end of his announcement of victory echoed in every-one's ears, 'Long live the cause of freedom!' Freedom would be toasted and cherished long into the night, from London to Highclere and all over the world.

Epilogue

When the formal celebrations of Victory in Europe Day were held, Lieutenant Lord Porchester of the Blues and Royals was second in command of the sovereigns' escort in the procession to St Paul's Cathedral and to the Houses of Parliament. Porchey and Catherine were deeply proud.

Robert Taylor had an arduous journey back from Germany. There were millions of people displaced across Europe, members of the armed forces heading home, or refugees looking for somewhere they might rebuild their lives. When he eventually made it to Highclere he told Joan little about his experiences, but he hugged her more fiercely than ever. He returned to Lord Carnarvon's service, as his butler, and he and Joan lived in a cottage at Highclere for the rest of their long lives. It was Robert who famously came to Henry, once he had become the 7th Earl, with a biscuit tin full of

Ancient Egyptian artefacts he had just found in a cupboard and said, 'Excuse me, my lord. I think there are some Egyptian treasures hidden in the castle.' Robert died in 1990 and a cedar of Lebanon is planted in his memory to the north front of the castle.

The war was over for Highclere's evacuee children and the teachers and nurses who had looked after them. Their belongings were packed back into small parcels and the children were bussed to the station where kindly railway staff thrust small white bags of sugar-coated almonds into their hands. They were almost as happy for them as the excited children were themselves. From Paddington they were taken by another bus to the Prince of Wales pub in Kilburn where their anxious parents and relatives were waiting for them. There were cheers and applause as the children clambered down the steep stairs from the coach and then mothers enfolded their daughters in a hug, fathers swung their sons round and round and lifted them onto their shoulders. In the midst of all this, one little boy, Terry, noticed that another small boy had not been claimed. Terry watched him quietly climb back onto the coach, clutching his brown leather satchel, and go to sit at the front next to the driver, ignoring everyone. Kind words from other mothers drifted past him. He stared ahead. As Terry's mother tugged on his hand to urge him home, Terry looked round. The little boy was still alone. What could have happened? Had his mother been killed by a doodlebug; was his father still in Belgium or Germany? In later years Terry told himself that someone must have gone to him, taken him home with them, but he never knew and always wondered.

By the end of 1946, most of the American GIs and Canadian troops that had been stationed in Britain had gone home. Some of them were accompanied by their British brides.

Even in the war's final days, everyone ran the risk of not making it back. On 5 May 1945 a B17 (nicknamed the 'flying fortress') from US Air Force 326th Squadron took off from Podington Air Base on a short training flight. The crew had completed their thirty-five missions and were looking forward to going back to the States. The pilot, First Lieutenant Reginald Hammond, got lost in low cloud and dense rain. He dropped down to see where he was, circled over Highclere Castle and set off towards the south, unknowingly approaching Siddown Hill. Too late he tried to pull the B-17 up but, despite his heroic efforts, he caught the trees. The wing tips sheared off before the plane crashed, belly down, and careered down the other side of the hill, catching fire as it went. The gamekeepers heard the rumble as it came over, as did the Stacey children in their cottage; the fog had increased the terrible sound of the flames. The local doctor, Dr Kendall, was not far away, and he and everyone in the area rushed up to help. One poor airman's body was found in the trees. The keepers went in among the smouldering wreckage and pulled out two badly burned airmen, but only one of them was still alive. Leonard Nitti, the radio operator, was the crew's sole survivor. The crash site is still discernible because of its lack of trees. There are remains of other planes buried across the estate. My husband and I plan to create a memorial to the men of the Second World War who died at Highclere, before their time, in the service of their country.

In July 1945, Porchey stepped down from his position with the Army Claims Commission, having been warmly compli-mented on his years of service. He retired with the honorary rank of Lieutenant Colonel. In the autumn he hosted several shooting weekends. Needless to say the first guests to be asked were Porchey's stalwart friends: the Duke and Duchess of Marlborough, Sidney Beer, Prince Aly Khan and his wife Princess

Joan, Cardie Montague and his new wife, and Peter and Poppy Thursby. Porchey and Sunny Marlborough resumed their highly acerbic games of bridge and returned to yelling cheerful insults at one another across their respective dining tables.

If some things at Highclere were the same, many more were not. The Second World War changed the social and economic framework in Britain; it marked the end of the era in which the country house was a symbol of power and privilege, and a cornerstone of the natural social order. While Highclere continued to be the home of the 6th Earl of Carnarvon, for the first few years after the war he found it increasingly difficult to make ends meet. It was the money from the flotation of Pyrotenax—the company Bro had urged him to invest in—that fundamentally redeemed his position in 1954. Porchey, and all the Carnarvons, were extremely lucky: it might have been very different. By 1955 a great house was being demolished every five days.

Porchey loved his home, the land and the people who worked there. His greatest wish was that Highclere would survive for future generations, and in this he was gratified. He lived in the castle until just before he died in 1987 and he lived all his years to the full. Witty and charming to the last, he remained an accomplished golfer and was a fine and competitive game shot. In 1955 his son Henry married a beautiful American girl, just as he had done. Her name was Jeanie Wallop and she and Henry lived across the park in Milford Lake House, so Porchey saw a great deal of his grandchildren. They grew up with an irrepressible if rather eccentric grandfather who loved to spoil them with generous gifts and meals of deliciously unhealthy food. Porchey adored the fine, old-fashioned dishes full of butter and cream that his great cook Ivy Rogers served for him in the 1970s and 1980s. He had a touch of the showman about him and was thrilled to appear on Michael Parkinson's prime-time TV chat show in 1976 and again in 1981, demonstrating his old-world charm and peppering the conversation with amusing stories from his life.

Brograve Beauchamp lost his seat as an MP in the 1945 General Election, which returned an unexpected landslide victory for the Labour Party. Winston Churchill immediately tendered his resignation as Prime Minister and Clement Attlee was appointed, with a mandate to build a 'cradle to grave' welfare state and a tax-funded National Health Service. The British electorate adored Churchill but distrusted what they remembered of his party's pre-war policies. Mrs Churchill commented that the Labour victory might be a 'blessing in disguise', to which her husband replied that it seemed 'quite effectively disguised'. Brograve's health had been shattered by the war but he lived until 1976 and continued to spend many enjoyable weekends with his wife, Eve, at Highclere playing bridge and golf. Their daughter, Patricia, delighted them by marrying Major Michael Leatham in 1949.

Henry succeeded his father in 1987 to become the 7th Earl of Carnarvon. He adored Highclere and the Hampshire countryside and, having completed an agricultural course at Cirencester College in 1947, he had started his farming career on the estate. Highclere continued to build its reputation for quality crops and livestock, winning a number of farm championships at the local county show. The farm continues to thrive under the 8th Earl, who has extended his father's legacy and expanded the business to grow and process oats for performance horses.

Like his father and grandfather before him, Henry had a passion for breeding thoroughbreds and loved the excitement of owning horses in training. He made a shrewd purchase when he bought his mare Jojo just after the war and bred a long line of winners such as Hiding Place, Smuggler and Little Wolf, who won the Gold Cup at Royal Ascot. He had an encyclopaedic knowledge of bloodlines and, through his membership of the Jockey Club, became a key figure in the modernisation of the racing industry. The 7th Earl shared this passion for the turf with his lifelong friend Her Majesty the Queen, whom he met as a child when she was Princess Elizabeth, and who is also a great authority on breeding racehorses. He became her Racing Manager in 1969, a post he held up to his death in 2001.

His life was underpinned by a deep sense of duty and public service. He was a member of Hampshire County Council for twenty-four years and served as Chairman from 1973 to 1977. After his father's death he took his place in the House of Lords, sitting on the cross benches (as an independent) and fighting the cause of rural interests.

Penelope van der Woude died in 1990, outlived by her husband and two sons. Her brother, who was by then the 7th Earl, and his wife, Jeanie, planted a grove of trees in her memory by the southwest lawns of the castle.

Tilly, Countess of Carnarvon, reinvented herself as an artist and achieved a certain measure of critical success. Having first tried her hand at watercolours, she began to paint seriously when she was encouraged by other artists. Her primary mentors were the ever loyal Cecil Beaton and John Spencer-Churchill, Winston's nephew. She produced a series of self-portraits in oil and portraits of subjects including Anita Loos, Kurt Weill and Lotte Lenya. As her work became more complex, it attracted considerable positive attention. She was sufficiently well regarded in her time to have paintings purchased by the Tate Gallery.

As might be expected, her marriage to the 6th Earl ended in divorce, with the first financial settlement achieved in 1946. She remained on cordial terms with Porchey (despite— or perhaps because of—the fact that it took until 1964 to complete the divorce) and even returned to stay at Highclere in 1950 and 1956. Tilly spent her remaining years commuting between London and New York, where she died of cancer in 1975. Porchey was among only a handful of mourners at her modest Catholic funeral, an event that, thirty years earlier, might well have filled Westminster Cathedral to overflowing. He never married again.

Almina closed her last nursing home, The Glebe, in 1943, and went to live in Somerset. She retained a particular dislike for budgets and taxes all her life. Porchey provided an allowance, which always proved insufficient. On one occasion, when she had a tax bill that she couldn't pay, he sent her the money. Almina promptly spent it on a marvellous party, and when Porchey remonstrated with her, she assured him that her party had been much more fun than paying the tax bill would have been, and for a great many more people. Over the years Almina worked her way through a vast fortune. She sold off most of the remaining Rothschild assets and much of her jewellery. In the end she was declared bankrupt. The judge commented that the reason for her sad situation was the role she had adopted as fairy godmother to so many others. Her grandson, Henry Porchester, bought her a house in Bristol where she lived the rest of her long life.

When she died the *Newbury Weekly News* printed an obituary signed 'C' (for her son, Carnarvon), recording that Almina's 'greatest joy in life was everything that contributed to the nursing of the sick . . . Courage and kindness were her greatest virtues and I think that is the context in which she would wish to be remembered by her many devoted friends and patients.' She received letters throughout her life from the friends and family of those she nursed. Almina had in many cases literally fought for their lives with all her love, care and experience. She died in 1969, so her great-grandchildren knew her well and still remember her fondly.

Ten years after the death of Geoffrey, Catherine married Don Momand and spent the last part of her life living peacefully in Switzerland. She would return to visit her son and his wife Jeanie at Milford Lake House, Highclere, and her daughter and Gerrit in Kent; she was a much-loved grandmother.

One of Catherine's inadvertent but crucial legacies to Highclere was the pledge for security given to her by Porchey when they divorced. During the lean years just after the war, Porchey survived by selling off parcels of land, but he was prevented from whittling Highclere's assets away to nothing by the terms of the agreement. The pay-out from the sale of Pyrotenax arrived just in the nick of time, but it was Catherine's divorce settlement that ensured there was still something to save, and that eventually ensured that her son Henry and her grandson Geordie could continue to farm much of the agricultural land at Highclere.

When she died, at the age of 79, Catherine was buried next to her adored brother Reggie and their mother, Gar, in the Cemetery Chapel in the park at Highclere. Porchey was moved to tears at her funeral. The whole family mourned the loss of a woman who had impressed her many friends and admirers with her infectious sense of fun, her dignity even at moments of great personal pain and her unfailing kindness.

Catherine's portrait, painted in 1929 when she was at her loveliest, still hangs in her sitting room next to Almina's likeness. It is one of my favourite of all the paintings in the castle.

Through a combination of determination, dedication and sheer love, Highclere Castle still stands today. My husband and I remain bound to the castle and its landscape, our lives and hearts belong to the place. An architectural witness to so much history, it is nevertheless both a home and a business. The focus of all our endeavours is to preserve the past for the generations to come.

Acknowledgements

Thank you to my husband, Geordie, ever patient as I struggle with deadlines and schedules. Helen Coyle is a great and calm editor, and her father Chris Coyle provided objective first feedback. And I have had subsequent help from Geordie and David Rymill to edit and check facts. David was and is unfailingly patient, helping me yet again as I mislay another date or pile of papers. He is a wonderful archivist. Robin Mann has been a great help researching and collating information and has now changed from academic research to join our team of gardeners.

Mr Ronan Donohoe—Portsmouth Athenaeum, USA has been incredibly helpful and I am so grateful for his time and research to help bring to light the Wendell and Fendall families. I am sure there are more stories and relationships to explore.

Patricia Leatham (Beauchamp) and June Prescott (Wendell) have been very kind to tell me about their family, the people they loved and knew. I have tried to tread the path of objectivity. Mrs Edith Eastment came and told me about her life as a nursing assistant during the Second World War. I was fortunate that Garry O'Connor had researched the HCR's part in the Italian campaign (O'Connor, Garry, *The 1st Household Cavalry 1943-44: in the Shadow of Monte Amaro*, The History Press: London, 2013), and John Walker, Chairman of the 92nd Bomber Group Memorial Association, has helped understand the last flight of a B17 and I hope it will lead to further research and a memorial.

Highclere is so full of stories and extraordinary visitors that it has been very difficult to narrow it down and choose whom to follow. The real cast is far larger than that of 'Downton Abbey', the fictional alter ego of Highclere.

I'd like to thank all the staff at Highclere for their support, in terms of coffees, tea, delicious suppers and John Gundill for his Mini Mars Bars in addition to consistent interruptions. Candice Bauval has tried to keep my diary clearer, thank you, and to beloved Nora Sutcliffe who has undertaken research expeditions with me. I am grateful to my sisters for their solicitous support, especially to Sarah for clarifying the beginning and the end. Steve Bohill Smith contributed knowledge and detail as I enthusiastically pursued my search for plane crashes and bomb sites around the woods and hills of the Highclere Estate. That should be a book and commemoration all of its own.

I am grateful that my publishers here in the UK and abroad have given me the opportunity to write another book about this inspiring castle and the people who have lived here.

The TV series 'Downton Abbey' has given us a profile that has helped us share this amazing home with millions of viewers, and, like the rest of the cast and crew, we consider ourselves both fortunate and grateful.

Picture Acknowledgements

Most of the photographs: © Highclere Castle Archive

Additional sources:

© Corbis: 3 (top right), 16 (top left) & 77 (text)/photos Bettmann. © Getty Images: 21 (bottom right)/photo Popperfoto, 32 (top)/photo David Montgomery, 127 (text)/ photo Fox Photos, 143 (text)/photo Topical Press Agency, 177 (text)/photo Central Press, 213 (text)/photo Walter Stoneman/Hulton Archive, 251 (text)/photo Roger Viollet, 315 (text)/photo Reg Speller. © Mary Evans: 3 (top left), 14 (top right) & 15 (middle right)/photos Illustrated London News, 13 (bottom)/photo Yevonde Portrait Archive/ILN, 14 (top left)/photo Everett Collection. © Newbury News Ltd: 30 (top left). © Rex Features: 31 (top)/photo Associated Newspapers, 31 (middle left)/photo Pierre Manevy/ Associated Newspapers. © TopFoto.co.uk: 7 (bottom), 11 (top and bottom left), 12 (middle right), 14 (bottom), 15 (top left and right).

Every reasonable effort has been made to contact the copyright holders, but if there are any errors or omissions, Hodder & Stoughton will be pleased to insert the appropriate acknowledgement in any subsequent printing of this publication.

Bibliography

This is not an exclusive list but the following may interest those who wish to pursue this period of history further.

Bailey, Catherine, *Black Diamonds*, Penguin: London, 2008

Beevor, Anthony, *D-Day*, Penguin: London, 2012

Beevor, Anthony, *The Second World War*, Weidenfeld & Nicolson: London, 2012

Brassey, Paul, Burchardt, Jeremy, Thompson, Lynne, Ed, *The English Countryside between the War*, Boydell & Brewer: Suffolk, 2006

Buchan, Ursula, *Green and Pleasant Land*, Random House Publishing: London, 2013

Cooper, Duff, *Old Men Forget*, Ulan Press, 2012

Courcy, Anne de, *Debs at War*, Phoenix Publishing Group: San Diego, 2006

Day-Lewis, Tamsin, Ed, *Last Letters Home*, Macmillan: London, 2005

Ferguson, Niall, *The War of the World*, Penguin: London, 2009

Hattersley, Roy, *Borrowed Time*, Abacus: London, 2009

James, Edward, *Philip Purser*, Quaret Books: London, 1991

James, Edward, *Schwäne spiegeln Elefanten*, Schirmer Publishing: Munich, 2012

Jenkins, Roy, *Baldwin*, William Collins: London, 1987

Jenkins, Roy, *Churchill*, Macmillan: London, 2001

Kiste, John van der, *George V's Children*, Sutton Publishing: London, 2003

Leatham, P. E., *The Short Story of a Long Life*, Wilton 65 Publishing: Windsor, 2009

Loelia, Lindsay, *Grace and Favour: The Memoirs of Lolelia Duchess of Westminster*, Weidenfeld & Nicolson: London, 1961

Lovell, Mary, *The Churchills*, Abacus: London, 2012

Lukacs, John, *Five Days in London May 1940*, Yale University Press: Yale: 2001

Macintyre, Ben, *Double Cross*, Bloomsbury Publishing: London, 2012

Middleboe, Fry, Donald, Grace, Christopher, Penelope, *We shall never surrender: Wartime diaries 1939–1945*, Macmillan: London, 2011

Mulvalgh, Jane, *Madresfield*, Random House Publishing: London, 2009

Norwich, Lord John Julius, *The Duff Cooper Dairies*, Phoenix Publishing Group: San Diego, 2006

O'Connor, Garry, *Household Cavalry Regiment 1943–44: In the Shadow of Monte Amaro*, The History Press: Gloucestershire, 2013

Olson, Lynne, *Troublesome young Men*, Macmillan: 2008

Perry, John, *Pershing: Commander of the Great War*, Thomas Nelson Publishing: London, 2011

Purser, Philip, *Final Quest of Edward James*, Quartet Books: London, 1991

Reid, Charles, *Malcolm Sargent*, Penguin: London, 1968

Rhodes, Margaret, *The Final Curtsey*, Brilinn Publishing: Edinburgh, 2012

Roberts, Andrew, *Master and Commanders*, Penguin: London, 2009

Roberts, Andrew, *The Storm of War*, Harper Perennial: London, 2012

Sebba, Anne, *The Life of Wallis Simpson Duchess of Windsor*, Phoelix Publishing Group: San Diego, 2012

Self, Robert, *Neville Chamberlain*, Ashgate Publishing Limited: Aldershot, 1988

Smith, Sally B., *Reflected Glory*, Simon & Schuster: London, 1997

Soames, Mary, Ed, *Speaking for Themselves: The personal letters of Winston and Clementine Churchill*, Black Swan Publishing: London, 1999

Taylor, D.J., *Bright Young People*, Random House Publishing: London, 2008

Warwick, Christopher, *George and Marina*, Weidenfeld & Nicholson: London, 1988

Young, Gordon, *Golden Prince*, Robert Hale Publishing: Kent, 1955

Ziegler, Philip, *Diana Cooper*, Faber and Faber: London, 2011

Ziegler, Philip, *King Edward VIII*, Sutton Publishing: London, 2001

The novels of Evelyn Waugh are an excellent commentary as well as great literature. *Brideshead Revisited* never fails to entrance.

I have used our own archives at Highclere Castle extensively, and above all need to thank David Rymill our excellent archivist who has been able to help me here as well as draw on any references and records from Winchester Archives and other sources.

Index

Lady Catherine, the Earl, AND THE
Real Downton Abbey

www.highclerecastle.co.uk

INTRODUCTION

A captivating follow-up to the bestselling *Lady Almina and the Real Downton Abbey,* this is the story of Catherine Wendell, the American beauty who married the man who would become the 6th Earl of Carnarvon and presided over Highclere Castle during the Jazz Age. Catherine first met Lady Almina's son, Lord Porchester (Porchey), in Gibraltar, where she immediately caught the eye of the dashing twenty-four-year-old aide-de-camp. He was one of British society's most eligible bachelors, and she was one of its favorite young ladies; she had already turned down several proposals.

The 5th Earl of Carnarvon died in Egypt not long after Porchey and Catherine's 1922 wedding. *Lady Catherine, the Earl, and the Real Downton Abbey* captures the tumultuous transition as Porchey discovered how precarious his father's financial situation had been. Just as the Crawley family must cope with financial jeopardy on the hit PBS show inspired by Highclere Castle, the 6th Earl was unsure if he could afford to keep the beloved family estate. The book captures his wrenching decision to auction off the Castle's most valuable assets, including the family pearls. Yet he was able to keep Highclere itself and maintain a modern version of his ancestors' lifestyle.

With candor and sensitivity, the current countess of Carnarvon also captures the subsequent unraveling of Catherine and Porchey's marriage. Drawing on the Castle's splendid archive—including diaries and scrapbooks—she then traces the tragedies and triumphs experienced by the family and staff as World War II erupted. Highclere Castle and the estate were turned into homes for evacuee children as well as lodging for soldiers, and the divorced Catherine and Porchey found common ground as their son, Henry, set off for the frontline. His sister, Penelope, along with their parents, volunteered for service on the home front.

A stirring portrait of history, *Lady Catherine, the Earl, and the Real Downton Abbey* will captivate your reading group. We hope the questions that follow will enrich your journey to this extraordinary time and place.

QUESTIONS AND TOPICS FOR DISCUSSION

1. How does Lady Catherine's world compare to the societies depicted in *Lady Almina and the Real Downton Abbey*? Who had the greater freedom—wealthy Almina or modern Catherine? What can both women teach us about resilience?

2. *Downton Abbey*'s characters cope with romantic rivalries and economic crises, just as Porchey and Catherine did. In what other ways does the PBS show echo the book? In what ways was life at Highclere Castle even more dramatic than at Downton Abbey?

3. How did *Lady Catherine, the Earl, and the Real Downton Abbey* enhance your understanding of the British experience during World War II? What historical details surprised you the most?

4. The author artfully weaves Henry's frontline experience with Robert Taylor's. How did World War II transform Britain's social divisions? Who in your family was part of the Greatest Generation?

5. Catherine's widowed mother decided to move her family to London, but Porchey's new bride, Tilly, ensconced herself in the States. How did transatlantic connections shape the culture of the early twentieth century? How were the American and British identities perceived on both sides of the Atlantic?

6. In chapter fourteen, we learn about George, the valet and acting butler who was dismissed after shirking his duties and trying to have a taste of his lord's lavish lifestyle. Compare him to Robert Taylor, whose lifelong career outside the military was to be a devoted servant at Highclere. If you had lived during that time period, which role would you have been more likely to take?

7. What did Porchey and Catherine ultimately seek in their other spouses? Why was Catherine able to find a match with a stable man who cherished her, while Porchey pursued women who could not commit to him?

8. Just as Lady Almina transformed Highclere Castle into a hospital for wounded officers during World War I, Porchey and Tilly saw the estate transformed into a shelter for children and, later, for soldiers' quarters. Does this spirit of hands-on generosity exist among today's upper classes?

9. Like *Downton Abbey*'s Robert Crawley, Catherine's father lost his fortune by staking the family's future in a single stock. On the other hand, Porchey's investment in Pyrotenax helped secure his future. What do these decisions tell us about the balance of luck and wisdom in building—and keeping—wealth?

10. The book begins with depictions of an opulent life for Catherine and her children. It shifts to a life of service as each member of the family begins supporting the war effort. Despite the trauma of war, how was the family enhanced by the immersion in working-class duties?

11. The author reminds us that Catherine's divorce stipulation secured Highclere Castle for her son, and for future earls of Carnarvon. In doing so, what did she preserve besides architecture and a place of shelter? What are the intangible benefits of maintaining the Castle and its owner's noble title?

12. What do you predict for the future of Britain's aristocracy and the new generation of royals? Will their network be as powerful as Porchey's friendships with future kings and queens?

Guide written by Amy Clements

Also by the Countess of Carnarvon

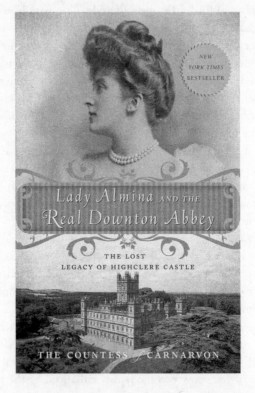

"Gives the juicy backstory behind last year's Emmy-winning Masterpiece Theatre drama."
—*New York Times*

"[A] fascinating insight into how the seriously rich once lived."
—*Newsweek Daily Beast*

B\D\W\Y
AVAILABLE WHEREVER BOOKS ARE SOLD